Technique, Discourse,
and Consciousness

Technique, Discourse, and Consciousness

An Introduction to the Philosophy of Jacques Ellul

David Lovekin

Bethlehem: Lehigh University Press
London and Toronto: Associated University Presses

Associated University Presses
440 Forsgate Drive
Cranbury, NJ 08512

Associated University Presses
25 Sicilian Avenue
London WC1A 2QH, England

Associated University Presses
P.O. Box 39, Clarkson Pstl. Stn.
Mississauga, Ontario,
Canada L5J 3X9

The paper used in this publication meets the requirements
of the American National Standard for Permanence of Paper
for Printed Library Materials Z39.48-1984.

Library of Congress Cataloging-in-Publication Data

Lovekin, David.
    Technique, discourse, and consciousness: an introduction to the philosophy of Jacques Ellul/David Lovekin.
        p.   cm.
    Includes bibliographical references.
    ISBN 0-934223-01-7 (alk. paper)
    1. Ellul, Jacques.   I. Title.
BX4827.E5L68 1991
194—dc20   89-85467
                                                                        CIP

PRINTED IN THE UNITED STATES OF AMERICA

To Donald Phillip Verene

Contents

Preface

My interest in Jacques Ellul began in a hallway at Northern Illinois University in the spring of 1969. While teaching philosophy at Sauk Valley College in Dixon, Illinois, I was also auditing a Hegel seminar at Northern Illinois University that was being given by Donald Phillip Verene, with whom I had done a master's thesis seven years earlier, "Ernst Cassirer's Concept of Man." At the end of one seminar session, Verene asked me if I knew of Jacques Ellul's *La Technique ou l'enjeu du siècle* (1954) *The Technological Society* (1965), mentioning that the translator, John Wilkinson, had claimed that Ellul's work could be compared with Hegel's *Phänomenologie des Geistes*. Wilkinson believed that in this work Ellul had produced a "phenomenology of the technical state of mind."[1] The following week I bought a copy of *The Technological Society* and began a twenty-one year study of Ellul and of the problems related to a philosophical consideration of technological society.

The background for my reading of Ellul was Cassirer, Hegel, and Verene's voice, still remembered from that Northern Illinois University hallway. From Cassirer I learned to view culture as a structure of symbolic forms—myth, religion, language, art, history, and science. From Hegel, I understood epistemology as a dialectic of consciousness and object. And from Verene, I learned to consider Hegel and Cassirer jointly—to see culture as a dialectical process of symbol formations and transformations.

At a time when most critics and commentators were explicating the more obvious neo-Kantian features of Cassirer's thought, Verene insisted on the Hegelian dimension to Cassirer's system. Cassirer's Kantian readers were more interested in the categories in Cassirer's work; Verene was interested in the dialectic *between* the categories, in seeing Cassirer's system as open-ended and as revealing the epistemological presuppositions of a cultural-social scheme.[2] A culture reveals what it believes to be true in its practices. A culture's metaphysics is lived; it does not reside outside of space and time. This is a perspective well worked out by R. G. Collingwood in *An Essay on Metaphysics* (1939).[3] Every action, Collingwood claimed, could be shown to reveal a metaphysical depth, an "absolute presupposition,'' a notion that has greatly influenced my reading of Ellul. On this reading, Ellul's notion of *technique* is to be understood as the absolute presupposition of our time.

I came to Ellul's analysis hoping partially to fulfill Cassirer's claim in the second volume of the *Philosophie der symbolishchen Formen* that technology might be construed as a symbolic form, as a distinctive way of forming symbols, a way with its own specific structure parallel to the other forms.[4] Having reviewed the critical literature, I realized that I was very much alone in this attempt. Ellul's critics were, in the main, interested in his religious views only, or in his theories about propaganda in a modern state dominated by mass media, or in what many were calling his "technophobia." With scant exception, Ellul's critics did not consider his thought philosophically, or see his works as a constituting a coherent whole. Superficially read, Ellul himself abets such a response. In the foreword to *Le Vouloir et le faire: Recherches éthiques pour les Chrétiens* (1964) [*To Will and to Do: An Ethical Research for Christians* (1969)], Ellul writes:

> I am neither a theologian nor a philosopher by profession. I possess none of the specialist's qualifications, for in our day philosophy has become a technique, and one is disqualified if he has not climbed all the steps of that edifice in a university program. I am trying only to be a human being. I am trying to live fully in this age. I feel the anguish of those around me. I am acquainted with our general laxity in a society without structure and without rules. My trade is to reflect, and I have undertaken to do that as a man, nothing more. I shall run into many a problem which the specialists have studied hundreds of times. I approach these in innocence and with the fresh outlook of the incompetent. I shall take care not to give a definition of ethics. The reader will choose any one among the thousands available, since all these definitions are partly accurate, but only partly. The specialists will shrug their shoulders. Perhaps a man will pay attention. ... [5]

Professional philosophers and theologians have become intellectual technicians who claim to find truth in rational and efficient method-ologies. Ellul rejects such a possibility and so disclaims professional identification as a philosopher. Nevertheless, I believe that the philosophy Ellul claims not to have reflects a holistic philosophy of culture, one more fully and explicitly developed in the writings of Cassirer and Hegel.

More recently I began to relate Ellul to the eighteenth-century Italian philosopher of history and culture Giambattista Vico, who, in Cassirer's view, founded the science of mythology. Mythology, for Ellul, is humanity's attempt to construct, using symbols, a meaningful world out of the particularities of experience. These myths provide people with a sense of origins, meaningful action, and transcendence. Both Vico and Ellul hold that the founding of communities in the temporal world is a poetic act and that recollecting this act is of profound consequence for humanity in every stage of cultural development. Both Vico and Ellul hold that communal decadence and disarray follow the forgetting of these origins.[6]

In my study of Ellul, I approach technology as a symbol construction following the path of a specific form of rationality. The role of the imagination in symbol construction, for Vico, is crucial; for Ellul, the imagination is problematic. Ellul develops no clear theory of the imagination, although he values its dialectical possibilities. He understands that spontaneity for the individual and in the social world are expressions of the imagination, and he values the Roman myths as expressions of a collective imagination. Imagination is thus a dialectical obstacle for technical reason. But, likely, Ellul regards the imagination as fundamentally limited by the power of the Wholly Other, his notion of God. In my article "Giambattista Vico and Jacques Ellul: The Intelligible Universal and the Technical Phenomenon," I laid the foundations for future work that must confront more directly the imagination as a response to technique. It would be useful, in relation to Ellul's critique of modern art in *L'Empire du non-sens*, to show how the imagination has been coopted. In this book, however, I have tried to avoid comparing Ellul to other thinkers to explain Ellul's importance, although I have used other thinkers, among them Cassirer and Hegel, to explicate some areas of Ellul's thought.

There are some exegeses and analyses of Ellul's thought from which I have profited greatly. Of the few dissertations on Ellul, I found Katherine C. Temple's "The Task of Jacques Ellul: A Proclamation of Biblical Faith as a Requisite for Understanding the Modern Project" (1976) the most useful of those in which Ellul's theological and sociological thinking is examined.[7] Temple shows the independence and at the same time the interdependence of both of these, reflecting one aspect of the dialectical life within Ellul's work. Particularly valuable are her interviews with Ellul. Darrell J. Fashing's *The Thought of Jacques Ellul: A Systematic Exposition* (1981) is a well-managed exposition of the varied elements of Ellul's thought, with an eye, however, to reconciling Ellul with Gabriel Vahanian; this, in my view, is the least valuable aspect of the book.[8] Fashing's is the first systematic study of Ellul in print—in English, nonetheless—and is useful in clarifying the misreadings of Ellul promulgated by Lewis Mumford, Harvey Cox, and Samuel Florman. Clifford Christians and Jay M. Van Hook, editors of *Jacques Ellul: Interpretive Essays* (1981), have collected a volume of essays on Ellul's intellectual influences, his sociopolitical views, and his ethical-theological perspective, but the majority of the essays are expository or comparative.[9] None attempt to break any new philosophical ground or to treat Ellul's importance as a systematic thinker in the history of Western thought. Finally, *Religion, Société et politique: Melanges en hommage a Jacques Ellul* (1983) is a 900-page festschrift of mostly appreciative attempts to apply, to explicate, or to commend Ellul's thought.[10]

My concern is this book, over and against these other studies, is to address three questions: (1) In what sense does Ellul have a philosophy of technology? (2) What does Ellul mean by "technology"? (3) What is Ellul's answer to the problems posed by technique in the contemporary age? In developing answers to these questions I have sometimes used examples taken from contemporary events. A problem any writer on technical consciousness, even Ellul, faces is that such events, which are vivid examples at the moment, fade quickly from memory and from the social context that had made them seem important. This difficulty of having to use examples that may quickly become outmoded for a future reader is itself evidence that the outer life of technical consciousness is constant change. Yet, the inner life of technical consciousness depends upon certain permanent structures. To understand these structures is the aim of the three questions I have posed.

This book began as a dissertation at the University of Texas at Dallas in 1986, and chapters 4, 5, and 6 are revisions of chapters 2, 3, and 4 of that dissertation. I thank Paul Monaco, Harvey J. Graff, Zsuzsanna Ozsvath, Michael Simpson, and Robert Corrigan, members of my dissertation committee, for their judicious and empathic criticism of that stage of my work. Donald Phillip Verene, then chair of the Philosophy Department of Emory University, served as an outside member of the committee, and I owe him a special thanks. His passionate objectivity helped me to focus, in 1986, work that began in 1964 under his influence. For many years his friendship and wisdom have meant much to me.

For nine years Carl Mitcham, of the Polytechnic University of New York, and I carried on a letter and telephone correspondence in matters of Ellul scholarship that has greatly influenced my perspective. The formulation of this perspective was made possible by the access Carl provided to microfilms of Ellul's little-known or impossible-to-find work. To Carl, a thousand thanks.

Steven L. Goldman, Andrew W. Mellon Professor in the Humanities at Lehigh University, saw the strengths and weaknesses in my manuscript and gave me a sound and friendly criticism that has occupied me for the last year and one-half. I thank Steven for the many hours he gave to my writing, and I am grateful for what I feel has become a profound friendship.

I also thank Amy Sherman and Kelly Arnold, who helped with the typing of many revisions, and my colleague, Professor Anne Fairbanks, who helped in proofreading my manuscript and in steadying my sometimes wobbly prose.

Introduction

There is little question that the works of Jacques Ellul are among the most important in what has become a vast literature on the nature of technological society and on the effects of technology on human life. His influence is great if only by sheer weight of response to it. Ellul's name is usually mentioned as representative of those thinkers hostile to technology. As such a thinker he is villified or praised, depending on whether the writer values or deprecates technology's incursions in human history. Ellul's readers, as I will show, are often not objective readers. Typically, Ellul is judged to be a conservative Christian opposed to progress; a pessimist who overgeneralizes technology's power and presence in the twentieth century; an insightful critic of the effects of media, propaganda, bureaucracy, and state power; a committed voice for the preservation of human freedom and choice against the dehumanizing forces in the modern age. These views, while justified, fundamentally miss Ellul's mark. They miss the important philosophical dimension that surrounds Ellul's writing.

In *Le système technicien* (1977) [*The Technological System* (1980)], Ellul writes:

> Man's central, his—I might say—metaphysical problem is no longer the existence of God and his own existence in terms of that sacred mystery. The problem is now the conflict between that absolute rationality (*rationalité absolue*) and what has hitherto constituted his person. That is the pivot of all present-day reflection, and, for a long time, it will remain the only philosophical issue.[1]

The question of God was the concern of philosophical reflection in the medieval world, in its quest for an ultimate reality that was beyond the *hic et nunc*, the here and now. What is ultimately real, however, is just what humanity decides to respect above all else beyond question. It is the ultimate presupposition, inevitably mysterious—that which humanity decides it cannot be without. In modern society the ultimately real is absolute rationality, *la technique*. Technique thus becomes the current mystery. The central

15

problem that technique poses for society is its denial of mystery to the sacred. The sacred becomes the familiar technical here and now. The irony of this denial is central to Ellul's writing, especially in *Les Nouveaux Possédés* (1973) [*The New Demons* (1975)].[2] Technique—that is, as scientific-technical rationality—denies the possibility of a transcendent reality that is inaccessible to measurement, experiment, and quantification. In this denial, technique becomes an absolute in its most troublesome form: technique denies absolutes absolutely, while claiming absolute validity for such denials. The medieval pursuit of meaning in universal terms is reduced to meaningful moments. The meaning of the world *becomes* its appearances, and thus a nominalism, in which the universal is reduced to the particular or to its names.

This aspect of Ellul's thought is closed to those many readers who fail to understand technology, *la technique*, as a form of consciousness, but precisely this thesis is the central concern of *The Technological Society*.[3] Ellul does not say that technology is mere mentality, that the real is just an idea. At the same time, however, the real cannot be separated from its being known and thus cannot be separated from the modality and expression of knowledge. Many of Ellul's critics, as I will show, are the equivalents of naïve realists for whom the world is purely present, simply before the eyes in pristine clarity. Ellul is not such a realist. The world appears to a specifically intended and specifically focused awareness that shapes that world through symbolic interaction with it.

The symbol is the means of interaction between consciousness and its world. It is the form of mediation that that consciousness takes, which leads it out to the world and back toward itself. The symbol is of great importance in self-knowledge and in knowledge of the world; the symbol makes such knowledge possible. Self-knowledge and knowledge of the external object break down when the distance between mind and its object collapses into the symbol, which then fails to serve as a mediator. The symbol loses the capacity to refer when it becomes reality itself. The symbol is the condition in which the idea and the object remain reciprocally *other* albeit correlated. Understanding this is central to my interpretation of Ellul's thought and especially to *La Parole humiliée* (1981) [*The Humiliation of the Word* (1985)],[4] *L'Empire du non-sens: L'Art et la société technicienne* (1980),[5] and "Symbolic Function, Technology, and Society" (1978).[6]

The Symbol is the great unexplored territory in Ellul scholarship, the ground linking his social and historical studies with his theological studies—a corpus of some 40 books and 800 articles.[7]

Ellul's critique of technology is unique in this sense: he approaches technology as a symbol construction, to be understood as a specific moment in time, which has ultimate meaning only in relation to a God who is at once *Wholly Other* and yet immanent and having no meaning beyond itself. A wholly immanent god, Ellul believes is incoherent, a false absolute.

Ellul's God is both outside and beyond His creation, which humanity has rejected, while remaining present in that creation. God, for Ellul, in *Sans feu ni lieu: Signification biblique de la Grand Ville* (1975) [*The Meaning of the City* (1970)],[8] allows this break in His fondness for freedom. Before the rupture, God's creation is whole and perfect, which Ellul takes on faith in the Bible, the revealed word of God. After the rupture, the world is known apart. Humanity can only stand before it at a distance, grasping it in names and in buildings, edifices that challenge and to a degree mock God. This distance and alienation is not known only by faith; it is actually revealed in history and in society, in which humanity attempts to make its own place and time in symbolic activity that is essential to the freedom that God allows. The symbol, in its capacity to refer and to point to an *other* enables humanity to deal with its own limitations, to see that its knowledge is contingent and conditioned by otherness, while at the same time going beyond the *other*. Knowledge does not advance unless the critical distance between humanity and its world is obtained. The *other* can only be transcended if it is first acknowledged. In the past, God, nature, and society provided humanity with its essential meetings with the *other*, but these are now mediated by the machinations of *la technique*.

In *The Technological System*, Ellul writes:

> The symbol in the technological system has changed meaning and value for the plain reason that the symbolized object or the object provoking the reference to symbols is not what it used to be. It is no longer an object both alien to man and belonging to a "natural" universe in which everything *had* to be symbolized. The object of the technological world now has its own efficiency, its power, it can obtain results, it is a work of man and yet alien. Hence, the symbol no longer plays the same role as earlier in regard to the object.[9]

In traditional societies, it is the natural object, beyond and behind which the gods and God hides; it is this object with a transcendent dimension that calls out to be named. The objects of the technological society—the genuine imitations—do not mediate once named. They do not point beyond themselves but degenerate into signs, objects, and icons—into degenerate symbols. Ellul's historical, theological, and sociological analyses chronicle this degeneration.

In his multivolume *L'Histoire des institutions* (1955–80),[10] Ellul shows that the ancient Roman Empire, like pretechnological societies in general, was not founded by force, by laws per se, or by praxis. It was established in relation to the ancient gods and heroes. Religious and poetic symbology pointed beyond the here and now to establish meaning and truth, the dimension that surrounds a reality, that gives meaning and order to those lives. By the eighteenth century, Ellul notes, legal institutions became realities and truths in and of themselves, thereby losing their symbolic nature. The state, like truth, was determined solely by reason and method. The philosophy of Descartes is everywhere applied. As discussed in *The Discourse on Method*, this involves putting the fables and stories of the past aside, in favor of clear and distinct truths.[11]

In *The Technological Society*, Ellul demonstrates that the rationalization of Western society, beginning around 1750, culminates in the appearance of *le phénomènon technique*.[12] In pretechnological societies, techniques are confined by custom, by religious, aesthetic, and philosophical preference, by the individual worker's ability, and by the worker's knowledge and care directed toward the object of work, often the object at hand. Tools and time-honored methods of production extended the worker's will in the world. But when tools and rituals are rationalized, they embody an abstract technical intention, no longer the measure of individual care, concern, knowledge, and ability. The bulldozer levels everything in its path; *it* does the work, needing only to be started and guided, and now even these functions are being taken over by computers and servomechanisms. The tool and ritual no longer mediate, are no longer symbolic, but have become the means and measure of reality itself. The natural world and the worker's body are likewise coopted as technical intention projects itself and makes a new world, one that it no longer knows it has made, which constitutes the ultimate in symbolic collapse.

In *La Subversion du Christianisme* (1984) [*The Subversion of Christianity* (1986)] Ellul states that the Church begins its secularization in the fourth century A.D.[13] when it becomes an institution promulgating dogma, wealth, and power, all worldly concerns rather than an iconoclastic force. Christianity is not a morality, for Ellul; it provides a symbolic text and a challenge: the Bible is a book of questions to be asked while God enters history, an occurrence fraught with contradiction. The Bible does not encourage belief (*doxa*), as Ellul reads it, but disbelief, doubt, faith, imagination, reason, and courage, which is the reason it is written in parables.[14] The reader is forced through the parables to participate in the text's symbolic dimension. Ellul writes:

> The Christian God makes himself known in Jesus Christ and not elsewhere. ... Outside Jesus Christ God is totally unknowable and inaccessible. As I have said above, the only possible theology relative to God is what much later (from the twelfth to the fifteenth century) will be called negative theology, that is, declaring what God is not. There is no possibility of saying positively what He is. This means that the condemnation of the visible in religious domain receives emphasis. There can be no demonstration of either the divine mystery or God's revelation. The Christian God is a *hidden* God. Nor can any image of Jesus be preserved or imagined. We have here a religion of the Word alone, and Jesus is himself the totality of the Word, living and not ritualized.[15]

Critical tensions play between the image and the word, between reality and truth, and between the finite and the infinite. God is a Wholly Other, and not a Wholly Other. He is an infinite, who yet effects and participates in the finite. He is a truth beyond reality, which is nevertheless known. This paradox, a truth expressed in contradiction, cannot be expressed in rational, scientific language. It is not a rational truth, nor is it an irrational denial. It is a truth expressed in metaphor and allegory. An expression of truth requires that the tensions between the image and the word remain. At issue is the logic of the metaphor whose importance is broader than biblical concern.

Symbolic tensions and their forms of expression are fundamental to Ellul's dialectic, to which little attention has been paid, although he insists that it is central to his work.[16] Ellul's dialectic is not a method, but a way of understanding, a type of knowing. No specific truths result. Ellul is clear that in dialectical tension no syntheses are impossible. Dialectic resists the scientific conceptual discourse of technique in which synthesis of opposition is the goal and requirement.

In *The Humiliation of the Word*, Ellul contends that the word, essential to dialectical language, opens the human to time, ambiguity, personal decision, goals, and freedoms. He writes:

> [Language] can command an action. It gives birth to institutions. But reality is not where its specificity lies. We have mentioned myths and symbols, allegories and metaphors, analogies and history, as spheres in which language moves about easily. In these contexts it takes on its full stature and becomes truly the word. In other words, it is true to itself when it refers to Truth instead of Reality.[17]

The word and the image are inextricably related although they point to different domains. The image moves to the real; the word attempts the true. They are two radically different sides of what can never be the same question. The true and the real can only be double-edged.

The image evokes the world of the certain—a reality—a that-which-is-before-one; it is personal but at the same time objective. It can also be before others. The view outside a window is available to all in principle but not exactly as it is available to any one personal view. One may see the same tree as an *other*, but the actual fact of seeing is personal and private, although it is an experience, nonetheless, of a certain. The image is part and parcel of what most mean by reality. It stands forth in its homogeneity and its sameness, giving birth, as Ellul notes, to the logical principles of noncontradiction and identity.[18] For good reason, Ellul concludes, Western philosophers since Plato have identified "idea" with some form of what is to be seen either by the bodily eye or by the mind's eye.[19]

The word provides an opening to another dimension. The word is not private but evokes paradox, discussion, and debate. An idea as a word must be spoken or written, but once embodied, it requires controversy and contradiction. The word, as distinct from the that-which-is-before-one as an image, is a scene that surrounds, a place in time and duration, which shifts like the Heraclitean flux. A sound heard requires, almost with gravitational necessity, a turn of the head, a movement to fix and to locate, to focus with an image. The word, by contrast, opens the individual up to a community existing in time and duration and to a sense of destiny as process. The image, that other domain, seeks to halt the flux, to stop the flow, and to replace uncertainty, a feature of the word, with certainty. If the image leads to affirming the principles of identity and noncontradiction, the word leads to their denial.[20] Both domains, however, are required, and understanding this is what grounds Ellul's dialectic.

When the dialectic ceases to function as a tension between idea and object, image and word, reality and truth, then freedom is lost. An essential freedom is the freedom to symbolize. As stated above, symbolization reveals the possibility of freedom, a freedom that is at stake in the technological society.

In the technological society, to summarize my analysis so far, all becomes a technical phenomenon. Humanity's mediations in tools, rituals, art objects, institutions, and so on were symbolic in that they were directed by limiting forms of otherness. These symbolic mediations were spontaneous expressions of a community and of its philosophical, religious, artistic sensibilities, outpourings of inspired imaginations and intellects of individuals, or crafty modifications of natural objects met on terms of their own necessities. Before technique, symbols reached beyond the mundane and worldly, even though the powers of symbolization are fragile. Technological symbols—*les phénomèna technique*—do not reach but replicate. Technology becomes the sacred, replacing the religious dimension in its appearance as the infinite that appears as the technical system itself. Images proliferate as the meaning of the technological society becomes another moment of it. The Prime Mover becomes the prime motor that empowers the assembly line that furnishes the contemporary life world. The best is the new, and all must become useful. These fundamental laws for technological growth and productivity are a metaphysic: that which can be done, will be done. With this pronouncement, technique ceases to be meaningful, understood as specific means to determinate ends; technique is now the ensemble of all means and ends, forming an endless continuum without closure or limit.

The world that the technical mind conceives is the world that thenceforth appears. The world ceases to appear as a natural world, as a communal world, as a world divinely inspired. The modern world is the world Descartes envisions as he looks out of his window:

> So I may by chance look out of a window and notice some men passing in the street, at the sight of whom I do not fail to say that I see men, just as I say that I see wax; and nevertheless what do I see from this window except hats and cloaks which might cover ghosts, or automata which move only by springs? But I judge that they are men, and thus I comprehend, solely by the faculty of judgement which resides in my mind, that which I believed I saw with my eyes.[21]

Descartes's world is a world he sees. His sight and his judgment move together. He sees and he judges. He looks out from his own private world—a world haunted by his solitary ego ranging about anonymous extended objects—and sees, not people, but apparitions, or automata moved by springs, which he *judges* to be people. He knows he can only understand these phenomena—spring-powered hats and cloaks—by the faculty of judgment, of reason. Here, Descartes in the seventeenth century is a momentary witness to the world in which we live, a world of images and clear and distinct ideas, a world of solitary confinement attempting to derive community.

Ellul writes in *The Technological Society*, "The principles established by Descartes were applied and resulted not only in a philosophy but in an intellectual technique."[22] It is useless, Ellul believes, to try to understand social, cultural, or intellectual developments after 1750, apart from the movements of *la technique*. Descartes's beliefs in the clear and distinct, his trust in methodology, and his reduction of the individual to a thinking rational being, a full one hundred years before 1750, places him, nonetheless, very much in technique's service. However, there is another side to the famous Cartesian certitude. With the aid of his marvelous imaginative construction, an evil genius, *"un mauvais génie,"*[23] Descartes doubts, and he also believes in a good and orderly God, who guarantees the clear and distinct verities and those ideas which are modeled after them.

The twentieth-century person does not sit in a room and imagine, as Descartes did, a mechanical landscape; the individual's doubt is not framed over and against an eternal God, who is the pattern and meaning of creation. The modern person is certain of a truth simply before the eyes, a truth that is the expression of technique. The computer is just one manifestation of this truth, of meaning itself. Ellul adds, "Gone is the doubt of Descartes, and also the doubt with faith. It is, however, only the fascinated person, dispossesed of himself who can be so convinced."[24]

Without a sense of personal identity, personal interest, without an "I" fashioned through doubt and honed by introspection, the individual gives up to a life of momentary fascination. Such people, Ellul observes, with deference to Pascal,[25] live a life of distraction, wonder reduced to the stare straight ahead. To be fascinated is not to be interested. To be fascinated is to be held by the image at hand. Even the Cartesian reflexivity is gone, leaving only the method without the capacity for selectively applying it. It is, after all, not to be everywhere applied, in all areas and in all ways.

Ellul turns to Kierkegaard for philosophical advice:

> As Kierkegaard points out, the self or person cannot become freely itself without entering an interplay between the possible and the necessary, freedom and necessity. There is no individual, no human person, no self, if there is no freedom, no possibility, before him. There is no meaning to life unless there is some latitude of freedom in which the self is constituted. Conversely, there is no meaning to this freedom if it does not rest on and run up against some necessity or a whole ensemble of necessities. It is the dialectic between these two realities that constitutes human existence. Man is caught in a network of determinations, but he is formed to dominate them, to use them, and to constitute his freedom in this use.[26]

Ellul's philosophy and his theology combine in a dialectic of otherness within a symbolic order—the condition of humanity's freedom, biblically, historically, and sociologically understood.

To repeat, Ellul's dialectic is no methodology. Method involves synthesis. Ellul insists that humanity is commanded to live in a world apart, in a cultural world that is always to some extent humanity's own making, which arises out of encounters with otherness. Herein lies Ellul's so-called pessimism, which, from another side, appears as the recognition of tragedy. Ellul's thought evokes the narrative that human events are revealed in history as they move toward ends. For him, the ultimate end is God's judgment; for the citizen of the technological world, however, progress is provided by technique, which has become its own end.

From both perspectives there are ends. In Ellul's eschatological understanding, real, external, ends exist. Humanity will finally have to face God's judgment and His forgiveness. For the technological mind there are no external ends; there is only an infinity of moments, each proclaiming an end, each a goal finitely conceived. The technical sense of infinity Ellul judges as meaningless and ultimately deterministic: there is nothing outside of technical intention against which to struggle. Ellul writes:

> There is freedom only starting from necessity and in terms of it, but also there is actuality (known, recognized by man) only in his struggle for freedom. This is true for a society just as much as the individual. Being itself is the necessary; before becoming itself, it is a possibility. It is here that the dialectical play has been fundamentally disturbed by the universalization of technique. ...[27]

Technique is determined from within by becoming the universal, by providing all the answers for human meaning and survival. Technique thus becomes the necessary without which nothing is possible, which is never more than the technically possible. Quoting Kierkegaard again, Ellul concludes: "'The loss of possibility signifies: either that everything has become necessary ... or that everything has become trivial.' In fact, with modern technology, both happen at once."[28]

Although Ellul denies officially that he is a metaphysician,[29] he raises a time-honored metaphysical problem between external and internal relations. One individual is not simply meaningful to another because one is to the left of the other, because one is taller than the other, or because one is plant foreman and the other is a worker. These qualities contribute meaning but only in relation to a larger standard of meaning and measure. A plant foreman is meaningful within the context of a factory. The factory's meaning may be sought in relation to the context of a society. And the society's meaning must be sought in relation to other societies. The part is always constituted in a relation to a whole. The current "whole" of a technological society, Ellul offers, is what has become problematic. As I will show, in the next chapter, a number of Ellul's critics are most concerned with Ellul's "reductionist tendencies," with his reductions of all problems to "*la technique*." But this is exactly *not* Ellul's concern. It is technique that reduces the real to the rational within its own methodological scheme and thereby becomes a totality, embracing all within its systematic purview. Relations, in fact, become systematically defined. Ellul focuses this problem above within the framework of freedom and necessity.

Meaning, as Ellul wants it, is always outside an internal relation. His theory of communication, logic, and dialectic—his entire notion of the symbol—rests on the meaningfulness of the negative, which is never really negative. The negative, as negative, is in relation to a positive, as positive, inasmuch as both the positive and negative remain. God as ultimate meaning, for Ellul, is the true infinite, which is inside and outside His creation at once. This is not an idea friendly to, or even possible in, scientific or technological logic. It is only expressible in metaphors and analogies and able to be postulated in terms of this theory of relations. *La technique*, importantly, is a metaphor for understanding the technological system.

Hegel struggled with the notion of infinity as an external and internal relation in his *Wissenschaft der Logik* (*Science of Logic*), and it is my contention that Hegel's efforts are very useful to understanding Ellul's concerns. As I will demonstrate in what follows, Ellul is much influenced by Hegel; in his "On Dialectic,"[30] Ellul acknowledges the importance of Hegelian dialectical negativity to his own dialectic, and in *The Technological System* Ellul understands that Hegel's dialectic, with its insistence on the negative, comes to a full stop for technological consciousness.[31] For technical consciousness, the important Hegelian tension between the subject of experience and the object of experience does not exist. Ellul is critical of Hegel to the extent that he finds Hegel's own dialectic canceled in a final synthesis in the Absolute Idea, an idea of the Absolute finally and fully formed.

I will not debate Ellul's reading of Hegel on this point, although I do not agree with it. Instead I wish to focus on Hegel's remarks in the *Science of Logic*, which help to illuminate Ellul's thesis. There, Hegel insists on the negativity of the dialectic in consciousnesses' attempts to think of infinity. Consciousness, as I will discuss more

fully in chapter 2, makes two mistakes in its labor toward the infinite:
(1) it posits the infinite simply as other than the finite, and the infinite
is then just one finite away, a moment that never comes; and (2) the
infinite is that which is absolutely beyond all finitude—it is what the
finite as a totality is not. In the first mistake, all relations become
internal, raising the question as to how they could be known. In the
second mistake, the infinite is absolutely external, and is thus
unknowable as well. This is Hegel's problem of the "bad infinity."

Technique is a bad infinity in the sense that it posits the abso-
luteness of merely internal relations. Whether Ellul's notion of God
as an infinity that is both finite and infinite—a true infinity—resolves
Hegel's problem will not be my concern. I am interested in Ellul's
idea of God as an essential form of otherness that keeps the dialectic
moving and that avoids a vicious relativism. I do not, in short, wish
to argue Ellul's religious case, although I think his notion of God as
an external *other* is important.

I am interested in Ellul's idea of technique itself, an idea that
technique does not form. Many of Ellul's critics clearly reveal their
parochialism in their denial that a whole beyond its particular
moments can be formed. That is, they deny the notion of "technique
as a whole," a notion central to Ellul's writing. I am interested in
Ellul's claim that meaning is constituted in the act of constructing
meaning; I am interested in uncovering how the idea of technique,
for Ellul, arises by considering consciousnesses' symbolic relations to
its own constructions and to those appearances of otherness out of
which symbols are formed. Finally, I am interested in the "life-
world" that technique generates. Ellul's theory of technology is no
simple intellectual construction. Technique is a specific form of life
and labor at a historical moment, one with its own thought,
language, and structure. The humiliated word—the symbol in its
degenerate form as technical phenomenon—is couched in the
concepts and the clichés of the language of authority, in a form
suggestive of Orwell's *Newspeak* but even more insidious. Technical
discourse is an anonymous memo to automata passing in the
Cartesian street, at most fascinating but rarely engaging. Technical
discourse is the monologue, not a dialogue, of the rational mind,
directed toward spring-powered hats and cloaks, abstract extensions
of the rational ego's dream, the sleep of *la technique*. Technique, it
will be suggested, is a form of forgetting, resulting in a displacement
from the past and the future. Human history is currently told from
the standpoint of technique, as if it were a universal aspect of human
culture and arrangement. Technique is an eternal present, coming
from nowhere and going nowhere, all for the sake of progress—its
image as a denuded word.

Technique, Discourse, and Consciousness

1

Ellul and the Critics

The Sociological, Historical, Political Perspective

In France Jacques Ellul is known as a historian of legal institutions, a lay minister and biblical exegete, and a political activist. In America he is known as an analyst of propaganda and as a critic of technology, which he regards as an autonomous force. Ellul gained much of his American audience during the late 1960s during its brief period of cultural upheaval when, according to William Stringfellow, Ellul's voice as prophetic critic of bureaucracy was finally heard.[1]

In 1960, Robert M. Hutchins and Scott Buchanan, speaking for the Center for the Study of Democratic Institutions, asked Aldous Huxley, then Regents' Professor at the University of California, to suggest some important contemporary works on technology. Above all others Huxley recommended Jacques Ellul's *La Technique ou l' enjeu du siècle* (1954), comparing it to Spengler's *Der Untergang des Abendlandes* (1918–22). Huxley confessed that Ellul had achieved in *La Technique* what he had attempted in *Brave New World* (1932).[2] Further, John Wilkinson, the translator of *La Technique*, states that Huxley had believed, "... that the book would become one of the 20th century's most authentic documents of social criticism against that fake liberalism that had fastened onto the world the totally technocratic society and its age of total wars."[3]

La Technique was published in Paris in 1954, and it received little attention. As a result of the Center's interest, however, an American edition was published in New York in 1964 with the title *The Technological Society*. The publication was not, apparently, easy. As Alfred A. Knopf wrote in an introduction to the second printing: "I committed our firm to an undertaking that I soon began to call Knopf's Folly."[4] Knopf refers to the difficulty of bringing out a complicated text in often convoluted French, to translator Wilkinson's extraordinary expenses, to the tactical problems of going to Greece to meet Ellul, and to the preparations of a special

29

introduction and final chapter for the American edition.[5] These
difficulties are only an anticipation of the intellectual difficulties the
text poses.

The Technological Society, the book that earned Ellul his
American audience for his social studies, was initially greeted with
great interest in America. The distinguished sociologist Robert K.
Merton wrote an introduction for the American edition, echoing
Huxley's enthusiasm and also comparing Ellul's book to the writing
of Spengler as well as to the studies of Veblen and Mumford. Merton
states:

> Less penetrating than Thorstein Veblen's *The Engineers and the Price
> System*, it nevertheless widens the scope of the inquiry into the
> consequences of having a society pervaded by technicians. Ellul's book
> is more colorful and incisive than Oswald Spengler's *Man and
> Technics*—which by contrast seems faded and unperceptive—although
> Ellul handles the historical evidence much more sparingly and with less
> assurance than Mumford. And it is more far-ranging and systematic than
> Siegfried Giedion's *Mechanization Takes Command*, which, of all the
> books overlapping Ellul's subject, comes close to giving the reader a sense
> of what the dominance of technique might mean for the present and the
> future of man. In short, whatever its occasional deficiencies, *The
> Technological Society* requires us to examine anew what the author
> describes as the essential tragedy of a civilization increasingly dominated
> by technique.[6]

Merton understands that this is no typical sociologist and not a
typical historical study. He is aware of Ellul's concern for
illumination and for the large picture. Moreover, he is aware of what
many of Ellul's subsequent critics never quite grasped:

> By *technique* ... [Ellul] means far more than machine technology.
> Technique refers to any complex of standardized means for attaining a
> predetermined result. Thus, it converts spontaneous and unreflective
> behavior into behavior that is deliberate and rationalized. The Technical
> Man is fascinated by results, by the immediate consequences of setting
> standardized devices into motion. He cannot help admiring the
> spectacular effectiveness of nuclear weapons of war. Above all, he is
> committed to the neverending search for "the one best way" to achieve
> any designated objective.[7]

Merton makes it quite clear that Ellul's discussion of technology
considers more than machines. Instead, Ellul places before the
reader a specifically human type—Technical Man—the reality behind
the machine, who seeks results that are the product of rationalized

calculation, eschewing spontaneous and unreflective behavior. Technique, embodied in Technical Man, moves toward "the one best way," toward absolute perfection. Technique, Merton seems to understand, is a disposition of consciousness.

Merton concludes his introduction:

> In proposing and expanding this thesis, Ellul re-opens the great debate over the social, political, economic, and philosophical meaning of technique in the modern age. We need not agree with Ellul to learn from him. He has given us a provocative book, in the sense that he has provoked us to re-examine our assumptions and to search out the flaws in his own gloomy forecasts. By doing so, he helps us to see beyond the banal assertion that ours has become a mass society.[8]

Merton's words were largely ignored. Instead of opening up a perspective beyond the commonplace, Ellul's work triggered a barrage of banal responses. Typically, Ellul's readers responded favorably or unfavorably to his work, depending on how they valued technology's incursions in human history. The notion of technique as a form of consciousness, the master key behind Ellul's social studies, remains, as I will show, unexplored.

The lack of objectivity and perception in Ellul criticism is nicely reflected in the following example. Eugene S. Ferguson, in his prestigious *Bibliography of the History of Technology* (1968), announced that *The Technological Society*, "... has been taken seriously, but the reviews have been generally unfavorable."[9] He cites Howard Falk's review in *Technology and Culture* (1965) as representative of this "generally unfavorable" reaction. Ferguson's charge, however, is difficult to maintain. Of the thirty-two reviews written in French and English up to and including 1968, only seven are truly negative, while twenty-two are distinctly positive and three are neutral.[10]

Ferguson's counting is questionable: thirty-one percent is not a majority. Worse, however, is his standard of measurement. Falk's article reflects the misreading and presumption to which Ellul's dense work falls prey. According to Falk, Ellul's case

> centers on an entity he labels "technique." By this he means not only the apparatus of modern science, technology, and production but also industrial and commercial techniques of all orders, insurance and banking techniques, organizational techniques, psychological techniques, artistic techniques, scientific techniques, planning techniques, biological techniques, sociological techniques (p. 253).[11]

The "entity" of technique, on this reading, is all-encompassing, "like a live organism [that] grows and transforms everything it meets into its own substance."[12] Thus, he claims, "Once the existence of technique is assumed independent of man's control, a general framework for an extended series of insights and conclusions is created."[13]

Falk then refers to Ellul's remarks in the Foreword to the revised American edition in which Ellul asks that his readers judge the objectivity of his account before they brand him a pessimist. But, if technique is an entity out of control, then the posture of pessimism would seem warranted. Falk's position is that pessimism is not warranted and that Ellul has simply overdrawn his case for the autonomy of technique.

Falk first notes Ellul's claim that "in the United States scientists are eager to work for the state in view of the low salaries paid university professors." "In fact," Ellul says, "the federal government has been having a difficult time attracting and holding scientists in governmental laboratories."[14] If true, Ellul has made an error in fact, missed a detail, though Falk does not consider the gulf between 1954 and 1968.

Falk cites a further problem:

> After reading a 38-page review of historical developments (which can be ignored without danger of loss), we are told: "Those who claim to deduce from man's technical situation in past centuries his situation in this one show that they have grasped nothing of the technical phenomenon" (p. 146). Later we learn that "modern man surrounded by technique is in the same situation as prehistoric man in the midst of nature" (p. 306).[15]

Falk understands Ellul to have contradicted himself.

Finally, Falk attacks the lack of currency of Ellul's critique, for not adequately considering, for example, advances in computer technology. Ellul's understanding rests too much, Falk feels, on the realities of industrial technology and neglects the artist, the university, and social protest as providing effective responses to technique.

Falk concludes:

> Ellul has actually played a neat trick on us and on himself. By using the word "technique" as a synonym for both "organized society" and "technology" he has lumped the whole of human social development into the process of refining the instruments of production—by definition. Human society certainly exists apart from individual man, but social

development is the very process by which tensions and relations between the individual and society are continually aggravated and resolved. The fact that Jacques Ellul wrote his book is, in itself, proof that social development is richer and broader than the mere refinements of production techniques.[16]

Ellul is castigated for including too much in his definition of technique and for not trusting in the powers of the written word. Ellul's own writing is offered as evidence of the possibility of challenging and transcending technique. But, Falk's understanding of Ellul's writing is also evidence, evidence of the frailty of the word in its reduction to the written sign.

Falk misses the following essentials in Ellul's case. Technique is neither an entity nor a specific process, but the mentality that makes each process and the entire ensemble of technical processes possible: technique is this totality of mentality and process. Technique is an ensemble. Technique has moved from the laboratory and the factory to encompass the entire life-world, which includes the university, the home, state parks, and all manner of leisure-time activity; the state and the factory are merely the most obvious forms of technique. Techniques of the past and techniques of the present are both similar and different in degree and kind: that is, they include technical operations such as manually punching buttons or chipping stone, but they logically entail a different stance toward the world, a different view of the object. Technique has become the nature—the environment—that surrounds. Technique coopts all movements that attempt to transcend it, an understanding that is anticipated in the chapter "Human Techniques" in *The Technological Society* and that is developed more fully in *The Humiliation of the Word* and *L'Empire du non-sens*. The artist either panders to the consumer or utters meaningless ejaculations (or draws lines on the floor, to be later explained by a museum guide or some other authority); the university relies upon government and/or commercial funding; protesting students rally not against bureaucracy but against their powerlessness to join it, often being satisfied when they were placed on university committees. The "counterculture" typically has moved behind counters of their own, joining the world of bureaucracy and business.

Behind Falk's misunderstandings are the following assumptions: Technology is this or that technique, this or that device, a physical, discrete, and neutral extension of the human being's will; the true is revealed in a particular instance and should not result in contradiction; the most nearly adequate account of reality is the current account. There is also a resistance to Ellul's pessimism and an annoyance with the notion of technique as a universal that is too inclusive.

Ellul's work, regarded as pessimistic, has generated a whole literature of optimism. For Victor Ferkiss, in *Technological Man* (1969), technology creates no problems that cannot be handled with care. We must be cautious to use technology wisely, self-consciously.[17] Alvin Toffler, in the much-discussed *Future Shock* (1970), argues that Ellul is simply pessimistic and insensitive to the endlessly varied life that technology has to offer. Humanity must learn to choose more rapidly from the technological menu. Toffler claims that human freedom is not at risk as Ellul thinks it is. On the contrary, now human beings have too many choices: an endless supply of cigarettes—all brands imaginable—many styles of automobiles, eight different blends of Sunoco gasoline, and so on.[18] Samuel Florman in his famous *Harper's* article, "In Praise of Technology" (1975), agrees with Toffler. Florman claims that Ellul is simply wrong in ignoring the ever-increasing amount of freedom gained through technology.[19] Technology is not an external force in culture. Rather, the problems attributed to technology are the results of humanity's infinite capacity to desire.

Florman expands his critique in *The Existential Pleasures of Engineering* (1976). He attempts to answer the following anti-technological charges that, for him, are exemplified by Ellul's work: that technology is an all-determining influence; that technicians are to blame for the public's tastes; that there is a technocratic elite; that technology is dehumanizing.[20] He answers these claims in a chapter ironically titled "I Refute It Thus," referring to Dr. Johnson's famous *ad lapidum* attack on Bishop Berkeley's idealism. Johnson, of course, misunderstood Berkeley. Johnson was trying to refute Berkeley's claim that all was an idea by kicking a rock. Johnson misunderstood that Berkeley was not denying the existence of objects but that he was instead claiming that an object of consciousness requires a subject for that object. Florman too fails to understand Ellul's point that technological objects similarly entail a mode of consciousness.

Florman argues that technology is not an all-powerful force because it is an *extension* of basic human desire, a universal feature of the human condition.[21] Technicians are not responsible for the public's tastes, he contends; "If people are vulgar, foolish, and selfish in their choice of purchases, is it not the worst copout to blame this on 'the economy,' 'society,' or 'the suave technocracy?'"[22] Technicians are not the elitists. The elitists are the antitechnologists themselves.[23] People are not forced to work against their wills at grueling jobs they hate. Eighty to ninety percent enjoy their jobs, according to a Gallup poll, Florman reports.[24]

Again Florman misunderstands Ellul's claim that technique has become desire itself, a specific and unique direction of desire for absolute certainty and efficiency. Florman does not grasp technique as a modality of consciousness, a specific mentality forming that object first in preconsciousness, then in consciousness, and finally in action. It is Ellul's hope that once recognized as a form of consciousness and desire, technical necessity might be weakened. The commonplace that technique is neutral while desire is strong only strengthens technique's hold. It is the lie of technical consciousness's neutrality that maintains the specific form of our addiction to, and dependency on, technique.

It is unclear what Florman understands by "taste" in the above quote. How would it be separate from an economic/social milieu? Ellul does not blame technology for current taste, although he does insist that taste is no *a priori* and that it has to be understood in relation to technique. Surely the current taste for frozen and fast food, for digital watches, for personal computers, and for microwaves reflects the available technologies and the minds receptive to them. Ellul contends that taste determined by social status reflects society in an "aristocratic infancy." With technique and mass production, taste moves to what is "off the rack." Designer jeans offer the semblance of an aristocratic posture, being at the same time a feature of a carefully planned mass market. Florman's language reflects that mass market in the commonplace language of two generations—"vulgar" and "copout." Significantly, Florman has adopted clichés—keys to technical consciousness, as I will later argue—with their capacity to appear as thought itself, while sidestepping the labor of thought. The cliché is language and thought purchased "off the rack" of technique. Statistics from the Gallop poll serve as another type of modern commonplace. The truth is reduced to quantifiable, repeatable fact reported by an authority. Doubt is dispersed and the evidence of personal experience is eschewed. Florman's presumptions themselves reveal the object of Ellul's attack.

Most interesting is Florman's defense of technology against the charge of dehumanization:

> I have seen early morning crowds pouring into a Park Avenue office building, into a spacious lobby, via a smooth-riding elevator to comfortable offices with thick carpets and dazzling window views. I have heard them chattering of personal concerns, a boyfriend who called, a

child who scratched his knee, a movie seen, an aunt visiting from out of town. These people are no more dehumanized by their environment than are a group of native women doing their laundry on the bank of a river.[25]

Florman grasps the marvels of contemporary civilization: carpets, spacious offices, elevators , movies, phone conversations, relations at a distance. Ellul challenges these as distractions, as flights from the disembodied tedium that is technique. For Florman, these distractions are presumed values, which, as values, affirm Ellul's point: the modern citizen loses the capacity to choose value apart from those provided by technique.

Of further interest in uncovering the presumptions of Ellul's critics is Florman's view of the primitives who, like the office workers, are happy at their tasks. Technology has always been with us, he argues, improving our lives in its advance. The primitive world is presumed to be identical in principle to the modern world. He states:

> I leaf through ... *The Family of Man*, a book reproducing the photographic exhibition assembled in 1955 by Edward Steichen. I see 503 pictures from 68 countries, representing man in every cultural state from primitive to industrial. I see lovers embracing, mothers with infants, children at play, people eating, dancing, working, grieving, consoling. Everything really important seems eternally the same—in cities and in jungles, in slums and on farms. Carl Sandburg's prologue attempts to put it into words: "Alike and ever alike, we are on all continents in the need of love, food, clothing, work, speech. ... From tropics to arctics humanity lives with these needs so alike, so inexorably alike." A few moments spent studying these photos make the attitudes of the antitechnologists seem peevish and carping. These are real people with real faces that give the lie to the antitechnologists' snobbish generalizations.[26]

Florman's people are not real people. Florman looks at a picture book. He counts all of the faces. They are real to him. He says as much. He counts them and he looks at them. Florman lives in a world where pictures are reality and where the past is not fundamentally different from the present. This feature of presentmindedness that is tied to the visual is essential to the consciousness Ellul understands as technique.

Ellul's pessimism is a problem to those of his readers who, in varying degrees, presuppose the commonplace that technology and progress are synonymous. Ellul's methodology is a greater problem. Merton warns that Ellul's sociology is not typical, that it requires an analysis behind the fact, that "the facts" of modern life are themselves being called into question by Ellul. Nevertheless, many readers already had their own paths to follow. Daniel Lerner, reviewing Ellul's book *Propaganda* in the *American Sociological Review* (1964), writes:

> What this book tells us about propaganda is less interesting than what it tells us about Jacques Ellul, about the present state of mind of French social scientists, and about the "Cartesian method" today. ... Among recent French generations, this preference for dialectical interpretation of reality has signified mainly an evasion of the grubbier activities of data-collection and data-analysis.[27]

It is remarkable to see the Cartesian method conjoined with dialectical analysis. Perhaps Lerner intends this ironically. His precise meaning is obscured by a lack of clarity about the nature of Ellul's dialectical method. Ellul does, in fact, consider himself a dialectician, but it is likely that Lerner's charge is simply an *ad hominem*, directed against analysis found wanting in fact.

Rupert Hall, in his review of *The Technological Society* for the *Scientific American* (1965), is also put off by the absence of empirical detail and by what appears to him irresponsible assertion. He states: "*The Technological Society* is to be thoroughly commended to all those who still imagine that social problems can be tackled with can openers; it is a cure for unreasoning euphoria."[28] Ellul is predictably criticized for not seeing the positive side to technical development. Hall commends instead Lynn White, Jr.'s more balanced studies, which give technology its proper place in the great march toward progress.[29] Put in other terms, Ellul is chastised for not repeating the commonplace, for not listing the marvels technology has provided.

Critic Charles Silberman, like Hall, is concerned with Ellul's facts and his methodologies. In his 1966 article "Is Technology Taking Over?" he begins by saying that Ellul's faulty methodologies and his lack of convincing evidence are wedded to a paranoid style.[30] Ellul's notion of technology is never clear to Silberman. He understands only the conventional view of technology as bureaucracy, tools, and machine use. Typical of Silberman's criticisms are the following:

> The politician, [Ellul] tells us, "no longer has any real choice; decision follows automatically from the preparatory technical labors." The evidence? In the U.S., we are informed, on the authority of a German writer, "unchallengeable decisions have already been made by 'electronic brains' in the service of the National Bureau of Standards; for example by the EAC, surnamed the 'Washington Oracle.' The EAC is said to have

been the machine which made the decision to recall General MacArthur after it had solved equations containing all the strategic and economic variables of his plan." The fact, of course, is that Harry S. Truman made the decision. The Bureau of Standards did then have a computer (its correct name was SEAC), which did make some decisions for the Pentagon—for example, how many army raincoats to order, and in what sizes.[31]

This revision of facts leaves Ellul's case undisturbed. If we extend Ellul's point to include what Silberman does not quote, we read:

This example, which must be given with all possible reservation, is confirmed by the fact that the American government has submitted to such computing devices a large number of economic problems that border on the political. Even admitting that we are not yet at this stage, we must recognize that every advance made in the techniques of inquiry, administration, and organization in itself reduces the power and the role of politics.[32]

Ellul offers the example with reservations. He is concerned not with the facts but with what they signify. He understands that it is the nature of technical consciousness to rationalize a procedure that in turn affects the content and form of other procedures. Inquiry, administration, and organization have ceased to be separate from technique. The capacity of technique to permeate all domains is Ellul's concern. Could the Pentagon decide not to use computers or could officials make choices using other than a logic modeled on computer computation?

In their criticisms of Ellul, Falk, Florman, Lerner, Hall, and Silberman reflect the commonplaces that *are* technical consciousness. These critics, in the main, are in favor of technical progress, which they understand as the material accumulations of society that are directed toward making life more efficient and more rational. Technology lifts the burdens of life. Technology is assumed to be a neutral extension of rational, though often misguided, will and desire. The problems posed by technology, these critics would conclude, require greater rationality and more determined will.

The genius of Ellul's account, as Merton understands, is its capacity to challenge the commonplace. As Ellul writes in *Exégèse des nouveaux lieux communs* (1966) [*A Critique of the New Commonplaces (1968)*]:

The commonplace will be formulated at the point of confluence of the philosophy, the ideologies, the religions that are being prepared in the intellectual crucible, and the average man's concrete activity to earn his living and to survive. Analyze the commonplace and you will find the nourishment of that society: its intellectual or spiritual nourishment as well as its material or economic nourishment, its insubstantial bread and dreams as well as its hard technical and political realities.[33]

The commonplace is thus more than tired, worn-out expression. It provides a repository for enacted beliefs, a *topos* that situates the facts of daily life. The commonplace is specific to each society and yet provides the general tenor and outlook that directs the intellectual and the common person alike. Ellul lists the following as representative of a technological society: "Man is free"; "Progress is always positive"; "Work is freedom"; "The machine is a neutral object and man its master"; "We must follow the current of history"; "Anyway it's a fact."[34] These commonplaces are at the heart of the above criticisms; they are what the common person and the intellectual share but never talk about—the presuppositions of daily life that direct the material-spiritual focus.

When these critics call for more facts, for sharper analysis, for less pessimism, and for less generalization, they are really calling for Ellul to adopt their facts and methodologies, their optimism, and their generalizations that generalizations are impossible. Unlike Toffler, Ellul does not see greater choice of goods in the marketplace as expressing a freedom that matters. These choices instead bind the citizen more strongly to that marketplace. Unlike Silberman, Ellul understands the making of technical decisions to become more and more tied to the technical system. The fact that computers would be used to purchase raincoats is further evidence that nothing is too insignificant to escape technical concern. Technique clearly is not simply a matter of machines but is also a movement of mentality. The failure to understand this unites all of the above critics. To conflate the life world of the carpeted, air-conditioned office with that of the banks of the Ganges is a confusion of monumental proportion. Florman's notion that "folks are folks" empties the material world of the specific mentalities that make it meaningful.

The neutrality of technique and its pervasiveness in human culture are themes that run through much thinking about technology. Technology is commonly depicted as neither moral nor immoral. Moral value is held to be independent of use and usefulness. Technique becomes a matter for empirical investigation, both historically and socially. In "The Importance of Technology in Human Affairs," the lead article in the influential *Technology in Western Civilization* (1967), to which Hall and Ferguson are contributors, editors Melvin Kranzberg and Carrol W. Pursell Jr. write:

> Man has always lived in a "Technological Age," even though we sense that this is particularly true in our time. The modern tractor-driven plow represents a higher level of technology than the heavy crooked stick with which primitive man—or rather woman—scratched the soil; and the hydrogen bomb is an infinitely more complex and lethal weapon of destruction than the bow and arrow. Nevertheless, the stick-plow and the bow-and-arrow weapon represented the advanced technology of an earlier era.[35]

Thus, technology is taken as an essential feature of the human condition, present in every culture at every time, and yet it is relative to that time. Technology differs in various cultures in degree, but not in kind. Technology that is an extension of the body is simply more complex than advanced machine-computer technologies. Modern people are not, in principle, unique.

Curiously, although Kranzberg and Pursell hold that technology is essential to culture, they also claim that technology, "cannot be defined with precision."[36] As evidence, they offer the following definition:

> Technology, in a sense, is nothing more than the area of interaction between ourselves, as individuals, and our environment, whether material or spiritual, natural or man-made. Being the most fundamental aspect of man's condition, his technology has always had critical implications for the status quo of whatever epoch or era. Changes have always rearranged the relationships of men—or at least of some men—with respect to the world about them. Not a few of the historic outcries against technology (or, more properly, against some changes in technology) have been essentially protests against a rearrangement of the world's goods disadvantageous to those who complain.[37]

Technique is an essential feature of human culture and yet is only understandable in relation to specific cultures. Therefore, no general and precise definition is possible, which is, of course, a definition. Why, however, is technique pervasive? How could technique be known as not possessing defining characteristics? If technology were defined as the sum of all human-world interactions, the notion would become meaningless. By contrast, Ellul's concept of technique would appear quite restrictive. Kranzberg and Pursell understand technique to be something that is revealed in history, a history that takes shape with data collection and empirical analysis. But how, exactly, is technique's shape revealed? To an objective observer? Where would such an observer be found?

The Kranzberg and Pursell view, which predominates in much thinking about technology, raises many questions. How is the notion of a specific culture or society possible, if a culture is to be reduced simply to its material elements? What is this notion of individuality that seems presupposed? If "folks are folks," as Florman also supposes, the notion of a truly specific culture would seem violated. Cultural difference would be no real difference, if cultures were merely different in degree. As Leibniz observed in his principle of the identity of indiscernibles, a true difference must be both a difference in degree *and* a difference in kind. The very notion of materiality and individuality is begged in favor of what Ellul would call a technical disposition, in which individuality is a matter of system shuffling. The individual becomes this system. For Kranzberg and Pursell, all cultures are technical cultures waiting to be born. Cultures are technical in essence. The absolute as technique enters history backward. The technical particular is merely reified. The form of technique is presupposed, while its reality, as form, is denied.

The Kranzberg/Pursell position raises the crucial question: Why are not the technical interactions of primitives, wielding fundamentally body-extended techniques, held to be fundamentally different from the interactions of those in technologically advanced cultures? Watching is surely different from doing, although in technological cultures watching has *become* doing: a visit to a modern factory confirms the necessity of workers observing, while machines do the work. Watching highway workers working is to participate in a spectacle—the observer observes workers observing the work being done by men riding atop machines. The keeping of records and data is a modern technology that would seem to have made modern life fundamentally different from, not merely more complex than, primitive life. The concern with technology itself is a modern concern. The *Oxford English Dictionary* locates the use of the word *technology* in the seventeenth and eighteenth centuries as a discourse on technique. From my perspective, the problem rests with critics' not understanding technique as a mentality socially embodied.

In his keynote address at the International Symposium on the History and Philosophy of Technology, 14 May 1973, Kranzberg responds to Ellul's claim that *la technique* has come to dominate life, that technical mechanisms have become the goals of modern life, thus losing their neutrality.[38] Kranzberg states:

My own view on this matter is embodied in what I call "Kranzberg's Law.". . . "Technology is neither good nor bad—nor is it neutral." By that I mean that technology interacts with society in ways which do not seem necessarily inherent in the technology itself. Thus, for example, by the very scale of its use the automobile has "locked" American society into certain spatial distribution patterns, life-styles, and economic activities.

Values become attached to particular technologies and hence serve to determine the lines of future political, social, and, yes, technological action itself. The task of both history and philosophy is to make clear the interactions which transform technological instrumentalities to social phenomena and value-laden decisions and activities.[39]

"Kranzberg's Law," like his definition of technology, is curiously vague, strangely lacking in circumspection. If technology is neither good, nor bad, nor neutral, what is it? Is all value somehow beyond it? Do cars command society because there are so many cars or because cars have become the good? Where is the domain of value? Philosophy, traditionally seeking such a domain, is encouraged to "clarify social interactions." History, too, is to have its eyes on the social ground. The transcendent apparently becomes the immanent. Finally, if technique is value free, what does it mean to call it essential?

Ellul's critics, at least those examined so far, have represented technical rationality. They are either in favor of technological advance, which is assumed to be progress, or they ignore the epistemological-philosophical dimensions of the notion of technique. Problems that arise can be solved by refining techniques, by better planning, and by becoming more objective. There is no receptivity to the notion that technique has become objectivity itself.

Ellul's readers typically do not engage his work. Often, even as devotees, they simply explicate and/or apply his ideas uncritically to contemporary issues. *Introducing Jacques Ellul* (1970) is an example of this. Edited by James Y. Holloway, it is a collection of essays originally appearing in the theological journal *Katalgante*. This first book in English on Ellul is, by and large, a devotional. Christopher Lasch's contribution is an exception. He writes:

> In itself, Ellul's analysis of modern society is unoriginal (except for one or two sharp insights) and in some respects even misleading. Moreover, the work for which he is best known, *The Technological Society*, is the weakest of his three sociological treatises, although it is also the most ambitious. In large part, it repeats what has been said by Max Weber, by Veblen, and by the theorists of the managerial revolution, the "new class" and "mass society."[40]

Ellul's sociological writing is ambitious, yet unoriginal and flawed, apparently in what is borrowed from Weber, Veblen, and other theorists of mass society. *The Technological Society* is the weakest and the most ambitious. The issue raised by this claim is the problem of whether Elull's sociological writing can be read alone.

As I reflect, I find, it is Lasch's claim, his reading of Ellul, that is unoriginal. The technological society, as he understands it, is simply an overwhelming and overpowering social structure, overly committed to machines, bureaucracy, and automation.[41] For Lasch, it is structure. This is only the surface region of Ellul's notion of technique. Lasch approves of Ellul's analysis of modern communications, which he calls "brilliant," but he does not understand Ellul's claim that all areas of culture and society are assimilated by technique as a form of intentionality, which motivates the structure. Lasch, like many readers, criticizes Ellul for not giving politics enough power in the face of technique.[42] Lasch assumes that technique and politics can be separated, without clearly showing how this is possible. It is the claim of *The Technological Society*, *Propaganda*, and *The Political Illusion* that communications, politics, and technique form a nexus. Lasch rejects this claim without either acknowledging or examining it. Most important, he fails to recognize the centrality of technical intention.[43]

Lasch moves to important ground, however, when he writes: "What is valuable in his social writings takes on meaning only when one considers the ethical, cultural, and philosophical position they intend to support."[44] Lasch does not venture beyond this remark. He recognizes that Ellul's Christianity expresses an important tension between the state and the individual, and between other individuals and the individual. Lasch recognizes the importance of tension in Ellul's thought. He understands that Ellul's God provides a sense of coherence and a moral perspective that brackets the state and the society.[45] God is a principle of ultimate tension that forbids a collapse into apathy, a fall into meaninglessness, incoherence, and discontinuity. God offers Ellul a critical distance, a vantage point, from which to view the social world.

Although not explicitly a commentary on Ellul, Langdon Winner's *Autonomous Technology: Technics-Out-of-Control as a Theme in Political Thought* (1977) is, nonetheless, one of the most sustained, thoughtful, and appreciative accounts of Ellul's thought.[46] Winner values Ellul's work, understands its breadth and depth, and sees that the notion of *la technique* is more than a concept of machines, gadgets, and gewgaws. Technique, he allows, is a sweeping form of intentionality, one productive of the technical system.[47] The sweep of Ellul's thought thus both fascinates and offends. Winner, like Lasch, understands the apparent generality of the notion of technique as reductionism. Winner, however, fails to encounter his own reductionisms.

Winner writes:

> His [Ellul's] work stands as an elaborate hall of mirrors, deliberately designed to leave no passage out. From the building of skyscrapers to roller skating, Ellul's ubiquitous concept of technique expands to encompass any subject and to resist contrary examples. Planning and public opinion, for instance, which might be taken as possible forces counter to unbridled technical advance, are shown to be mere products of technique itself. *The Technological Society* is less an attempt at systematic theory than a wholesale catalog of assertions and illustrations buzzing around a particular point. The book is one that its readers rave against, refute in dozens of ways, and then lose sleep over.[48]

Winner is correct that Ellul's text is a labyrinth that one cannot simply approach. It must be responded to and directly engaged. Ellul's critics, however, as I have been suggesting, often bring to their reading the intentionality of technique while denying its reality. In the end, Winner is no exception to this. His fails to understand technical *intention* as that which motivates technological or institutional structures.

Winner writes:

> It is an odd state of affairs that a thinker so wary of mechanism should have produced so mechanical a theory. This reductionist tendency in his thinking, common to philosophers searching for the flaw in Western culture, leads to a badly distorted reading of recent history. Indeed, techniques of communication, propaganda, and police work have played an important part in the rise of modern totalitarian states. Refinement in techniques of warfare definitely has something to do with the frequency and destructiveness of war in the twentieth century. But to explain war, totalitarianism, or any other fact of the times wholly or substantially by reference to the culture's obsession with technique is certainly to overstate the case.[49]

Winner's argument is that, "... technology itself is a political phenomenon."[50] Ironically, Winner is the reductionist, ignoring the conclusions that Ellul draws in the *L'Illusion Politique: Essai* (1965) [*Political Illusion* (1967)], which I will examine more fully later. In brief, Ellul writes that the first stage of the political illusion is to claim that politics is the most important of all human activities, that all activity is essentially political. This is Winner's error—the assumption that all is ultimately political. The next stage in Ellul's account of the political illusion is the reduction of *le politique* to *la politique*, the reduction of the general concern for the welfare of humankind to the social mechanisms, institutions, and techniques that bring these about—as if political freedom were effected by the pull of the level on the voting machine. The political illusion is finally achieved when *le politique* on longer exists, when attention to means supplants the consideration of ends. This is Winner's second error—the belief in the primacy of social structures. Technique cannot be understood apart from its institutional structures and artifactual embodiments, although it is no one of these. Winner, like Lasch, is troubled by this persistent ellusiveness of technique in spite of the ubiquity of the technological.

Winner argues that to regain control of technology in the political realm we must find (1) less oppressive technics, (2) technics subject to democratic, social control, and (3) smaller scale and highly flexible solutions to technical problems. In other words, more people must become involved in technical matters, which thereby become an even more pervasive, albeit smaller and more democratic, social reality. Technical problems still require technical solutions for Winner, an example of the mentality Ellul warns against. Winner adds, however: "Finally, I could suggest a supremely important step—that we return to the original understanding of technology as a means that, like all other means available to us, must only be employed with a fully informed sense of *what is appropriate*. Here, the ancients knew, was the meeting point at which ethics, politics, and technics came together."[51] But how is this sense of what is appropriate to be gained? Is all, ultimately, a political problem? It is Ellul's charge that technique is an essentially reductionistic intentionality and that reducing all to the political is the first phase of its dominance. If technique is all-encompassing, that is not Ellul's fault. It is telling that Winner's solutions to the problems of technique involve more technique, more involvement with the technical, more planning. Winner is right to be concerned about a loss of sleep, about the mirrored labyrinths of Ellul's account of technology, an account that is not a system but a deliberate response to a system, *le système technicien*. Winner's engagement of Ellul's charge is, in the end, a looking-glass exercise.

Winner discusses with some thoroughness aspects of what I have called the logic of technique—e.g., the principles of self-augmentation and autonomy.[52] He finds some incorrect facts, some misinterpretations, and some gross generalizations. Winner disagrees with Ellul's apparent indentifications of science with technique, with his lack of precision regarding the process of technical invention and technical implementation, but values the risk Ellul takes, "... the willingness to offer a complete, uncompromising statement."[53] Ellul has taken a chance, over and against a piecemeal sociological approach, "to notice the elements of dynamism, necessity, and ineluctability built in to the *origins* of the process."[54] Technique is unique, having its own laws, its own necessities, which are endemic to the system it establishes. Ultimately, Winner believes that these necessities may be abrogated as a result of consciousness raising and democratized planning. He is, finally, unclear about why these political goals and desires are not simply also concerns for a more efficient ordering of society. If the life-world has been restructured, as Winner often admits it has, how would the "wisdom of what is appropriate," the wisdom of the ancients, arise without a restructuring of that life-world and its specific intentionality?

Winner offers what he calls "Epistemological Luddism" as an entrée to such wisdom: "The idea is that in certain instances it may be useful to dismantle or unplug a technological system in order to create the space and opportunity for learning."[55] Unplugging the toaster and turning off the television for a week will hopefully disengage and reorient the technologically addicted. However, the most important aspects of the technological system that concern Ellul can neither be avoided nor unplugged. Pulling up a TV dinner tray to a suburban picture window might reorient one to one's neighbors, but it will not turn off the needs for system, spectacle, rationality, and reinforcement—all critical aspects of technique that Winner needs to reevaluate. Winner's presumption that technical problems require technical solutions conflicts with the notion of Luddic Epistemology. Winner assumes that technology can be avoided, that it can be unplugged. Ellul charges that it is a feature of technical intentionality to assume that there are only technical solutions to technical problems. Luddic Epistemology requires a larger epistemology than this one, which distances itself from technique as a way of knowing. Winner's concern for fact and consistency, his distrust of philosophical generalizations, and his need to understand problems in terms of solutions and structures is exemplary of technical knowing, from Ellul's perspective. Nonetheless, within Winner's account there is quite another direction: a concern for origins, for dimensions that surround the social and the practical, for a wisdom of that which is appropriate. This is Ellul's direction of concern, a fact that Winner, curiously, does not grasp. Ellul lays bare the structures of technique and provides a schema that reveals how those structures are possible, as expressions of a mentality seeking methodologies of efficient ordering. Winner's discussion of some of the logic of technique—for example, self-augmentation, autonomy, and rationality—founders on Winner's own presumptions. Winner refuses to accept Ellul's challenge that technique is an outgrowth of rationality, of the desire to reduce problems to discourse, and of the belief in progress and material success.

Finally, for Winner, Ellul is the Christian, for whom technology is sinful, expressive of finite human pride. He writes:

> His eye ... is that of a Christian theologian. Through his rendering of psychologtical, sociological, and political scientific data we can see Ellul's conviction that the rich and marvelous complexity of God's creation, including the human species, is being supplanted by this reckless, rigid complexity of a myriad of harebrained schemes. Technique in his view is truly *sin*, exactly the kind of sin one would expect from a being that had eaten of the tree of knowledge. But the tree of absolute knowledge and the works that spring from it carry the marks of inevitable ignorance. "For we never know whether there is not something in man which our analyses and scientific apparatus are unable to grasp." Thus as Karl Jaspers also observed, man lives in a world of self-created imperfections, many of which become an integral part of his character, yet he believes and cannot be convinced otherwise that technology is perfect.[56]

Ellul is indeed a Christian, although he would resist the label of theologian, that is, one who attempts a systematic account of God's ways, of God's nature. Theology as system, for Ellul, runs much in line with the ways of technique. While technique is an expression of humanity's disobedience to God, to call it sin is too simple. Better, technique is humanity's attempt to establish its own absolute. Here Winner is on the mark. In my view, technique is a form of wisdom out of touch with its own ignorance, which is endemic to its very enterprise: the positing of absolutes in the face of their denial. Winner and Lasch, both mindful of the Christian dimension to Ellul's thought, do not probe its philosophical significance, although their criticisms call for such an approach.

Carl Mitcham and Robert Mackey, in "Jacques Ellul and the Technological Society" (1971), are among the first critics to begin to take seriously the philosophical dimension of Ellul's writing. They argue that Ellul does not distinguish between technique and technology as well as he might, that technology is not necessarily incompatible with human choice, and that if, as Ellul claims, technology establishes a system of internal relations such that the relata acquire reality through their relations, then the determination of any individual's essence becomes problematic. In one sense, the essence of human being would be determined through these finite technical relations and, in another sense, human being would ultimately be determined by God.[57] Mitcham and Mackey thus identify an apparent contradiction in Ellul's thought.

To the first charge, one can respond that Ellul's case is based on technique and technology becoming interchangeable in the technical system, a matter I discuss more fully in chapter 4. In brief, technique as mere means, clearly distinguishable from goals and discourse, is a feature of pretechnological cultures. In technological cultures this distinction is eroded, and freedom is only available in the shadow of technique. Nontechnical choices are, to be sure, in principle, possible, but Ellul's point is that as a matter of fact they are not made, because technique becomes choice itself. Freedom becomes an abstraction. Freedom, from Ellul's Christian perseptive, is what God grants to His creation. It is essential to Ellul's dialectic, the subject of my next chapter, that being and essence be worked out in a tension through time. Following humanity's disobedience, humanity's break with God, which God allows, trial ensues, in which false absolutes are placed before God, the true absolute. Ellul, as a Christian, exposes these attempts that, in the modern age, take the form of technique in its multiple manifestations. Mitcham and Mackey are quite correct in reminding us of the classical problem that arises from accepting God's creation as perfect and finished, which Ellul does accept, together with the idea of that creation as free and partially indeterminate, which Ellul also accepts.

In part, Ellul treats the problem of freedom and determinism within God's creation by regarding the Bible as an *Urtext* and by refusing to regard the text as ever completely revealed. The Bible is God's word, and in Genesis it is stated that God created all things and that they were good.[58] His creation was perfect and complete. Yet, part of that perfection requires freedom within the creation. God grants the creation similar powers to his own. The creation is not a machine.[59] Ellul states this emphatically. Creative possibility and play are allowed. Machines require power, force, design, creativity beyond their own. They are not the cause of their own being. Humanity and its creations always herald a beyond, a that-which-they-are-not and a that-by-the-sake-of-which-they-are. God speaks to humanity through the Word, which, like the creation itself, is never fully revealed. Knowing requires interpreting.

Ellul does not see his work as metaphysical or theological; he does not discuss at any length why he avoids these concerns. Nonetheless a metaphysical and theological dimension is implied, one that is consistent with Ellul's methodology of no method in the Cartesian sense of that word. Ellul's dialectic, his substitute for method, is an expression of the power of the symbol, and that is what Ellul's readers unfortunately have read past. The notion of the symbol has its source in Ellul's reading of the Bible and in his refusal to confuse the True, *Le Vrai*, with the Real, *Le Réel*, and the image, *l'image*, with the word, *la parole*.[60] The tension between the True and the Real, between the image and the word, powers his social critique as well. The problems of personal freedom and determinism can also be seen within these distinctions. While this will be discussed more fully in chapter 2, some brief clarification is necessary here.

The Theological-Philosophical Perspective

Although Ellul claims to be neither philosopher nor theologian, a crucial theological-metaphysical dimension surrounds his writings. As stated above, this dimension is located around the tension between the True and the Real and the image and the word. God's Word is the True. This I take as a limiting condition, an Absolute that is never known absolutely but one that makes possible the particular, the relative. God is a universality that surrounds all that is particular, the Real, the totality of God's creation. God's Word is known in the gospels and in the person of Jesus Christ. God cannot be known as a pure Wholly Other but is revealed as a truth that is known in reality. His revelation, however, can never be known adequately as an image, as that which is merely real. The image lacks the ambiguity of the word, the power to appear as that which is and is not.[61] God's Reality, His Truth, is known indirectly, for example, through the True as it is situated in the Real, in the True and the Real as they are given in the human world. The entrance to the True is through the word; the image is the domain of the Real. The word indicates the true that surrounds, ultimately indicating the True; the word, unlike the image, is no sensual present before which one stands. The image is tied to the Real. The word, as it indicates the True, is what the image is not. The word is what the image is about. The word can indicate the Real but it must not be confused with it, yet just this state of confusion is the state of affairs in the technological society where the word is humiliated.[62]

In the particular world the true is relative to the false; they indicate each other. The image is not the false *per se*, any more than the word is the True *per se*. In the human world after the break with God, this totality is bifurcated. This bifurcation, like the prior totality, is a given. I take this also as a limiting condition, an absolute presupposition. Humanity's symbols after this break lack the totality of expression that Adam's words had.[63] Here is another limiting condition: humanity's symbols, as bifurcated, seek the totality they both express and lack; they are unifications of contradictions that are the present reality that can only indicate the true and, ultimately, the Truth. In this sense, humankind is both free and determined. Humanity as part of God's plan is given the freedom to challenge that plan. God's creation, once finished, is opened to freedom and play. Relativity is the reality after the break with God. Symbols are humanity's attempts to bridge that break, attempts that partially succeed but finally fail. Ellul's social critiques are chronicles of those failures, as humanity attempts to determine its own freedom over and against a fixed essence, a fixed form. Typically, Ellul contends, human beings cannot live with that freedom. In anguish, they posit their own absolutes that, as absolutes, fail. Technique is such an absolute.

For technical consciousness the Real is before the eyes. The True is reduced to the Real. Words are meaningful for technique inasmuch as they can be lodged in the Real. The Bible is thus crucial for Ellul as a model. As a book to be held in the hands it is worthless. As a set of formulas or prophecies forecasting answers, rules, and laws, it is meaningless. The biblical word, as Ellul understands it, resists such reduction. Ellul is not proposing a mere matter of exegetical technique. In my view of Ellul's thought, the Bible is an epistemological reminder that any specific reality is surrounded by ultimate purpose, which is shadowed by the Word and by the words of commentators and readers profering and seeking illumination. The Bible forces the epistemology of technique to its limits. For technique, knowing takes place on the side of the clear and distinct. The truth must be noncontradictory and yet must be a sensuous present. The Bible presents another kind of knowing. The Bible portends a truth that surrounds, a God who is imminent and transcendent at once—neither one nor the other considered separately.

Ellul writes:

We have to realize that *everything* in the Bible is contradictory. Yet there is revelation only as the contradictions are held together. God the Wholly Other is incarnate in a man. He is still the Wholly Other. And we have to understand—I repeat this because it is essential—that the truth is made up of the actual contradictions. Each aspect of the truth is true only because it is linked to its radical opposite. If I say that God is transcendent and stop there, this is not the Biblical God. If I say only that Jesus Christ is God, this is not the gospel. This way of speaking is basically contrary or contradictory to the mind. I do not say the human mind, but at any rate that of the Western world. From six centuries before Christ we have been functioning in the mode of "either-or." What is black is not white. What is true is not false. What is act is not thought, etc. We think analytically with an admirable rigor. We sometimes forget great syntheses. But (I would say almost ontologically) we are unable to accept the existence of opposites or to hold together two ends of a chain that are logically exclusive.[64]

"Knowing in a great synthesis" is not the knowing of technique, which is a "knowing that" something is the case, a knowledge of disjunction and exclusion. Something is either true or false for this cast of mind.

"Knowing that," Ellul contends, involves seeking the larger context against which such claim is possible. Knowing that something is the case for technique involves knowing that a sensuously and logically consistent particular has appeared. "Knowing that" is reduced to knowing here and now. Consistency in the here and now is purchased, however, at the price of the suppression of difference, of opposition, of time, all of which are, ironically, the conditions of human knowing. Only God's knowledge, we would suppose, is knowledge of the wholly true outside of time.

All human truth is in opposition to God's truth, and yet such opposition is part of God's plan. God's plan is no technical diagram. The diagram is a consistent image, a representation of reality surrounded by the true, an opposition expressible in the word, which admits of contradiction. God can be no mere abstraction nor any pure particular. God is the concrete universal, to speak in philosophical terms. God is both within and without time, who yet decides to appear in time. Ellul's version of Christianity takes this contradiction seriously and gives him a perspective outside of the landscape of technique.

The Christian God does not appear in a philosophical tract. Ellul's continual disagreement with philosophy stems from his regarding philosophy as tied to Aristotelian logic and to the primacy of the image and the visible.[65] The Christian God is no idea, and Ellul congratulates the death-of-God theologians for putting an end to the notion.[66] The Christian God appears in the persona of a man. "Persona," Ellul reminds us, means mask, a visibility that hides, that reveals and conceals.[67] God's appearance is an is not this reality. He appears in a text that is a nontext, founding a religion that is a nonreligion. Christianity, as Ellul understands it, is an enemy to religion and morality, to fixed documents and doctrines. Ellul writes:

> From the beginning of Genesis we learn a stupefying fact whose implications have seldom been grasped. What Adam and Eve acquire

when they take the fruit is the knowledge of good and evil, that is, knowledge in the sense of the ability to state, as God does, that this is good and that is bad. ... There is no transcendent good and evil as we constantly think when *we* judge that the Old Testament God is wrong when, for example, he orders Abraham to sacrifice his son. To be like God is to be able to declare that this is good and that is bad. This is what Adam and Eve acquired, and this was the cause of the break, for there is absolutely nothing to guarantee that our declaration will correspond to God's. Thus to establish morality is necessarily to do wrong. This does not mean that a mere suppression of morality (current, banal, social, etc.) will restore the good. God himself frees us from morality and places us in the only true ethical situation, that of personal choice, of responsibility, of the invention and imagination that we must exercise if we are to find the concrete form of obedience to our Father. Thus all morality is annulled. The Old Testament commandments and Paul's admonitions are not in any sense morality. On the one side they are the frontier between what brings life and what brings death, on the other side they are examples, metaphors, analogies, or parables that incite us to invention. When Jesus consciously and deliberately breaks the commandments that have become moral, when he makes of transgression a kind of constant conduct that his disciples must adopt, and when Paul brutally asks why we should keep commandments that have become merely human commandments, they are aiming not just at the Jewish law but at all morality.[68]

Ellul is clear: imagination and invention are required as a duty toward God who enters history, masked, in the persona of a man and in the metaphors, analogies, and the parables of the Jewish people. Consistency and analysis, seeking the image, will always lack scope and the proper methodology of no methodology, which only the word and its openness to the contradictory, to the ambiguous and ambivalent, can provide. An appeal to the irrational and to the abandonment of concern and morality are useless responses, although they are understandable in the predicament in which humanity is placed—each individual fending for his or her own solution.

Although morality is annulled, the search for it is required. Humanity, in breaking with God, takes on God's task of stating, of declaring, what is right or what is wrong. We have declared ourselves to be God, Ellul maintains, and with that decision we must remain. With the mention of Abraham, we are reminded of Ellul's chief theological influence, Kierkegaard, and of his notion of the teleological suspension of the ethical. Moral choice involves, ultimately, an abandonment of the conventional and the commonplace, of what often passes for moral worth. Instead, humanity must stand before the Wholly Other, ready to imagine and interpret as well as to reason and understand. Reasoning and understanding break down as they approach the ambiguous, the contradictory, and the paradoxical, though they are at home with the image and the concept. Ellul reminds us continually—in his reading of the Bible in relation to his own life and his own historical social context—that Christian knowing requires a grasp of the image surrounded by the word, of the particular and its relation to matters of ultimate concern. Ellul's reading of the Bible and the technological society reveals the imaginative grasp of humanity's attempts to construct their own absolutes in an absolute fervor, with the absolute reaffirmed in its every denial.

Faith and hope come in relation to questions of God's grace and His judgment and love at the end of time. These are matters of hope and faith. The approach to social and biblical analysis requires more rigor, the rigors of imagination and its appreciation of metaphors and parables and the powers of reason as they move the story, the metaphor, and the narrative to current social concern. Because of humanity's break with God, reality and the knowledge of reality is unremittingly dialectical: a knowing of anything is never constructive of or identical to the thing itself; absolutes are sought but never gained absolutely; appearance and reality—the image and the word—forever face off in opposition. Ellul's dialectic of oppositions that never resolve is located in the immediate world, in the social/historical world, and in the theological world. Beyond these confrontations is a peace that inspires the desire for synthesis, a peace that is only achieved by God in His own time and His own way.

Ellul writes:

The visual world involves stopping; I must freeze and frame things. But the word stops no more than time does. No instant can last, nor can time be suspended. The word is the same. We must move ahead to meet what is advancing toward us: the great eschatological recapitulation of Human history. . . . We live in dialectic what will be the calm of the lotus flower. We live in conflict the life that promises reconciliation. We must not refuse this single possible mode of living: division, tension, and dialectic, as they are expressed and implied by the word. For apart from this mode all that exists is petrification, rigidity, decomposition, and death. We can live this life only to the degree that we know that the reconciliation is already won, and that in Jesus Christ word and sight, proclamation and experience, space and time, are united. We need to know that we will see this reconciliation, that we "will understand fully, even as [we] have been fully understood," that we will see "face to face" what we have heard about (1 Cor. 13:12). Job says: "I had heard of thee by the hearing of the ear, but now my eye sees thee" (Job 42:5). Based on this certainty, without which we have nothing to live for and without which the conflict would be intolerable, we can return to the daily struggle to make the word resound, alone and unshackled. During the space of time that separates us from this final sight, may the word resound for human freedom and for God's truth.

Dedicated to the memory of my friend
Yves Hébert
who died July 12, 1979,
as I was writing this last page.[69]

Here is an expression of Ellul's hope as he contemplates ends—the final end, the end of the dialectic, and the end of a friendship. Ellul considers the universal way very much in concrete terms, his words and his images struggling for unification. His struggle as an individual recapitulates the human condition in fancy and in fact. Fact must be faced. The actual end of the dialectic cannot be known in the here and now; to attempt falsely to stop the clash of forces and worldly powers is to risk petrification and death, and yet the cessation of this strife and chaos is the goal of life. Ellul remains dialectical and ironic to the end.

It is not my concern to treat Ellul's theological thought theologically. It is beyond the scope and interest of this study to trace Ellul's theology—its influence and its implications—beyond its philosophical importance, and even there my interest is narrow. I am interested only in his notions of the image and the word, in his theory of the symbol and its metaphysical and epistemological implications for his philosophy of technology. Ellul's critics, as I have been arguing, typically bypass the philosophical implications of his thought. They ignore his notion of the consciousness of technique that I will work through in the next chapter. They have not understood his theory of the symbol in relation to his notion of social structure. They have, in short, failed to grasp what I call the logic of technique. Ellul's theology, to the extent that it illuminates the logic of technique, is my concern. Technique, I will show in the next chapter, engenders what Hegel would call a bad infinity. Ellul understands this sense of technique, although he does not name it such. He does understand the hubris of technical consciousness as it posits itself as an absolute, as it reduces the infinite to the finite, and as it thereby becomes the sacred. Religion, seemingly destroyed by the powers of reason and understanding, is simply replaced by the technical.

A number of Ellul's theological critics, like his social critics, call for greater consistency and for more clarity, which misses the purpose of Ellul's critique. In *Jacques Ellul: Interpretive Essays*, a collection largely of expository essays, Gene Outka examines what he calls Ellul's ethics of discontinuity. In the main, he charges Ellul with vague and obscure language,[70] with undeveloped claims,[71] and with a "bewildering pastiche" of seemingly contradictory assertions.[72] He begins his essay with the following remarks:

> Of course Ellul's version of discontinuity may appear on examination to be idiosyncratic or unduly obscure at crucial points. Even so, certain basic questions will surface periodically in reference to his work. For example, how are we to understand the insistence that a believer's freedom be wholly unprecedented? Why must the distinction—between worldy and Christian accounts of love, justice, goodness, and religion itself—not be elided in any way? *Can* such a program be executed successfully? Does Ellul himself succeed, or do we find hints of continuity that the program officially forbids?[73]

That is, does Ellul posit a range of consistency that his ethics of discontinuity would seem to forbid? Outka does not seem to consider that continuity and discontinuity are both possible—and even likely—on some level in Ellul's account, which is systematic without being a system, inclusive and yet open-ended.

Outka observes the problems of consistency in Ellul's *To Will and to Do, Violence: Reflections from a Christian Perspective* (1969), and *Ethique de la liberté* (1975) [*The Ethics of Freedom* (1976)]. He outlines the difficulties of Ellul's case: that God places the burden of freedom on the shoulders of humanity as a crushing weight that, paradoxically, seems inescapable; that although God creates *in toto*, humanity is confined to the relative, which is also necessary; that the ethics and morality of the state, while fragmented and failed, are necessary; that the necessary is the great enemy of freedom, while at the same time necessity remains freedom's primary condition; that although all humans are saved, nonetheless a greater moral burden falls on the Christian; that freedom oscillates between the spiritual and material—i.e., as desire exceeds gain—making hope an essential totality; that the Christian, while seeking absolute guidance in revelation, nonetheless must keep a careful eye and ear to the finite, to each ethical problem as it occurs in time and place. On my reading of Ellul, Outka finds a pastiche because he ignores the discontinuity in the continuity of discontinuity that Ellul claims. That is, for Ellul, to seek continuity is to find discontinuity, and to find discontinuity is to seek continuity. His notion of technique is a case in point. Technique becomes a necessity when it is thought to be so; and technique becomes even more of a necessity when humanity thinks that it is beyond technique.

Outka, after all, is right. Ellul requires that the notion of freedom and morality be understood as problematic. Ellul implores the Christian, or any other seeker of transcendent values, to understand ethical and moral questions sociologically and historically. The Christian's duty to God is no mere ringing of bells and burning of incense. The Christian, as all humanity, is found with dirty hands, unavoidable stains, which living in the world in a specific place and at a specific time makes inevitable. But in this, where is the problem? Ellul posits that there is a radical inconsistency between ultimate reality and human understanding and that humanity must live with this inconsistency. Life is not simply a matter of logic. The infinite is, of necessity, beyond the finite. For Ellul to lay out a concrete plan, an ideology, a workable format, as one suspects Outka would wish, would be to usher in a greater inconsistency. It would reduce the infinite to the merely finite.

On another level, if Ellul were required to justify his knowledge that reality is discontinuous with God's infinity, he would turn to the Bible and to his interpretations of sociology and history, which he feels indicate parallel dialectical patterns of human challenge, hubris, and failure, all in the human desire to achieve the Absolute. Ellul, however, is careful to regard his readings of the Bible, history, and sociology as relative and contingent. He is consistent with his view of reality as a balancing act between the consistent and the inconsistent.

Outka is concerned that, in one way, Ellul is too sociological and that, in another way, he is too deterministic.[74] This concern is commonplace among Ellul's critics, who do not examine their own commonplaces. Ellul's task is to find the commonplace—the symbol structures, no matter how decadent—of the modern age, a place that is at once material, intellectual, and rhetorical. All contemporary commonplaces, Ellul urges, issue from the workshop of technique, which is the current absolute, the modern sacred. Ellul writes:

> Although I have deliberately not gone beyond description, the reader may perhaps receive an impression of pessimism. I am neither by nature, nor doctrinally, a pessimist, nor have I pessimistic prejudices. I am concerned only with knowing whether things are so or not. The reader tempted to brand me a pessimist should begin to examine his own conscience, and ask himself what causes him to make such a judgment. For behind this judgment, I believe, will always be found previous metaphysical value judgments, such as: "Man is free"; "Man is lord of creation"; "Man has always overcome challenges" (so why not this one too?); "Man is good,"

or again: "Progress is always positive"; "Man has an eternal soul, and so cannot be put in jeopardy." Those who hold such convictions will say that my description of technological civilization is incorrect and pessimistic. I ask only that the reader place himself on the factual level and address himself to these questions: "Are the facts analyzed here false?" "Is the analysis inaccurate?" "Are the conclusions unwarranted?" "Are there substantial gaps and omissions?" It will not do for him to challenge factual analysis on the basis of his own ethical or metaphysical presuppositions.[75]

Ellul warns that to challenge facts without examining metaphysical presuppositions is unwarranted and unrevealing. He implies that the fact carries with it a metaphysical warrant.

The metaphysics to which Ellul alludes is not an ontological or a classical metaphysics, but a sociocultural metaphysics, a sense of reality given in and by the lived world. It is a sense of reality, for example, embedded in the cliché, in such commonplaces as "Man is free," "Progress is always positive," which Ellul analyzes more completely in his *A Critique of the New Commonplaces*.[76] The commonplace, so often disdained by the intellectual in its overt form, is nonetheless a type of metaphysical ground for culture on a level of presupposition.

Ellul's thought seeks the universal in the concrete, and in this he is deeply philosophical, although he never discourses on a level of pure abstraction. Issues of free will and determinism are placed in a sociohistorical context, without remaining merely on a descriptive level. Ellul describes while he reveals the frame for his description. He works toward the presuppositions that make the description possible. Practicality and measured efficiency are the presumptions the technical mind makes in approaching reality. Is it so or not, Ellul asks? Outka's question regarding Ellul's ethics of discontinuity rings clearly: "Can such a program be executed successfully?" Is it so or not, we need ask.

Arthur F. Holmes, in "Ellul on Natural Law," also from the *Jacques Ellul: Interpretive Essays* volume, objects to what he calls Ellul's "voluntaristic nominalism."[77] Most simply, Holmes finds untenable Ellul's claim that there are no absolute ethical moral values. He rejects Ellul's apparent disjunction between divine will and intellect, between God's commandments and His creation. Holmes thinks it unlikely that God would command humanity to a meaningless, trivial existence, cut off from necessary sustaining values. Holmes states his assumptions clearly: "Consequently, fixed moral standards destroy neither an individual response to God's particular will for him nor the spontaneity of personal freedom.

Rather, both are essential to the guidance of Christian liberty and the knowledge of divine will."[78] In other words, a Christian is unfree and adrift without the guarantee of fixed essential truths. Holmes allows for a notion of "value-potentiality" and "action projects," which open up value to the relative. He states: "Murder, adultery, theft, and every inhumanity can only be considered evil, because life and marriage and property are neither value-neutral nor fully value-actualized. Evil denies to their value-potentialities the actualization sought. Not everything automatically turns out all right in the end."[79] Of course Holmes is right. Times can be tough, and the freedom to seek value in the potential would seem to be a good, even in Ellul's analysis. But Holmes's criticism takes place in the abstract. Property is not a notion to be spun out *a priori*. In early modern Europe hunting quickly became poaching as a result of enclosure acts, as the reaction to property removed from the commons to the side of the wealthy and the powerful. Murder, likewise, cannot fully be defined apart from the society that determines it. A nuclear power plant "accident" that kills countless workers would not be considered murder. Murder, Ellul would urge, is now defined by technique, such that moral judgment is inherent in use. A nuclear power plant accident could never evoke the charge of murder because power plants were not designed to kill. Thus, the moral must always be sought in the relative.

Holmes seemingly sees no other alternatives than these: either one is a Christian believing in timeless ethical, moral, and religious truth, or one is a skeptical, existential, empiricist, embracing a form of scientism. Scientism, Holmes correctly observes, is counter to Ellul's perspective. Holmes locates an essential tension in Ellul's thought: "... without knowledge of the good he still makes universal his value judgments about technological law and society."[80] Holmes, in summary, very much regrets in Ellul's work what he believes to be a disjunction in fact and value. He interprets Ellul's attack on natural law and natural theology as opening the doors to positivism.

Holmes's objections are valuable. It is good to rethink the problems posed by relativism and absolutism, and useful to ponder how God's creation—in the beginning perfect—could become less than perfect. Holmes is correct that Ellul disdains theoretical discussion while such discussion is nonetheless warranted by Ellul's claims. But Holmes ignores the treatment of Ellul's real epistemological concern that appears in Ellul's theory of the symbol. Ellul does not deny value in God's creation; he does not take the natural and cultural worlds as pits of decadence. He does not deny the presence of absolute value to embrace instead the view that all is arbitrary and relative. What Ellul claims, however, is that the cultural world challenges the primacy of the natural world in the creation and perpetuation of its own values, which are then taken to be absolute, and that God permits this. This value is not located simply in the creation but is always held in relation to the human in a process of emergence. The symbol—manifest in cultural institutions, languages, and laws—is the evidence of this emergence. God as the true infinite is also finitely connected. But the infinities humanity projects are either abstract infinities or are merely immanent and finite. The Christian's duty is to remain aware of this and to bear witness to God as the Wholly Other and transcendent, who is at the same time immanent. With this awareness humanity's symbolic constructions remain symbolic in a reach always exceeded by a grasp. The idealist-empiricist dichotomy that concerns Holmes does not concern Ellul, who understands that the human world is never a "given" world. The human world is, after the fall, symbolic and mediated.

Daniel B. Clendenin, in *Theological Method in Jacques Ellul* (1987), sets out to show to what extent Ellul is (a) a theological positivist, holding to the primacy of biblical revelation, (b) a follower of Calvin, Kierkegaard, and Barth, (c) an existentialist, (d) a prophet, and (e) a dialectician.[81] First and foremost, Clendenin urges, Ellul is dialectician in his emphasis on oppositional encounter in reality, epistemology, and theology.[82] Freedom is the positive pole of the dialectic, Clendenin realizes, which he summarizes as follows:

> It is what I would call "synergistic." That is, freedom, for [Ellul] requires the co-operative interaction of two discrete agencies, God and man. According to Ellul, God never acts without man. He loves man, "hence he never regards him as a mere object. He respects man. Hence he never acts on him from outside." It is equally true, though, he goes on to say in this passage, that freedom does not depend only on man. There is an objective reality which is given in Jesus Christ. Elsewhere, Ellul has called this a "twofold movement" of man's obedience and God's free grace.[83]

From my reading of Clendenin's account, God is the reality who keeps humanity from accepting the world, the individual self, and social institutions as abiding necessities. Clendenin sees Ellul's sociological studies of technique, the state, and propaganda as serving this end, although he does not analyze this to any extent. As his title indicates, he is concerned with Ellul's theological methodology. His discussion of "dialectic" relies on the *Encylopedia of Philosophy* article "Dialectic" by Roland Hall and on John Boli-

Bennet's article "The Absolute Dialectics of Jacques Ellul," which is likewise indebted to the *Encylopedia of Philosophy*.[84] Clendenin concludes that Ellul's dialectic stands on its own, although it is related to traditional practitioners such as Zeno, Plato, Aristotle, Fichte, Hegel, and Marx. Ellul departs from the tradition in his emphases on reality, on the Bible, and on a tension between "the eschatological Already and the Not Yet, in the constant renewal of promise and fulfillment."[85] On an existential level, Clendenin further understands, lies Ellul's commitment to individual encounter. The dialectic must be lived; it is no abstract movement, no school of study. The dialectic is human life in its encounter with its own absolutes and ultimate limits.

Clendenin's perspective, however, is not mine. He is correct to remind Ellul's readers of the importance of the dialectic and of Ellul's application of it on three levels: reality, epistemology, and theology. His discussion of Ellul's theological influences in useful. His treatment of the levels of reality and epistemology are wanting, however, and are likely beyond the scope of his study. But, in his overall grasp of the dialectic, certainly in its epistemological dimensions, he gives no real attention to the role that the symbol plays in Ellul's writing. Clendenin also takes Ellul's dialectic as Ellul's methodology. In my view, Ellul's dialectic is not a methodology. This is the point at which Ellul most clearly departs from his philosophic predecessors, for whom thought ought to end in a system, which is closed and complete. For Ellul the system is technique.

In the final analysis, Clendenin believes that he has located an inconsistency in Ellul's work, in what he understands to be Ellul's "universalist" tendency. Clendenin writes:

> The most glaring inconsistency in Ellul's theological dialectic is his nearly unqualified affirmation of the universal salvation of all people beyond history, a doctrine which Ellul says he accepted as a result of his reading of Barth. As we noted in Chapter Two, some dialectics are what Gurvitch described as "ascending" or Taubes called "synthetic." In Hegel, for example, the dialectic ends in the perfect freedom of the state, while in Marx it ends in the classless, stateless society. For Ellul, the dialectic is similarly ascending or synthetic, for it comes to an end in what he has called "the calm of the lotus." The mode of dialectic, with all its tensions, contradictions and divisions, looks forward to a time of complete peace, balance, unity and calm. Thus, Ellul's dialectic is really only penultimate.[86]

Clendenin refers to the passage I cited earlier where Ellul is considering ends—the final page of *The Humiliation of the Word*, the death of his friend, and the *eschaton* promised in the Bible at the end of time. The peace at the end of time is achieved by God and only by God. It offers Ellul a hope for resuming the daily dialectical struggle. Ellul never believes that the dialectic can be final. The calm of the lotus is of the same order as the perfection of God's creation—beyond human comprehension and yet within the here and now as a sense of lack to be overcome. It is not clear that Clendenin understands this. In one sense, for Ellul, the dialectic achieves nothing. It is no method. And yet, in another sense, it is the affirmation of human freedom, which is a condition God grants to humanity. It is this same freedom that humanity continually tries to give up.

Ellul never regards his dialectic as final. This should come as no surprise to Clendenin. The dialectic in the finite and incomplete world takes place against the positings of completeness, in which the object for the human is beheld simultaneously as a presence and a lack. The order of God is absolutely what the human lacks, whereas in the broken world after the Fall, lack and presence are both contingent and relative. In the human world the absolute is only relatively present and relatively absent. Thus the notion of his dialectic "ascending" as if there were progress toward this absolute, makes no sense on Ellul's terms. Of course, it is difficult to imagine how God's creation can be at the same time both complete and permitting of play. This, however, is an essential paradox, which can be revealed in a text and by a symbol but which is incomprehensible to the image and to mere particularity alone. Ellul's words on this matter invite us to recall the tension between the image and the word. Clendenin, on my reading, tries to reduce Ellul's words to the logic of the image, to the conceptually consistent. The calm of the lotus will never posses the degree of "actuality" the desire for it will have as long as God's order remains Wholly Other. God's order of completeness, what Ellul hopes will return with God's judgment and grace, is the calm of the lotus. Completeness is what the human word seeks and is what God's Word more completely portends. The True, *Le Vrai*, is the goal of the word, whereas the Real, *le Réel*, is the focus of the image. This tension is critical, without which the reading of Ellul's texts suffers. Ellul is consistent in understanding that completeness, *le Vrai*, what the word seeks, is of a wholly different order than the actual, *le Réel*, what the image seeks. That is, he is consistent in positing a fundamental inconsistency working between the two orders. Inconsistency is to be understood as a correlation, but this is a notion that dogs the conceptually committed mind.

Only God would know what was at the end of time. God's knowledge is not human knowledge, and yet, somehow, God's transcendent perspective—at least that it is transcendent—is known. The word and the Word are humanity's contacts with transcendence. The text is the key to Ellul's notion of immanence; it is what prevents his understanding of God from being hopelessly alienated and abstract. The text is the reminder that the True can only be the whole and that the whole contains both the image and the word. God as Wholly Other is a philosophical reminder of the provisionality of all accounts, even our accounts of God. Accounts that are more confined to the particular, the image, and, hence, the Real, are more provisional than understandings fueled by the paradoxical, the word, and the True. The mentality of technique places all on the side of the particular, the image and the Real. Technique is a conceptual mentality that distrusts the metaphor and the parable. In this way, Ellul's biblical studies are critical for his social studies. The understanding needed to read the Bible on Ellul's terms is not technical understanding with its obsession with consistency. Needed is an imaginative understanding.

Ellul's specific readings of biblical texts, as I have been saying, are not my concern, although I am interested in them as openings to the powers of imagination, memory, and metaphor to a narrative discourse that overflows the here and the now. Ellul's seemingly paradoxical attacks on morality and ethics truly are paradoxes. The truly moral sense in which all accounts are provisional is corrupted by a technical mentality that reduces the true to the lawful and the orderly. The Bible as a kind of *Urtext* is more paradoxical than most texts. Ellul writes:

> Revelation is an attack on all morality, as is wonderfully shown by the parables of the kingdom of heaven, that of the prodigal son, that of the talents, that of the eleventh-hour laborers, that of the unfaithful steward, and many others. In all the parables the person who serves as an example has not lived a moral life. The one who is rejected is the one who has lived a moral life. ... None of the great categories of revealed truth is relative to morality or can give birth to it; freedom, truth, light, Word, and holiness do not belong at all to the order of morality. What they evoke is a mode of *being*, a model of life that is very free, that involves constant risks, that is constantly renewed. The Christian life is contrary to morality because it is not repetitive.[87]

The conceptual mind seeks the consistent and typically is drawn to the cliché, which as I will show in my last chapter is more than lackluster language. The cliché is instead the embodiment of technique, a chrome-plated notion that the true can and must be written down and then reasoned about with a clear and single purpose. As what is true becomes what can be repeated, the true is reduced to an object. The True is not grasped as a "mode of being," whose reality overflows its embodiment.

The biblical text for Ellul is nondeductive: "We *never* find a single, logically connected truth followed by another truth deduced from it. There is no logic in the biblical revelation. There is no 'either or,' only 'both and.' We find this on every level."[88] The Bible is no adding machine. Truths are not spun out such that consequences follow of necessity from form and by definition. Conclusions are not simply contained in premises, to fall out by virtue of observation, craft, or intimidation.

The Bible, in Ellul's reading, makes a very complicated sense. It is the history of a people as they both encounter and attempt to construct absolutes. It is the history of a specific people and also a repository of general truths that resonate through time. It is a paradigm of paradox. The Hebrew people, the Bible tells Ellul, are the chosen people of God and yet they forever disobey Him and are punished in return. Their punishment is not the result of a *quod erat demonstratum* but is the expression of God's freedom and power. Ellul understands this as an ultimate surd, giving challenge to all aspects of *la technique*, taken as a will to power and force. Outside all elements of plan and purpose or reason and order there is an outer order, a *Wholly Other*, Jaweh, who is both immanent and transcendent. The Bible shows Ellul, at every step and turn, that there is nothing that cannot be opposed, and this even includes any one reading of the Bible or any notion of God. It is this sense of the Bible that provides Ellul with a perspective of irony and distance, which motivates his social critiques.

Norman O. Brown, in "Jacques Ellul: Beyond Geneva and Jerusalem," shows an appreciation for this irony, although he, like most critics, is disturbed by it. Between Ellul's *The Presence of the Kingdom* and *The Politics of God and the Politics of Man*, Brown finds a most difficult shift of intention.[89] In the *Presence*, Brown finds Ellul as a critic of technical society, positing the notion of God in a dimension beyond technique. This notion of God as Wholly Other, Brown feels, is demeaned in the *Politics*, with its more rigidly Calvinistic interpretation of the Bible. Brown is concerned that Ellul is reading the Bible too literally when, in regard to God's taking Israel as the chosen people, he says: "We have to make a decision here, a decision of faith. For my part I confess that Israel is the chosen people."[90]

On my reading, however, Ellul must opt for this view, and not simply because the Bible says it, because taking the Bible literally, for Ellul, is wrong. The Bible ought not to be reduced to formulas or images. Ellul is saying, I feel, that it must be believed because it is absurd but not irrational, because the particular is always grasped in a universal of paradox and contention. Israel is the paradigm of all nations, Ellul holds, in placing the state, human law, and technique above God's judgment. Israel is all nations, a notion that the conceptual mind cannot contain. Israel is clearly no groundless, nonspecific generality: nonetheless it represents what is wrong in all nation-states. And yet God does not wholly condemn it. It continues to resist and abide.

Brown, however, clearly grasps the complexity of Ellul's ultimate challenge to technique in the following remarks:

> In *Presence of the Kingdom* ... Ellul deduces from the unprecedented character of our present crisis the need for what from the theological point of view would amount to a new Pentecostal outpouring of the Holy Spirit, a new prophetic era, with a new language, and a new style of life. Christian intelligence is transformed into poetry: "But the characteristic work of the Christian intellectual is to discover a new language, a language which helps men to understand one another, in spite of publicity, a language which permits men to abandon their despairing solitude, and avoids both rational sterility and subjective emotionalism." Ellul even invokes the spirit of Mallarmé: "The search for the new language which will give a purer meaning to the words of the tribe." The last word in given, as it were not to John Calvin, or Karl Barth, but William Blake. Or Ernesto Cardenal, and *The Gospel in Soletiname*.[91]

Technique, I am arguing, is a discourse and a mentality that demeans the individual and the domain that surrounds. As Brown understands it, Ellul finds the technical to be a place of no place. The *sensus communis*, with its true speech—words seeking the True—is overcome by babble. I want to understand Ellul's words as important challenges to this babble—the clichés of science and technique. I turn now more directly to Ellul's words, which until now have been cloaked in critical misunderstanding. I do not claim, of course, that my interpretation is the true one. I simply hope that I offer a freedom of understanding that goes beyond the logic of technique.

2

Ellul and the Problem of
a Philosophy of Technology

I address three questions in the course of this study: (1) In what sense does Ellul have a philosophy of technology? (2) What does Ellul mean by technology? (3) What is Ellul's answer to the problems posed by technique in the contemporary age? I have already anticipated answers to these questions. I suggest that Ellul understands *la technique* to be a form of intentionality and symbol construction. Technique is a mentality, a system, a way of culture and society, and a way of life. Technique is a metaphysics, a manifestation of the ultimately real, an addiction and an obsession that we wish to do nothing about. Technique is the real confined to the here and now that is expressed in concepts and images. A transcendent reality beyond the contingently present is denied, and an ambiguous language powered by metaphor and myth is consigned to meaninglessness. However, an irony results. The more a noncontingent absolute reality is denied, the more the contingent and the relative become absolutes. This recognition is the central concern of Ellul's theological, historical, and sociological works. Ellul believes in the power and the efficacy of freedom as it is worked out in history, society, and consciousness. For Ellul, freedom becomes the final necessity, which, in spite of being necessary, can be given up. Freedom is the ultimate stake and wager of the modern age.[1] Ellul's master work, *La Technique ou l'enjeu du siècle* (1954), makes this point clearly in its French title. Technique, it is claimed, is the game, the wager, of the century, a sense lost in the English translation, *The Technological Society*, published ten years later. "*Enjeu*" is a word associated with gambling, with games of chance, and here one may think of Pascal's famous wager, which is *un pari*. "*L'enjeu*," Ellul's wager, suggests taking a chance *in a game*—a matter of direct involvement. "*L'Pari*," Pascal's wager, suggests a more intellectual problem. Pascal realizes that he cannot prove the existence of God and that he cannot disprove that existence either. He writes:

"Dieu est, ou il n'est pas." Mais de quel Côté pencherons-nous? La raison n'y peut rien detérminer: il y a un chaos infini qui nous sépare. Il se joue un jeu, à l'extrémité de cette distance infinie, où il arriva croix ou pile. Que gagerez-vous? Par raison, vous ne pouvez faire ni l'un ni l'autre; par raison, vous ne pouvez défendre nul des deux.[2]

There is a game, *un jeu*, being played at the extremity of this infinite distance between possibilities, he says, where either heads or tails will turn up. How will we wager? By reason, we can defend neither position. He concludes: "On me force à parier, et je ne suis pas en liberté," which I translate as: "It forces me to wager, and I am not free."[3] Pascal realizes that he has to choose. Rather than choose the infinity of the natural world—a false infinity—he chooses God—the true infinity.

In the revised preface to the American edition of 1964, Ellul writes:

In my conception, freedom is not an immutable fact, graven in nature and on the heart of man. It is not inherent in man or in society, and it is meaningless to write it into law. The mathematical, physical, biological, sociological, and psychological sciences reveal nothing but necessities and determinisms on all sides. As a matter of fact, reality is itself a combination of determinisms, and freedom consists in overcoming and transcending these determinisms. Freedom is completely without meaning unless it is related to necessity, unless it represents victory over necessity. To say that freedom is graven in the nature of man, is to say that man is free because he obeys his nature, or, to put it another way, because he is conditioned by his nature. This is nonsense. We must not think of the problem in terms of a choice between being determined and being free. We must look at it dialectically, and say that man is indeed determined, but that it is open to him to overcome necessity, and that this *act* is freedom. Freedom is not static but dynamic; not a vested interest, but a prize continually to be won. The moment man stops and resigns himself, he becomes subject to determinism. He is most enslaved when he thinks he is comfortably settled in freedom.[4]

The nature of humanity is to remain importantly problematic after the break with God, who is committed to the freedom that humankind is willing to give up. Human beings, perversely, opt for false infinities, finite infinites, choices against which even God struggles in vain. God is an immanent infinity—directly involved in humanity's stake. This is the theological assumption behind the above remarks that have clear meaning in the secular domain. In the social world, nothing is given in absolute finality, although the human sciences, paradoxically, may have it otherwise. The human sciences discover determinisms on all levels. Certain Darwinians affirm that human nature is but a product of chance selection, while the Lamarckians emphasize genetic inheritance. Behavioral sciences claim the psyche to be a myth, while the gestaltists insist that the psyche is a whole—both mind and body. Historicism wars perpetually with relativism. In some sense, Ellul states, all these determinisms apply. Reality can be defined and worked out mathematically, although mathematicians do not always agree on proper formulation. Matter on the atomic level may indeed be losing energy, while matter on the organic plane may be increasing and moving toward greater complexity. The human sciences offer perspectives, Ellul is saying, that must be taken as provisional, and as partial, they give access to the real—*le Réel*—although these sciences never achieve the true—*le Vrai*. These distinctions and this understanding are critical for Ellul's dialectic.

In the preface, mentioned above, Ellul states that his "purpose is to arouse the reader to an awareness of technological necessity and what it means. It is a call to the sleeper to awake."[5] As mentioned in the last chapter, the reader is to ask, "Is it so, or isn't it?" While Ellul's method is avowedly descriptive, beneath the flow of facts is the form of technical necessity. Technique has coopted the human sciences and modern cultural and social life. This is Ellul's claim. Is it so, or not?

Typically, Ellul's readers do not get to this question. They knee-jerk in response to Ellul's pessimism, to his Christian perspective, and to his failure to offer solutions to technique, which they often find uncomfortingly general and all inclusive. In part, these criticisms are correct: Ellul is no patron of technical progress, which is held ipso facto to be of great good. He is indeed a Christian who believes in the primal efficacy of the Wholly Other. Like Kierkegaard, Ellul believes in a God who is always beyond systemic understanding and inclusion and, thus, in a value always beyond the *hic et nunc*, the here and now. The here and now must be reviewed in each age, Ellul contends, following Kierkegaard's Christianity further. Each age must locate its own demons, its own versions of necessity, to understand more deeply and fully what God is not. Ellul's wager, like Pascal's, involves the finite's relation to infinity. Ellul's wager, however, is no simple intellectual problem, although consciousness is involved. Even to make its wager, consciousness in the grip of technique must come to see itself as existentially embodied in the form of a bad infinity, as a false necessity. When consciousness breaks with technique, technique loses its hold as the all encompassing.

It is wrong to believe that Ellul regards technique as an entity in and of itself, as a thing-in-itself. *La technique* is a mentality within the society; it is the attitude of society toward technique. Ellul writes:

> Of course, if it is wrong to call modern society a mega-machine, we still should not forget that some people greatly desire to make it one. Here we are faced with the dilemma posed so magnificently by Kleist in "The Marionette Theatre." It is absolute alienation which allows mankind to receive grace—or else infinite consciousness. The latter being the attribute of God alone, man must be reduced to a puppet (and society to a machine) in order to find his original innocence and grace. Kleist does not appear to see *how* man will do that. But we know now. Thus, to achieve total liberty, exemption, and independence from natural as well as moral or social constraints, man must *be* in that state of perfect deindividualization, virtually of absence. The puppet acquires grace in absolute unconsciousness. (But for whom?) [6]

Ellul reminds the reader of Kleist's *Über das Marionettentheater* (1808), now likely forgotten, which was, nonetheless, of enormous influence throughout Europe during the 1930s and 1940s. Peter Gay suggests that the "Kleist Crusade" in Weimar Germany showed the intensity, the irrationality, and the confusion of the time, culminating in a blissful death wish.[7] Translated into French in 1937, in the wake of the Nazi rise to power, as *Essai sur les marionettes*, the popularity of this work was most ominous. Ellul in 1977 finds the work instructive.

As I interpret it, Kleist's fictional essay "On the Puppet Theatre" is about human choice, nature, and necessity. Kleist's story begins with a nameless man spending a winter in the town of M____ in 1801. Wishing to learn the key to the dancer's art, he consults the chief dancer of an opera company, the highly successful Mr. C. The key, Mr. C. offers, involves finding a mean between nature and artifice. The dancer must learn that the most beautiful movement, though contrived, must appear natural. This lesson is to be learned most clearly by observing the marionettes in the puppet theatre. This is, of course, a great irony. The puppet is dead wood, held up by strings. Nonetheless, the puppeteer's art involves bringing life to this dead mass. The grace of the puppet is not accomplished by many strings controlling each part of the limb. The puppeteer merely has to control the center of gravity of the limb, which then moves with extraordinary grace, albeit mechanically like a pendulum. The center is controlled by a straight line. When controlled, the limbs describe curves.

On one hand, C. states, the straight line to the center of the limb is very simple. A mere pull upward makes the limb move, a pull that seemingly requires little skill on the part of the manipulator. On the other hand, the line "... is something very mysterious. For it is nothing less than *the path of the dancer's soul.*"[8] The line, while simple outwardly, may be described as "something quite precise, rather like the relation of numbers to their logarithms or asymptotes to their hyperbola."[9] In principle, C. asserts, the art of dance could be entirely moved to the realm of mechanical reproduction.

The narrator learns that the mechanical construction would have a certain advantage over the human dancer. The mechanical construction lacks "affectation," the tendency of the soul to stray from the center of the business at hand.[10] The mechanical puppet also has the advantage of "counter-gravity."[11] The human must be supported by the ground, which the puppet only needs to "touch" on. C. concludes that the human would be no match for the puppet. Only a god could compete against it.

C. then invokes the third chapter of Genesis for further clues to the mystery of mechanical superiority. Consciousness continually gets in the human's way. He cites an example of a youth who is able to imitate a statue's pose only once. Subsequent attempts fail as the youth becomes too self-conscious. C. also narrates his fencing defeat by a bear who, by barely moving his body, was nonetheless able to deflect with his paws all of C.'s most ardent thrusts. Kleist concludes his essay:

> "Now then, my good friend, you are in possession of all you require to understand my point. We see how, in the organic world, as reflection grows darker and weaker, grace emerges ever more radiant and supreme. —But just as two intersecting lines, converging on one side of a point, reappear on the other after their passage through infinity, and just as our image, as we approach a concave mirror, vanishes to infinity only to reappear before our very eyes, so will grace, having likewise traversed the infinite, return to us once more, and so appear most purely in that bodily form that has either no consciousness at all or an infinite one, which is to say, either in the puppet or a god."
>
> "That means," said I, somewhat amused, "that we would have to eat of the tree of knowledge a second time to fall back into the state of innocence."
>
> "Of course," he answered, "and that is the final chapter in the history of the world."[12]

This remarkable story does not so much influence as inform Ellul's work, providing a focus for his entire philosophy of technique. The reference to the third chapter of Genesis is crucial. Ellul, as I mention in my introduction, singles out this chapter to explain the biblical response to technology. Here one learns of humankind's break with God. After this rupture the things in the world are *others* that stand apart. The gaze is alienated. Humanity's responses to the world are symbolic and mediated. The building of cities and the Tower of Babel are exemplars of this response, as is the rise of tyranny. The logics of mechanics and artifice are born. Human constructions become a world, which is part of and yet distant from God's creation. The natural world is a critical *topos* for Ellul; it is always other to the human's work and yet somehow a part—apart and a part. In this world that is both natural and artificial, fragmented and distant from God's original creation, the human becomes *other* to itself. The original unity can never, without God's grace, be achieved again. We may know, but in knowing, we learn that *what* we know is never wholly *that which* we know. Knowledge and the object are bifurcated. No amount of art, or *techné*, can bring them together. Grace becomes a metaphor, referring at once to God's kindness and forgiveness in response to humanity's transgressions and also to the human attempt to achieve grace and perfection in this world. *Techné*, after the break with God, is the basis of humanity's wager.

The word *technology* comes from the Greek word *techné*, which means "art." The word is connected both to making and to knowing. A *techné* is a form of know-how. But it is also a form of knowing that. For Plato, *techné* involves a knowledge of harmony and measure. To know how to build a bed is to know certain proportions and measurements as well as to know the purpose of the bed. The true artisan, on Plato's terms, must ultimately seek the Good and the True, upon which all particularity is dependent; the Good and the True are the ultimate goals of all measure. Clearly, *techné*, in the modern age, means something quite different. Still tied to measure, the goals of the True and the Good are abandoned or profoundly modified. From Ellul's view, the Good and the True have been reduced to the process of measuring. Measuring no longer implies a standard of measure beyond what is contingently determined.

This is the dilemma Pascal understands, the story Kleist relates, and the contingency that Ellul engages: the goal of wisdom is the infinite, which is somehow related to the finite. Technique or *techné*, for Ellul, is no longer a finite bridge for accomplishing finite tasks and is no longer a means for extending human consciousness into a world as *other*. Technique, as a form of consciousness, has become the world, paradoxically, of which technique is no longer conscious.

Wisdom, Kleist suggests, involves losing consciousness and artifice, paradoxically, by becoming artifice, which he prophetically describes in mathematical and geometric terms. Kleist's insight is exactly the metaphor that fits the reality Ellul describes. The technical phenomenon is the technical operation rationalized and objectified; it is the object purified by technical reason, which thrusts the knower back into the known that the knower has made. The knower has made the artificial, however, and is thereby separated from God's domain. We only attempt to return to the Garden and to the problem of Paradise, of God's grace or human grace; but the return cannot be effected: the technical phenomenon has become the mechanical puppet to which the puppeteer is tied.

The Consciousness of Technique

The history of the philosophy of technology has yet to be written. German philosopher Ernst Kapp coined the phrase "Philosophie der Technik" in his 1977 work, *Grundlinien einer Philosophie der Technik*.[13] Kapp was a neo-Hegelian, intent upon seeing Hegel's dialectic applied. He migrated to the central Texas hill country and became a farmer, inventor, founder of the philosophy of hydrotherapy (political aqua-geography was the central principle for his phenomenology of mind), and a theory of technology. Technology is the extension of human organs for Kapp: tools are extensions of the arms and the legs; the railroad is an extension of the circulatory system; and the telegraph is an extension of the nervous system.[14] Although a materialist, his Hegelian training teaches him the intimate connection between mind and nature, which he believed had to be protected from humanity's technological advance: "... everything is mediated through everything, law, religion, morality, art and sciences, one through the other ... into a multimembered organism of true humanity."[15] Technology can upset this balance, he realizes, producing a mechanical and nonorganistic state. Kapp writes: "... to the machine-man the state is also a machine, until it has destroyed him. ... Bureaucracy represents the misled and unhampered machine-side of the states. ... Every attack on bureaucracy from below strengthens and irritates it even more; for it is irritable, violent, irascible, sensitive, comparable to the weakened nervous system. ..."[16] Clearly, for Kapp, the philosophy of technology is the study of artifacts as they are *intended* in the world.

I link the origin of the notion of a philosophy of technology with the understanding of technology as a form of intention. Friedrich Dessauer, in his *Philosophie der Technik* of 1927, marks a further crucial development of this notion.[17] Dessauer was a research engineer, a pioneer in the development of X-ray therapy, and a Christian social democrat opposed to Nazism. He was concerned, in the above work, to extend Kantian criticism into what I would call a fourth critique.

Dessauer sees his advance on Kant in clear terms. The *Kritik der reinen Vernunft* (1788) [*Critique of Pure Reason*] examines the a priori conditions of experience, which are limited to the categorization of phenomena. The noumenal realm of the thing-in-itself is unavailable to scientific experience. In the *Kritik der Urteilskraft* (1790) [*Critique of Practical Reason*] the moral law is considered as transcendental to all phenomenal experience and is thus not subject to the causal and categorical world of science. The moral law is a law unto itself. In the *Critique of Judgment* the transcendental is approached from the side of the Beautiful, which is likewise beyond the realm of science. The thing-in-itself is unavailable—being either behind or above the realms of experience—to any of the three critiques. Dessauer thus posits the need of a fourth critique.

Dessauer writes:

> Accordingly, we encounter the thing-in-itself in the fourth realm in a special manner; it does not remain beyond perception as in the domain of natural experience. But the encounter is also constituted differently than in the second Kantian realm; it is more closely associated with the activity of our intellect. It is invention, more generally technology as act: a struggle to make the categories conform to the thing-in-itself.[18]

Technology is a form of knowing and making at once, in which that thing-in-itself is approached not as behind or above experience but as that which is invented, as that which in part conforms to natural law and as that which works. The technological thing-in-itself results as nature is overcome and transformed but yet is the result of an *inner working out* and fulfillment [*Erfüllung*] between ends and means.[19]

Of the process of invention, Dessauer writes:

> The work of the inventor consists of conceptualizing, selecting, combining, and ordering what is possible according to the laws of nature. This inner working out which precedes the external has a twofold characteristic: the participation of the subconscious in the inventing subject; and that encounter with an external power which demands and obtains complete subjugation, so that the way to the solution is experienced as the fitting of one's own imagination to this power.[20]

Technical invention requires a process of conceptualizing, selecting, combining, and ordering. Then the external object and its power is confronted, demanding complete subjugation. The result is an *inner working out* and fulfillment, an *Erfüllung*. The external object is met, overcome, conceptualized, and ordered. Compliance obtains.

Dessauer is clear that "... *the ordering of means is alien to nature*" and that the object of the imagination is tied to effecting a proper solution.[21] The process of technical order, if it is to work, must move outward toward the ideal object, at first asymptotically, as that which cannot be achieved. During this process, inventions seem quite vast and varied, marked by extraordinary diversity. But then, unlike mere abstract Platonic ideals, the invisible becomes visible as the object-that-works, *the third object*. With this third object diversity is canceled as the best approach to the problem is achieved. The third object is neither a natural object nor an object imagined, neither objective nor subjective, but objective and subjective at once. Dessauer writes:

> The airplane as thing-in-itself lies fixed in the absolute idea and comes into the empirical world as a new, autonomous essence when the inventor's subjective idea has sufficiently approached the being-such of the thing in the absolute idea. Then, for the first time, the thing works. In this fashion the inventor, in the course of an inner, experimental development, confronts the essence, the thing-in-itself, while seeking to "attain" it by modifying his own seeing and thinking. This takes place not only in the power of judgment, but also in scientific method. The thing-in-itself is thereby discovered, so to speak, in the (Platonic) idea. Then—and this is a powerful advantage—it is possible to verify to a certain extent whether the thing-in-itself or essence, has been captured in the technical object. If it has, then the thing works. Otherwise, it does not.[22]

The true is the made and the made is the true, all conceptually and experimentally determined. The pragmatic theory of truth is stood on its head: the true works not because it is true, but it is only true because it works and because it is made.

The great German philosopher Ernst Cassirer, deeply influenced by both Kant and Hegel, follows Kapp and Dessauer in understanding technology as a specific direction of human intentionality. Technology is no mere methodology, nor is it a collection of artifacts. But is a way of knowing, a symbolic form.

Cassirer founds the philosophy of culture, his major contribution to philosophy, on the insight that the human being is an *animal symbolicum*.[23] The world of immediacy—the mere animal world—is lost with the developments of myth, language, and science, the major symbolic forms that constitute the basis of human thought and culture. Wherever there is humanity there is myth, language, and science. Each symbolic form, however, reveals a special direction of human *Geist*, spirit. In myth, the world appears as a projection of an emotionally charged consciousness, full of gods, forces, and powers. The world, the cosmos, and the individual are intimately conjoined. The world of myth, first and foremost, exhibits the *Ausdrucksfunktion*, the expressive function, of consciousness. In language, the world stands apart as objects waiting to be named. Here the *Darstellungsfunktion*, the representative function, of consciousness prevails: the world is taken to be full of objects independent of consciousness. In science, the *Bedeutungsfunktion*, the conceptual function, takes over. The world is then understood in relation to conceptual activity. The true is the known and the known involves the cognitive faculties. Knowing is no simple act of perception but involves high-level powers of abstraction and synthesis.

In his three-volume work, *Die Philosophie der symbolischen Formen* (*The Philosophy of Symbolic Forms*), published from 1923 to 1929, Cassirer devotes one volume to each of the three symbolic forms: volume 1, *Die Sprache* (*Language*); volume 2, *Das mythsche Denken (Mythical Thought*); and volume 3, *Die Phänomenologie der Erkenntnis* (*Phenomenology of Knowledge*).[24] While there is a diachronic level of development suggested, with myth as the most primitive and basic form, and science the most advanced development of spirit; Cassirer, nevertheless, insists that all forms are everywhere present, at least nascently, Each form contains three stages—the mimetic, the analogic, and the symbolic.[24] A dialectical relationship between subject and object defines each stage. In the mimetic stage, the symbol and the symbolized express an identity. The primitive tribesman does not disturb the ground wantonly as the ground *is* his mother. In the mimetic stage, myths and symbols express these identities. The mimetic stage, however, passes over to the analogical as the force between the subject and the object is broken. The primitive learns that the earth is not really his mother, but that "mother" is what the earth can be called. The symbolic stage enters when consciousness learns that there is bireciprocal relation between all symbols and their referents, such that all things are potentially symbols and all symbols are potentially referents. The analogical stage thus corresponds most clearly to the symbolic form of language, and the symbolic stage most adequately represents the symbolic form of science. In this way, each symbolic form participates in the others. The symbolic stage of myth, for example, will lead to science, because science is already there implicitly. It is well known that alchemy is the basis of chemistry, both historically and phenomenologically.

At no time is there no language, no science, and no myth, although in a certain cultural social epoch, one form may predominate over the others. Cassirer was very much concerned with the force of myth as evidenced in Nazi Germany. In 1946, in *The Myth of the State*, he wrote:

> The new political myths do not grow up freely; they are not the wild fruits of an exuberant imagination. They are artificial things fabricated by very skillful and cunning artisans. It has been reserved for the twentieth century, our own great technical age, to develop a new technique of myth. Henceforth myths can be manufactured in the same sense and according to the same methods as any other modern weapons—as machine guns or airplanes.[25]

The myths of German supremacy, of the evil of the Jews, of the sacredness of Germany are not the spontaneous outpourings of the German imagination, Cassirer notes. They have been manufactured; they are the products of *Technik*. The expressive function of consciousness is not at work in these myths but neither is the conceptual mode directly in play. These modern myths, the products of technique, are somehow both rational and irrational at once.

Cassirer regards the number of symbolic forms as open-ended. By the 1944 publication of *An Essay on Man* he has added religion, art, and history. In the preface to *Das mythsche Denken*, volume 2 of *Die Philosophie der symbolischen Formen*, he indicates the possibility of ethics, law, and technology as symbolic forms.[26] Cassirer never develops these symbolic forms as he does myth, language, and science. He does write profoundly about technology, however. In the second volume on mythical thought, Cassirer states:

> For as soon as man seeks to influence things not by mere image magic or name magic but through implements, he has undergone an inner crisis— even if, for the present, this influence still operates through the customary channels of magic. The omnipotence of the mere desire is ended: action is now subject to certain objective conditions from which it cannot deviate. It is in the differentiation of these conditions that the outward world first takes on a determinate existence and articulation. Originally the world consists for him solely of what in some way touches his desire and his action. But now that a barrier is erected between the inward and outward worlds, a barrier that prevents any immediate leap from the sensory urge to its fulfillment, now that more and more intermediary steps are interpolated between the drive and its goal, a true distance

between subject and object is for the first time achieved. Man now differentiates a set sphere of objects which are designated precisely by the fact that they have a content peculiar to themselves, by which they resist man's immediate desire. It is the consciousness of the means indispensable for the attainment of a certain purpose that first teaches man to apprehened "inner" and "outward" as links in a *chain of causality* and to assign to each of them its own inalienable place within this chain—and from this consciousness gradually grows the empirical concrete intuition of a material world with objective attributes and states.[27]

With the use of implements, the first stage of technical development, the differentiation between "inner" and "outer," is objectified, literally. Desire is focused on an object that resists man's immediate desire. Desire is now linked to a "causal chain." Cassirer acknowledges Kapp's *Philosophie der Technik* and its notion of "organ projection."[28] Cassirer appreciates that this idea contains more than the idea of "technical mastery" and the "knowledge of nature."[29] A symbolic form, for Cassirer, is a type of knowing and being-in-the-world: perceptive, cognitive, and alive. Technique, he understands, is both a mode of apprehension and a mode of being; the artifactual side of technique has secondary importance.

In the 1930 essay "*Form und Technik*" Cassirer sketches out the mimetic, analogical, and symbolic stages of technique, which begin in magic, move to tool using, and culminate in scientific-technical constructions, wherein the world of nature is left far behind.[30] Basically, the essay is optimistic. For Cassirer, movement toward the conceptual, toward the scientific, always bodes well. But Cassirer is also a philosopher of harmony, believing in the virtue of balance, which, in the domain of symbolic forms, is easily disturbed. Cassirer continually acknowledges the importance of the whole of symbolic activity.

In *Zur Logic der Kulturwissenschaften* (1942) [*The Logic of the Humanities* (1961)] Cassirer notes that language—the basis of all symbolic forms—moves in a twofold way: (1) outwardly toward the object, in an indicative gesture producing nature concepts; and (2) inwardly toward the subject, in an expressive gesture exhibiting culture concepts.[31] From the indicative gesture grow the natural sciences (*Naturwissenschaften*), and from the expressive gesture come the humanities (*Kulturwissenschaften*). Culture as a totality requires both directions, a necessary dialectical tension. Each symbolic form reveals this twofold tendency. Recall how the implement serves to preserve the distinction between "inner" and "outer," which perhaps fires Cassirer's optimism regarding *Technik* as an expression of *Geist*, spirit. But Cassirer later feels forboding with the realization that *Technik* and myth have joined forces in the modern state.[32] The distinction between the outer and inner collapses. The rationality of technique becomes irrational, and the harmony of tension in culture turns to dissonance.

Cassirer ends *An Essay on Man* with a reference to Heraclitus: "The dissonant is in harmony with itself; the contraries are not mutually exclusive, but interdependent: 'harmony in contrariety, as in the case of the bow and the lyre.' "[33] The images of music and war, the humanities and technique, are haunting.

Humanity comes to know itself through culture, through the process of symbolization. This understanding harkens back to Pope's *Essay on Man*, whose title Cassirer borrowed, and to its conclusion that the proper study of mankind is man. Technology, Cassirer claimed in his 1930 essay "Form und Technik," may contribute to this self-understanding, a perception pioneered by Ernst Kapp. But Cassirer is also aware of *Technik*'s alienating capacity, of its stirring of desire and of its creation of an "inner crisis." The true is the whole, Cassirer believes, and there are no shortcuts to this totality, this infinity, this knowing of tension in symbolic constructs expressing both identity and difference. Cassirer writes:

> Here philosophical thinking must not content itself with a premature solution; there is nothing it can do but resolutely take this very contradiction upon itself [the dialectical opposition between inner and outer]. The paradise of immediacy is closed to it: it must—to quote a phrase from Kleist's article "On the Marionette Theatre"—". . . journey round the world and see whether [the world] may not be open somewhere in back." But this "journey round the world" must really embrace the whole of the *globus intellectualis*: we must seek not to determine the nature of the theoretical form through any one of its particular achievements, but rather to keep its total potentialities constantly in mind. And since any attempt simply to transcend the field of form is doomed to failure, this field should not be touched upon here and there but traveled from end to end. If thought cannot directly apprehend the infinite, it should at least explore the finite in all directions.[34]

The image of Kleist's marionette theater is invoked to recall the loss of immediacy suffered in the human world of culture—a symbolic world of things requiring names. Symbol creation is not simply an intellectual activity; it also has ethical and moral dimensions, a vital existential concern, that requires that symbolic energies not be blocked and that symbolic construction remain open-ended. Cassirer suggests that the cultural life of a society and of an individual are at stake in this activity. There is a moral dimension to cultural life that entails the embrace of an infinity that ever exceeds spirit's grasp and that is only revealed in *Geist*'s extension. Without the symbolic dimension—the designation of a thing that refuses to be fully and finally named—the infinite is closed and silent.

Ellul's theories of technology and culture have never been placed in this German philosophy of culture tradition. Although Hegel appears from time to time in Ellul's work—and then in relation to the importance of the dialectic—Ellul, on the one hand, would very much shy away from this German tradition that emphasizes the importance of the concept, the necessity of system, and the closure of analysis. On the other hand, Ellul is very much in this tradition in his taking technology as a form of intention, in his concern for the symbol, and in the importance he ascribes to the infinite. Ellul understands humanity's wager as tempting a loss of consciousness and symbolic display and as rejecting a false infinity for a true infinity. Ellul writes:

> The very important analyses of R. J. Lifton on the psychology of modern man exactly confirm these perspectives as do other studies by Erikson, Cassirer, and Boulding. He shows that modern man is one who changes. One cannot speak of his character or his personality because it no longer has any fixity or permanence. There is no longer a continuity of the person, which supposes a stable and intact relation between man, his symbols, and his institutions: this stability no longer exists. There is nothing but endless searches to find oneself. In this search we are all plunged into the same uncertainty, constituting a "universal mode of the becoming-self," a function of the structures of modern society. And Lifton characterizes this becoming self according to the following traits: the universal feeling, widely held, of "historical dislocation" provoked by the rupture from the relations with the symbols of a cultural tradition which nourish life. In the second place, the invasion of images, resulting from the extraordinary flood of neo-modern cultural influences discharged from the mass media, submerge the individual with badly-digested nourishment. Finally, the personality explodes between, on the one hand, a multiplicity of ideas, of metaphysics, of values, and, on the other hand, a chaos of unconnected and incoherent facts.[35]

Ellul is clear: the human being's sense of self, sense of historical location, and understanding of meaningful action are at stake in symbol creation. Like Cassirer, Ellul understands the human condition as centered on symbolic activity. Ellul understands that technique is a form of symbol construction. Further, as I will show, Ellul, like Cassirer, understands that a return to myth is an ominous inevitability. The free symbolizing consciousness risks dissolution and uncertainty as it separates from the object. Individual and cultural identity are at stake. Unlike Cassirer, however, Ellul locates the conditions of the wager in symbolic construction bracketed by God's infinity. This challenges the adequacy of all finite delineation and that reveals that All is not symbolic, even though all human knowing is expressed in symbolic terms. Cassirer, though, with Ellul, values the open-ended and disagrees with a Hegelian march toward the Absolute, unless that Absolute be understood as perpetually provisional. Cassirer, however, does not put this open-endedness in theological terms, which I, too, would like to avoid. As I stated earlier, I see Ellul's God in philosophical terms as the insistence upon the dimension that surrounds, upon that reality which always eludes complete confirmation. I am bringing Ellul together with this tradition of a *Philosophie der Technik* as a response to those critics of Ellul who completely avoid the consideration of technology as intention and who ignore the importance for Ellul of a symbolic dimension to technological activity.

There are other reasons for relating Ellul to the *Philosophie der Technik* tradition, to which his thought contributes a valuable counterpoint. Kapp understands technology as an organ projection, as an extension of the human body and will. Dessauer believes that *Technik* provides an entrance to the thing-in-itself by virtue of invention and practice. Cassirer holds out for *Technik* the possibility of furthering conceptual understanding. Kapp does fear the advent of the environmentally irresponsible "machine man"; Dessauer is aware of *Technik*'s alienating capacity; and Cassirer is wary of the couplings of myth and *Technik*. But, for all of these thinkers, *Technik* is joined to the concept, to an extension of human will, desire, and, at least in part, intelligence. None of these thinkers explores the possibility of *Technik* becoming intelligence itself, desire itself, will itself. None consider *Technik* as positing something wholly new, although Dessauer comes close when he moves *Technik* to the explicitly metaphysical, where *Technik* becomes the third object, a thing-in-itself.

Ellul, as I will show, regards the technical phenomenon—*le phénomènon technique*—as a wholly new moment in cultural social history, one that involves restructuring the relation of consciousness to the object. Technique is no mere extension of consciousness, in Ellul's understanding of it. The technical phenomenon, unlike Dessauer's third object, does not bring humanity closer to the thing-in-itself, although the technical artifact may have the character of the pure object for technical consciousness. Inasmuch as *La Technique* is the center of a new sacred, a new mythology, technique takes on a metaphysical character, which is the reason why Ellul mentions a return to metaphysics as stated above. *Le Phénomènon technique* heralds a new orientation of humanity to history and to science, which for Ellul become the major new mythologies justifying technique as the sacred. Science embodies an appeal to supreme rationality—one that masquerades as measuring—and history furthers the belief in progress and advance, helping the submyths of youth, novelty, and creativity to prosper.

Die Philosophie der Technik has an optimism not found in Ellul's work, which opts for the possibility of failure and tragedy, which holds out no hope for human rationality per se. Ellul, however, is no simple pessimist. He hopes for a return of a dialectical consciousness, the efficacy of which Cassirer never fully doubts; Ellul hopes for the intervention of the Wholly Other, who may change the terms of the wager; finally, Ellul tirelessly maps the phenomenon of *la technique* as a social, cultural, philosophical, theological force.

Although the philosophy of technology is yet to be written, Carl Mitcham has broken some important ground in his "What Is the Philosophy of Technology?"[36] He notes two clear traditions: a philosophy of technology that is technological philosophy, and a philosophy of technology that is humanistic in intention. Mitcham states:

> Technological philosophy emphasizes an analysis of the nature of technology itself—its concepts, its methodological procedures, its cognitive structures, and objective manifestations. It proceeds to interpret the larger world in predominantly technological terms. It thus may reasonably be said to increase or extend technological consciousness.[37]

This tendency would run counter to what I have termed the *Philosophie der Technik* tradition. Mitcham cites American mathematics teacher Timothy Walker's 1832 rebuttal of Thomas Carlyle's criticism of mechanistic thought and application in *Signs of the Times* as a telling example of technological philosophy. Walker claimed in "Defense of Mechanical Philosophy" that technology is man's great hope for freeing himself from the necessities of the natural world to which he is enslaved.[38] Many of Ellul's critics make similar claims.

Humanistic philosophy of technology, by contrast, searches for "... insight into the meaning of technology—its relationships to the human: art and literature, ethics and politics, religion. It thus seeks to reinforce an awareness of the non-technological."[39] It is clear that Ellul and the *Philosophie der Technik* tradition are on this side. I am here reminded of Cassirer's notion of the bidirectionality of human spirit: on the one side, toward the world as a collection of things; and on the other side, toward the world as an alter-body, as an expression of and/or for, human consciousness. From my view, it is important that this bidirectionality be maintained, which is the reason I wish to approach Ellul from this side.

Steven L. Goldman has also broken important ground in his "The Techne of Philosophy and the Philosophy of Technology."[40] Goldman understands the absurdity of denying technical intention that ". . . flies in the face of the obvious fact that artifacts always embody specifically intended ends of which they are means."[41] Further, he asks: "Why do we prefer this sort of action [technical] to be value-free when we ordinarily place so high a value on freedom of choice in action, which implies the freedom to exercise values in acting? With what in human experience is this flight from freedom and values cognate and with what outside the realm of technological action does it correspond?"[42] One might reply: if techniques are value neutral, they do not have to be assessed, at which point they achieve what Ellul would call the status of necessity.

Goldman is right in asking that philosophy of technology address traditional philosophical questions philosophically, that for example, philosophy should consider technology in relation to the mind/body problem, in relation to metaphysical questions. It will not do for a philosopher merely to give his opinion about the use of hydroelectric dams and for this to pass as philosophy of technology.

I consider Ellul as a philosopher of technology in the humanistic tradition, as a thinker who understands technology to be a form of intention for which the traditional mind-body relationship is altered; this alteration is evident as the human attempts to use both tools and language. The intentionality of *la technique* produces the technical phénomènon—*le phénomènon technique*—which is artifact, mentality, and symbol construction. To these concerns I now turn.

3

Ellul and the Consciousness of Technique

In Ellul's understanding, technology is neither neutral nor is the human's perspective on reality impermeable or unalterable. Instead, humanity's perspective on and vision of reality constitute a world made of symbols. Technology is a perspective, a mentality, a form of intentionality, embodied in the modern world and taking clear shape after 1750. Ellul states:

> The term *technique* [*la technique*] as I use it, does not mean machines, technology, or this or that procedure for attaining an end. In our technological society, *technique* is the *totality of methods rationally arrived at and having absolute efficiency* (for a given stage of development) in *every* field of human activity. Its characteristics are new; the technique of the present has no common measure with that of the past.[1]

Ellul's concept of technique does not mean a specific application of technology but refers to the concept of technology in its most general sense. In French, as in English, "technique" and "technology" may refer to "means" and "discourse," respectively. That is, *la technique*, an abstract noun, refers to the ensemble of procedures and methods of an activity. *La technologie* refers to the science or to the study of those procedures. Ellul's study of *la technique* is more a study of discourse than of procedures, although his central point is that technique-technology has now become a discourse, a language, and a world. Thus, by technique he means a totality stretching the bounds of ordinary language, perhaps one of the reasons he has taken to capitalizing it, showing that *technique* has indeed become something special. It should be noted that he is not consistent in this. In *La Technique* it is never capitalized, while in *Le Système Technicien* it is sporadically capitalized. I do not offer this as a criticism. His point should be clear, orthography aside. For the purposes of this study, by "technology" or "technique" I will mean what Ellul means above by *la technique*.

With some attention, Ellul's point is clear. Technique refers to the totality of methods, constructed with and by reason, that aim at absolute efficiency as a goal. Ellul does not claim that technique is efficient but only that efficiency is its *aim*. The search for absolute efficiency is a reaching for totality, which is also an aim, an intention, part of what I will discuss later in chapter 5 as the logic of technique. *Reason* is a *modus operandi*. Throughout *The Technological Society* Ellul writes of a "technical intention" (*d'une intention technique*), a "technical consciousness" (*la conscience technique*), and a "technical state of mind" (*l'état d'esprit technicien*).[2] It is incredible that the majority of his readers miss this. The claims by Ferkiss, Florman, and Toffler that technique can be altered miss this understanding—that technique has become a form of intention. To control technique would therefore require an intention that could go beyond it, to another level of objectivity, which is clearly a more formidable task than redesigning artifacts.

The technical object, *le phénomènon technique*, is far from neutral in that it embodies this intention from which humanity is unable to disengage. In the primitive world of the tool, employing what Ellul calls the technical operation (*l'operation technique*), objects in the natural world are worked upon and manipulated by tools that truly function as means.[3] That is, these objects are independent of the tool-user's grasp. In the technical operation—what all technical processes have in common—from computer programming to canoe building, the body serves as a mediator and the tool is the body's extension. With the transformation of the tool into a technical phenomenon, such objectivity is lost.[4]

Unlike the ancient artifact produced by a technical operation, the technical phenomenon is cut off from the fundamentals of normal, communal life—it is an object that is neither an extension of a cultural tradition nor the bodily wisdom of its maker. Instead, it is the product of the abstractive powers of reason and the understanding, a product of science. The atomic bomb is such a technical phenomenon, in all respects beyond the aim and purpose of its makers, but possible only as a result of scientific calculation. It was impossible not to use it, because it was the most efficient way to win the war, although "scientific opinion" was divided as to whether or not the world would be destroyed as a result of its use. Although produced by calculation, its use was governed by another force. The horror sustained by world opinion regarding its use still has not subsided. For many this act was a violation of all tradition and of any sense of human decency.

For the maker of the Samurai sword, in the world of the tool and the pretechnological, efficiency is beneath beauty and design, beneath the spontaneous intuitions and traditional sensitivities of its maker, which leave indelible marks in the temper and sharpening patterns of the blade.[5] Mathematical calculation does not enter in. The use of the sword is confined to the artist who wields it, to the artist's abilities and sensibilities, and to those who would get in its way. With the technical phenomenon, a whole system is involved. In modern warfare, all citizens join the military, as military functions and emplacements are inseparable from all areas of modern life. The distinction in atomic warfare between the civilian and the military becomes meaningless. Further, in the production of technical phenomena, all objects and processes must conform to a mathematics-like and efficiency-oriented methodology. Here reason produces objects from which the rational cannot separate. *Le phénomènon technique*, infinitely fascinating, is the amalgam of the goals for rationality, methodology, and efficiency. The technical phenomenon becomes the absolutely real, the aura of that which must, of necessity, be.

The distinction between the technical phenomenon and the technical operation is dialectical and presents an opposition basic to Ellul's thought. The technical operation refers to an operation on an object, given as an *other*, that resists the grasp, a point of both experience and logic. The tree returns the ax that is wielded against it; the clay-hard earth repels the hoe, sending shocks and vibrations a full arm's length. The intention to fell the tree or to turn the ground is adjusted in relation to the object against which it works and in relation to the society in which it works.

In the technical operation, the world is experienced as the body experiences it—muscle, skin, and bone against the resistant object. The basis of the technical operation is epistemological and lies in the experience of the object as a *not-me* , as that which stands apart and against the I that experiences it. The object is experienced as an other, *l'autre.* The object has an integrity of its own and appears before the subject, for which it is an object, as a *that-which-I-have-not-made*. Ellul understands the natural object as a dialectical *other* given in the technical operation. Inasmuch as it has a reality apart from the subject, the natural object returns the subject back to itself. The natural object encountered in tool use reminds the user of abundant limitations—more practice, more wisdom, more strength, more help, are often the lessons learned by an afternoon with an ax and an oak tree. The experience of the *otherness* of the object is canceled with the introduction of the technical phenomenon. Ellul's claim that technical consciousness is not dialectical begins here.

Ellul maintains that consciousness—after the Fall—is inherently dialectical, divided between an awareness and a that-of-which-it-is-aware. The subject—awareness—and the object are not identities. The object as *other* exceeds the grasp. Technique, however, proceeds as if that separation were negated; technique *is* that separation negated. The otherness of the object fades as technical reason intervenes to survey an operation and find the "one best way" of accomplishment according to a mathematically exact method having efficiency as an absolute. The technical phenomenon—reason objectified—is no other to technical consciousness, merely another moment of that awareness to itself.

In the world of the technical operation, moving huge amounts of stone requires suitable strength or the help of others, or both, the conviction that the stones do not mind being moved, and a conviction that the goal is worthy of the task. Only important reasons would motivate pretechnological tool-using people to clear a quarry of stone. But with the advent of the bulldozer, the resistance of the object, the amount of cooperation and concern, and the importance of the goal fall away as the actual is consumed by technical possibility. The bulldozer is the mentality that pushes away all that would resist. Astride this machine, the resistance of the object is transformed into the vibrations and the noise of the machine itself; the objections of onlookers would likely not be heard over this din—the onlookers themselves are likely mesmerized in the presence of such power; and the goal becomes technique itself, revealing the law of monism [*unicité*], which states that that which can be done will be done. The bulldozer in this example is both reality and metaphor. The silent operations of the computer are no less compelling. The key is understanding that the technical phenomenon is reason's commitment to itself.

Inasmuch as technique is a desire to objectify reason, technique is ". . . a means of apprehending reality, of action on the world, which allows us to neglect all individual differences, all subjectivity. . . . Today man lives by virtue of his participation in a truth become objective. Technique is no more than a neutral bridge between reality and the abstract man."[6] Technical logic is nondialectical. Individual subjectivity and individual difference are both abrogated and obscured as the objects for which they are subjects are transformed and turned into abstractions, into technical phenomena. With the technical phenomenon, the worker is the machine's limitation. The worker merely hangs from the device.

The natural object as *other* remains problematic. The body is the human's most intimate experience of that otherness, which technique continually tries to transform. Technique is a constant reminder that the human body cannot run fast enough, smoothly enough, or long enough and that it is necessary to revise standards of industrial production to accommodate the productive capacity of the machines. The embodied individual worker presents too many variables. The body makes one a different size from others, hampering the efficiency of the clothing industry. The body is unpredictable, becoming ill and ultimately dying. The body is, in short, filthy and finite, apt to lead the technical mind from its true and appointed rounds, apt to provoke a drift to an erotic daydream in the middle of an important calculation. The individual mind, embodied, often tacks an erratic course, likely to check in at a trout steam during a board meeting or to seek an arboreal bliss while talking to a valued customer about the relative merits of Japanese versus German transistors. The value of the body for technique is revealed in technique's disregard for the body, a disregard the first American astronaut, Alan Shepard, Jr., felt after four hours on the launch pad when he discovered there were no provisions for urination.

The calculator and the computer are ultimate technical phenomena, coopting the individual embodied human mind, examples *par excellence* of the triumph of technical logic, a nondialectical logic. Of the computer, Ellul writes: "The computer is fundamentally nondialectical, it is based on the exclusive principle of noncontradiction. With the binary system, a choice must be made, it is constantly *yes* or *no*. One cannot launch into a thinking that is evolutive and embraces opposites."[7] According to the principle of noncontradiction, something cannot be both *A* and *not A* at the same time. This invokes one of the so-called laws of thought, first enunciated by Aristotle. The law of noncontradiction leads inexorably to the law of identity, where *A* is identical to *A*—to itself—and to the law of the exluded middle, where *A* is either *A* or *not A*. Within this Aristotelian tradition, clearly the basis of computer logic, to think is to affirm these laws or principles.

And yet, from another direction, *A* is always what it is *and* what it is not. The object before one always exceeds one's reach and one's understanding. For human awareness, the body is the weight, the resistance, the guarantee of this physical and mental distance. Because one is here and the object is there, thought and object are not whole. The body is a key finite limitation. Temporal awareness is another limitation. When *A* is *A* is pronounced or thought, one *A* comes before the other in both space and time, and thus both are not identical. God, furthermore, is an absolute limitation. Only for an omniscent God would idea, subject, and object be identities. For such a God, *A* would be *A* and never not *not A*! For this God, reality would be complete, finished, and rational. For the computer, reality is a rational identity, a denial of the limitations of time and space. For Ellul, computer rationality has become reality, ultimate reality, the reality of a God who apprehends absolutely and for whom the idea of the object is the object itself.

The ideal of the computer, the completely rational machine, is no idea or ideal that humanity receives from God. From Ellul's perspective, this idea runs counter to the reality that God envisions. Though the creation, as related in Genesis, was once complete, humanity challenged it and disobeyed God, making perfection fractured and finite, which God permitted. God, however, is no machine, nor is His creation a machine. Ellul writes:

> God does not mechanize man. He gives him free play. He includes issues of every possible kind. Man is at the time independent. We cannot say free. Scripture everywhere reminds us that man's independence in relation to God is in the strict sense bondage as regards sin. This man is not free. He is under the burden of his body and his passions, the conditioning of society, culture, and function. He obeys its judgments and setting. He is controlled by its situation and psychology. Man is certainly not free in any degree. He is the slave of everything save God. God does not control or constrain him. God lets him remain independent in these conditions.[8]

The ideal of mechanization, by contrast, is humanity's version of God, for which humankind bears responsibility. God, as limit, allows the individual to discover his or her own limitation, which is the freedom of achievement. All other notions of freedom are abstract and unreal. Freedom is not a condition, but a response to a condition; freedom is achieved within the awareness and the overcoming of limitation and determinisms, in the recognition that necessities are in part the human's own makings.

The body, culture, society, are conditions and obstacles included in knowing. But they are never all there is to know, although they make knowing possible. They are mediations and burdens to be transcended but not denied. They are transcended in symbolic activity, in the realization that reality is never given per se, but is grasped indirectly, once the indirection becomes part of knowing. Reality known is reality mediated. To fully know the object is to engage it as mediated. The dilemma of the puppet theater returns. The human in the allegedly untroubled world of sheer immediacy is a myth, a past to which people never, by themselves, can return, although the creation of symbols signals nostalgic attempts. The technical phenomenon is the latest puppet from which people dangle in an inverted cultural gravity and of which they are no longer aware. Ellul writes:

> The technological system performs unintentionally. Hence, wherever it is applied, it produces a new kind of objectification which has nothing to do with Hegel's: it is no longer an objectification of the subject, and does not enter a subject-object dialectics. Now, anything that is incorporated, or seized, is treated as an object by the active system, which cannot develop or perform without acting upon a set of elements that have previously been rendered neutral and passive. Nothing can have an intrinsic sense; it is given meaning only by technological application.[9]

In the technical operation, consciousness is before an object as *other*, and subject-object dialectics apply, as I noted above in my discussion of the technical phenomenon. But with the technical phenomenon, the division between consciousness and the object is apparently canceled—it is canceled in consciousness but not in reality, understood as the True, what Ellul calls *le Vrai*. Technical consciousness has become an ultimate reality not because it apprehends what is ultimately real, but because it cannot obtain a reality beyond what it apprehends. And what it apprehends it objectifies; hence, the technical phenomenon. The technical phenomenon soon becomes the technical system, as the infinite is beheld in an infinity of grasps, what Hegel might call a "bad infinity."

Ellul notes above that technical objectification is not Hegel's objectification—a dance between the subject and the object that powers Hegel's dialectic. The technical phenomenon does not allow a dialectical distance between subject and object, such as is found in the technical operation, typically exemplified in tool use. Ellul appreciatively cites Hegel for an example of the dialectic of tool use. Quoting from Hegel's *Realphilosophie*, Ellul writes:

> The tool as such keeps back man's material annihilation; but in this respect it remains . . . his activity. . . . In the machine, man sublates this formal activity of his and lets it work fully for him. However, the deception he practices on Nature . . . takes its revenge on him; whatever he wins from Nature, the more he subjugates it, the lower he becomes himself. He may process Nature by means of various machines, but he does not sublate the necessity of his labor; he merely puts off his labor, removes it from Nature, and he does not erect himself as living upon Nature as living; instead, this negative livingness flees, and the labor that remains for him becomes more and more machinelike itself.[10]

Hegel marvelously anticipates Ellul's notion of the technical phenomenon that does not remove labor so much as it transforms work. The labor remains, but the laborer no longer works on the living *other* with an integrity and authenticity of its own. The laborer works on an extension of the laborer's self, which as self, the self does not recognize. The machine takes on the same necessity assumed by nature with one difference: the machine's necessity is humanity's own. It is through the machine that humanity becomes *other* to itself. But this form of *otherness* is not dialectically available. Ellul contends, adopting this logic, that the technical phenomenon is the advanced stage of mechanical necessity that goes beyond the machine and encompasses the entire technical system.

The Dialectic

The relationship between the technical phenomenon and the technical operation is fundamental to Ellul's notion of dialectic, which, as I have shown, is what his readers largely ignore. In tool use, as Hegel explains, consciousness struggles against the object and is aware of itself in and through the struggle. The technical phenomenon brings consciousness's collapse, what Ellul means when he says that technical consciousness is not dialectical. Ellul's concern for freedom is a hope to restart the dialectic, to return consciousness to itself, separated from its object. *La technique*, as consciousness, is still before an object taken as an object, but it does not face this object as a facet of its own awareness. This is the basis of the epistemological dimension to Ellul's thought. *La technique* is an objectification of technical desire resulting in the technical phenomenon. *La technique* then becomes desire itself, during which process the object of desire is lost. Subjectivity loses itself in this particular objectivity.

Ellul writes:

Man is progressively eliminated as a subject (apt to make decisions autonomously and singularly), by technical growth which imposes on him modes of life, attitudes, and calculated rules, more and more rigorous. Man is subjected to a progressive "reification" by this invasion of objects. He lives in a universe increasingly filled with these artificial objects and he has to situate himself in relation to them. He is, himself, treated as an object when the necessities of organization, society, and consumption demand it. And it is here that the famous "reification" is found, much more than in the labor of producing goods. The Marxist theory of goods for explaining this reification was correct a century ago. It is now only a detail. Reification now brings with it the whole of the many areas of man's activity, of the being of man himself. It concerns his family life as well as his leisure and his culture. And this reification includes as a corollary the progressive elimination of man by himself.[11]

The Marxist critique will not suffice inasmuch as there is no distance between the worker and the object—the machine, the factory, and the boss that alienate him. The suggestion box, for example, cancels this: the worker, like the boss, becomes concerned with efficiency, with the means of production. When the claim is articulated that a more efficient process or device may be brought to bear, all are silent. Technique is the locus of respect. The particular is reified—it becomes the universal itself. The technical phenomenon is the particular reified. This leads to the social dimension of the dialectic. As the subject collapses into the technical object, a true social critique is impossible. The goal of every critique becomes another version of efficient methodology. That an idea will not work, that a process is inefficient, that someone is not doing their job, will raise the greatest of scorn.

That consciousness is separated from its object is a ground for an alienation that Marx understood. Marx hoped that in the social world this alienation could be healed by placing the worker in charge of the process, by allowing the worker to identify with the means of production. Ellul forsees a greater alienation: that consciousness will no longer be able to know the terms of its alienation or even that it is indeed alienated. Behind this lies the metaphysical dimension of Ellul's thought. The given is that consciousness is fundamentally separated from the object after humanity's break with God. Ellul, however, is no ordinary metaphysician, and his God is no simple theological construct or another rational system. Ellul understands the break with God textually—through a certain reading of the Bible, historically and socially. Ellul begins with the understanding that God is both immanent and transcendent—the classic dilemma. The problem is: how is He to be known. A God that is a mere metaphysical construct is of no comfort, no value. Thus, Ellul's God must appear in time, while not being of time. He writes:

This historical process does not allow the revealed God to be metaphysical or to be constructed and known according to a metaphysical process. To define God as omniscient, omnipotent, impassible, imperturable, eternal, etc. is not to have understood the biblical revelation at all. One might say all this on the one side, but on the other the God of the biblical revelation enters time and history, suffers man's misery and sin, tolerates initiatives, limits his power, repents, revokes his condemnations, etc. Nor can we have one side without the other. A contradiction? Precisely. Logically insoluble, but it creates the biblical dialectic which makes man's relation to God not a repetition, a fixity, a ritual, a scrupulous submission, but a permanent invention, a new creation of the one with the other, a challenge, a love affair, an adventure whose outcome can never be known in advance.[12]

The biblical dialectic is located in paradoxes, which recount humanity's attempts to become God or God-like or to define God's nature. The Bible, for Ellul, is a book of questions without answers, a book of truths couched in metaphors that far outdistance conceptual confines, images of the clear and distinct. And yet, somehow, God's nature is revealed to Ellul: God is no mechanic or bureaucrat, no Puritan stick-in-the-mud, no dowdy Miss Grundy. God is found in love, challenge, and adventure, in suffering and forgiveness, in process and not in product.

Ellul reminds us that Moses's stone tablets are broken after he returns from the mountain, the inevitable consequence of trying to make God an image, to make Him visible. Ellul writes:

> ... the destruction of this single visible, material representation of God ought to remind us continually that the Bible in its materiality is not the Word of God made visible through reading. God did not become Jeremiah's secretary and write for him (Jer. 1:9). And he has not made his Word visible. Between the written word and speech there is the same distance we have discovered on the human plane. The phenomenon is exactly the same. The Bible is not a sort of visible representation of God.[13]

The word on the human plane mirrors and is mirrored by the biblical dialectic, wherein the true meaning is the meaning that surrounds, a meaning far greater than that expressed by the Aristotelian laws of thought geared for a conceptual understanding. Although the Bible is an *Urtext* for Ellul, it is no book of recipes, neither blue print nor outline; instead the Bible reminds us of the inadequacy of such denuded meanings and ushers in a permanant challenge to and critique of all attempts to reduce meaning and truth to the conceptual and to the image. The Bible is a reminder that God's medium is the Word and that the business of the word and the Word is to express the ineffable.

All words point on some level to the ineffable. They are reminders that we say that we mean and we mean what we say but also that if we knew what we fully and completely meant, we would not have to speak or write. On the human plane, thought, object, and word are never identities. We communicate because we do not know that we mean until we mean it, and meaning requires speaking or writing or both to some audience—the ear and eye of the *other*. I believe that this is Ellul's point when he writes:

> Because God speaks, when a person speaks a mysterious power is attached to what he says. Every human word is called on, more or less clearly, to express the Word of God, and there is a misuse of power, an abuse of words when this is not the case. Henceforth human language has an eternal reference from which it cannot escape without destroying itself or without stripping itself of all meaning. The value of the human word depends on the Word of God, from which it receives its decisive and ultimate character. This quality is expressed in its critical value and in ethical decision.[14]

The notion of God rescues human speech and communication from a dizzying relativity. Although human meaning is relative to other humans and to the human situation, God is the guarantor of ultimate meaning to which all meaning points and from which all meaning derives. God chooses to communicate in metaphors and symbols, reminding us that God's logic is not computer logic—the true, as A that is A and not *not A*. God, in the biblical account, both judges and forgives, and refuses to reduce the moral to an ethical formula. There are no such formulas; morality is revealed as the art of pointing and keeping the reference point moving, the art of realizing that the moral and the good are what are yet to be obtained. The moral is what is always beyond the common sense, although the moral is also therein revealed. The critical value of the word is in its reach beyond.

Ellul refuses to understand God outside of space and time as much as he refuses to reduce God to the spatial and temporal. In this sense he refuses to do metaphysics. The biblical text, in Ellul's reading, serves to identify this God as both in and out of time and space, but as one who establishes place. Ellul's reading of the 2 Kings in *Politique de Dieu, politiques de l'homme* (1966) [*The Politics of God and the Politics of Man* (1972)] shows dramatically the bi-directionality of God. It shows, as well, the power of the symbol to locate thought in two directions at once: back toward the mystery of biblical revelation in a time of the ancient Hebrews and forward to the secular mystifications in the technological society. The problem, then as now, is the reduction of God the infinite to God the finite, to a set of rules and conventional understandings. Currently, our finite deity is *la technique*. But the reduction of the infinite to the finite is an old game, an ancient wager.

Recall that Ellul's reading of 2 Kings drives Norman O. Brown to distraction, unable as he is to reconcile that Ellul of *The Politics of God* with the Ellul off *Présence au monde moderne: Problèmes de la civilization post-chrétienne* (1948) [*The Presence of the Kingdom* (1967)]. In *The Politics*, Ellul reveals a God that few want to face: a being who both forgives and judges. God seemingly allows the death of thousands and apparently uses political means to accomplish this. Why, the conventional wonder, does God permit the people of Israel to be so ravaged? Why, at any time, does God allow death and suffering? Ellul concludes that humanity chooses the ways of death and suffering and that God allows it to happen because He does not mechanize and plan out the future. God even permits His own son's death and joins in with the suffering. And only in paradox is there answer. The Bible forces a retelling, a reenactment, a reimagining, of these mysteries. The way, if there is one, is paved by narrative. Ellul writes:

> The text that encloses the truth of the Word of God is never so exact that it only bears repeating. This text invites me to retell the myth, to recreate it. And the recreated myth calls me to listen to the ultimate, absolute Word. The Word obliges me to speak. This indivisible process implies that the text should never be fixed, reduced to structures, enclosed within itself, or understood as if it were an exact and precise mathematical formula. No valid semiotic diagram exists that can exhaust the text that is a metaphor for the Word of God. Such a text must be spoken rather than dissected.[15]

Ellul, in this way, understands his own writings as words, not as finished clear and distinct formulas. His interpretations of the biblical narrative are narratives that encourage other voices and other views, which indeed require this otherness, an otherness which is too often silenced in the whine of technical authority. The semiotic trick of reducing meaning to a text, of defining language simply as more language, is part of the logic of technique masquerading as a truth on high, a truth of presumption. The true, for Ellul, does not appear in repetition, but in retelling. The logic of the cliché, which I discuss in chapter 5, is the logic of technique that silences a narrative of words that resist a reduction to images, to the here and now. A narrative is not a repetition but a movement from a beginning through a middle to an end, a story evincing notions of origins, development, and purpose. *A*, the subject of the narrative, typically becomes *not A* in time, because *A* never was simply *A*. Each human being is a unity of opposition, a reality open to the narrative but closed to the conceptual. The human world, to remain open and free, requires a narratival and dialectical understanding such as is imaged forth in the Bible and embodied in the everyday world on a material-epistemological level. Presently, this takes place between the polarities of the technical operation and the technical phenomenon.

Consider Ellul's examination of 2 Kings 5:1–9.[16] On the most simple level, we understand that the Syrian general Naaman, a leper, goes to Israel on the advice of an Israelite maid, captured on a raid. The maid tells Naaman of a famous prophet who will cure him. The Syrian king sends the Israelite king a letter of introduction, and Naaman departs carrying much wealth. When the Israelite king reads the letter asking for a cure for Naaman, the king rends his garments, declares he is not God, and looks for a point of quarrel. Elisha, the prophet, hears of the King's consternation and asks that Naaman be sent to him. Naaman arrives and is greeted by the prophet's messenger who tells him to wash seven times in the river Jordan. Naaman departs angrily, expecting a better and a more convincing show, and thinking that the rivers of Damascus are better than any of those in Israel. Naaman's servants, however, convince him to try the cure by reminding him that if the prophet had ordered a massive and complicated ritual, Naaman very likely would have complied. Naaman dips into the river seven times and is cured. He comes before Elisha to offer thanks and to affirm the God of Israel as the true God. Further, Naaman asks for some local soil to be given to him so that he might worship the true Lord in Syria, although he will also have to bow down to Rimmon, to his king's gods, for which Naaman asks forgiveness. The story ends.

Ellul retells the story in terms of a citizen of the technological society seeking a transcendent domain. The social analysis in *The Technological Society* is turned upside down. Ellul begins with the observation that in the Bible few are cured of leprosy. God chooses to cure, then, not a believer but an unbeliever; not a humble peaceful person but a great general of a nation that is the sworn enemy of Israel, God's chosen people.[17] God's purpose is cloaked in irony, eschewing common sense and obvious plan. Moreover, God's action makes no political sense; indeed, the political is portrayed as senseless.[18] The kings of both nations know only each other and only political solutions, which afford Naaman no cure. The prophet is not in the consciousness of either ruler. The prophet finally intervenes but then only indirectly—in some sense he does not act—and with the help of intermediaries. Servants convey the messages and force much of the action. They bring Elisha's words and convince Naaman to heed them. The kings are powerless. And Naaman, a general, believes only in magic and in the truth of the here and now. Nonetheless, he is cured. Even at the story's end, he wants to carry some local soil away; he has seen the Lord's power but he still believes in magic, and, likely he will remain a functionary of the state.[19]

Ellul understands, in his time, that the state has achieved absolute power and that the absolute is a plan invoked by a rational methodology. In this story he finds an inverted world where the powerful are powerless and where the powerless are powerful. In a time when technique and the power of secular magic revealed in the image prevail, Ellul discovers a time when only the word will work. Elisha works through the word. Naaman is only cured when he heeds the word. Common sense and conceptual thinking fail. Ellul writes:

> At every point the general has a decision to make. At every point this decision is not confronted by an irresistible constraint or by crushing evidence and certitude. He has to listen to what the little slave says. But why should he obey it? And even when the king of Israel sends him to Elisha, why should he not take umbrage and return to Syria to provoke the diplomatic incidents? In addition, the word Elisha speaks to him is certainly not a compelling or totalitarian word. He can refuse to listen to it, and this is exactly why Elisha does not appear, why he treats him thus. This kind of anonymity which does not break through the television screen nor stun the middle-class citizen is God's great respect for the liberty of the one he loves. Naaman, too, has to decide for himself.[20]

Only the individual can decide and that decision is never certain, never immediately given in the empirical world. The power of the state resting in the here and now is ultimately no power.

The individual in biblical revelation—as in life—is never given simply. The individual is revealed in opposition—an opposition within the individual, between individuals, between the individual and nature, and between the individual and the state. These oppositions drive the preceding story. The final opposition, Ellul concludes, is between the individual and God, opposition the individual continually effects by erecting means and methods as intermediaries, although God will not allow this break fully and finally to happen. Recall that for Ellul the break is narrated in Genesis, where he finds the origins of technique prefigured. Humanity challenges God, a wedge is driven between the human as subject and the creation as object, and symbolic powers are afforded humanity by God, who wants to maintain the relation. Ellul writes:

But because God wants his creature to live, he keeps the break from happening. Man absolutely cannot get rid of God because he cannot keep the subject of all things from really being that subject. He cannot keep himself, subject in the world, from being an object before God. Despite all the conspiracies that the trees in my garden may hatch up among themselves, they cannot keep me from calling them by their names and from picking their fruit when it is ripe. "Come," says God, and the subject is once again revealed as subject. But God does not smash or destroy. Babel does not crumble under the lightning flash. The problem is a spiritual one, and Babel is only a symbol. To man's desire to make a name for himself, God responds with the confusion of tongues. Its name is to be Babel. Confusion. Our text gives this etymology for Babel, but the experts say that this is not the true etymology. They are doubtlessly correct. But, if it is an error linguistically speaking it does make perfect sense in terms of the myth. That is exactly what the myth has in mind, that is the truth it must express.[21]

The truth of the symbol can only be revealed symbolically. Dialogue must overcome fact.

The Symbol

Ellul understands that the forming of the city is coterminous with a linguistic, symbolic act and with an epistemological break. Humanity's break with God is a break in fact, in language, and in consciousness. Myth is not a false story, but rather a framework for the conditions of the true that takes the shape of a narrative. Humanity tries to make the world object to its subjectivity using language and action—word and image—often to the neglect of that absolute subjectivity—God—for whom humanity would be object. Action points to the world as object and the word points to the world as subject. For humanity the object and the subject never fully come together, as they would be for God. Ultimately the result is Babel, although the symbols achieved are never fully meaningless. They need, however, to be interpreted in relation to what they are not—an infinitude that actually exceeds our grasp. What is grasped is always the finite.

God is, above all else, the reminder of the finitude of the human world that is revealed within the human's own attempts to understand it. Ellul writes, in "Symbolic Function, Technology and Society" (1979):

The interpretation of this world is already, by itself, the act of a subject who separates out himself and who deposits everything else into another universe of objects upon which he can, and is prepared to, act. This creation of an 'other world' furnishes him with a justification. And, finally, in the measure to which he is able to imagine a dimension other than that of the immediately sensible—a universe of which he is the constituent and where he continues to reinterpret and to institute new things—he becomes also the master of the real world.[22]

The symbolic world requires imagination and otherness. The dialectic between the individual and the world and between that subjectivity and what is expressed enables this "other world" to be achieved: it is both the condition of symbolic consciousness and its result. And again we turn to the problem of technical consciousness, which is nondialogical and nonsymbolic. Here is an irony. Technique, which is a symbolic construction, loses its symbolic dimension when it no longer points beyond itself, thereby becoming the beyond itself.

Because humanity in technique does not distance itself in relation to its own creations, it can no longer symbolize them. At this point humanity loses control of its own world, which it has created, a creation that humanity has forgotten but which it must not forget. A common world—a community—is formed on the basis of symbolic language and on that level it is maintained. Ellul writes:

> Man cannot have a relationship with another save by the intermediary of symbolization. Without mediating symbols, he would invariably be destroyed by raw physical contact alone. The 'other' is always the enemy, the menace. The 'other' represents an invasion of the personal world, unless, or until, the relationship is normalized through symbolization. Very concretely, to speak the same language is to recognize the 'other' has entered into the common interpretive universe; to display recognizable or identical tatoos, for example, is an expression of the same universe of discourse.[23]

The current *Other* is technique, which is no longer *Other* to itself. Object and subject collide and the dialectic collapses.

Human meaning that establishes and sustains cultures and societies is the symbolic transformation of otherness. Symbolic meaning requires a sense of the *other*, a designation that things are both what they are and what they are not. Naaman is cured and converted but remains a pagan and, likely, a man of violence. God forgives and judges and His ways are mysterious. Symbolic meaning includes and excludes simultaneously. Both are moments of meaning, without which meaning does not occur.

For Ellul, meaning is in the making and meaning is culturally shared, although all human meaning is bracketed by God's Wholly Otherness, which provides the reference point that halts an indefinite regress. Technical symbols are inimical to natural symbols because they disrupt shared meaning and deny all reference points that are *other*. On the one hand, technique is an acquired cultural social form and on the other hand, technical consciousness does not know itself as this shape. Technique is a form of forgetting, what Ellul calls *Lethotechny*.[24] For technique become an ideology, culture and meaning are arbitrary, contingent, and continuous; while, at the same time, technique becomes the nonarbitrary form of culture. Consciousness forgets that the technical phenomenon is the meaning that it has constructed. Human consciousness plays God. The technical phenomenon is not taken as contingent being but as necessary and contingent; the contingent becomes necessary and self-generating. The principle of *unicité* and monism, discussed further in chapter 4 and mentioned above, is applied: what can be done will be done. As Ellul states above, technique is a form of subjectivity that is not beheld as an object; objectivity is technique's grasp and desire. Objectivity is what technical consciousness determines. Technique denies the being of the Wholly Other—in any of its forms—and becomes the wholly other in the force of its denial.

Ellul's God, to repeat a critical point, is not a mere Wholly Other, but He is never wholly immanent either, unable to call the world into question. A God who is a complete Wholly Other would be useless: "The absolute affirmation that God is the *Wholly Other*, that he is so transcendent as to be a *complete* stranger to us, leads either to the terror-stricken crushing of those who dare not even live before God or to their total independence."[25] Such a God would be absolutely terrifying or absolutely irrelevant. God is a form of *otherness* mirrored in the natural object as *other*. The natural object is, significantly, what humanity does not make; God is absolutely what humanity does not make. God is the reference point for all making, a notion of ultimate purpose to which all finite purpose refers. For Ellul, God is of course more than notion, but to affirm this does not blunt the insight that otherness is required for consciousness's movement, for the all-important dialectic.

The Bad Infinity

Ellul always claims not to be doing metaphysics, which he understands as a merely rational construct, as a system, and as that which is, in principle, outside of space and time. At least, these are the typical objections he brings to Hegel's philosophy inasmuch as he thinks Hegel is a system builder.[26] Apparently uninterested in technical questions, Ellul does not engage in formal philosophical criticisms. Nonetheless, I find Ellul's contributions to social metaphysics of enormous value, especially as they relate to his notions of the dialectic, which are not as far from Hegel's as he sometimes states. As noted above, Ellul values the negativity of Hegel's dialectic, in Hegel's distinction between tool-using consciousness and machine-using consciousness. Even more importantly, he grasps a point of Hegelian logic with regard to consciousness's understanding of the infinite, which becomes, for me, a central conjunction for Ellul's theological, social, and historical studies. I am thinking of Hegel's discussion of a bad infinity, a *Schlecht-Unendliche*, which, in my understanding of Ellul, focuses the problem of technique in its social, historical, and theological dimensions. The notion of a bad infinity may help to focus Ellul's philosophical importance as well. As I read Ellul, technical consciousness is a manifestation of a bad infinity.

Hegel discusses the bad infinity in his *Science of Logic*. In simplest terms, a bad infinity is a merely negative infinity. It is taken as that which the finite is not. It is an infinity arrived at as a form of determinate being; in my reading, it appears either as the negation of that which is before consciousness as a single thing, or as the negation of the totality of finite things considered as a whole.

Of the first kind of infinity, Hegel writes:

> The infinite *is*; in this immediacy it is at the same time the negation of an other, of the finite. As thus in the form of simple being and at the same time as the *non-being* of an *other*, it has fallen back into the category of *something* as a determinate being in general.[27]

That is, I can understand the infinite in terms of the finite, a something that is before me, as that which is not before me. The infinite becomes a *not-this*. But, as a *not-this* it is both too abstract—merely negative—and too concrete—it loses its infinity by being so determined.

There is another sense of infinity that goes beyond the finite and the infinite, defined as mere others to themselves. Hegel writes:

> Finitude, namely, is limitation posited as limitation; determinate being is posited with the *determination* to pass over into its *in itself*, to *become* infinite. Infinity is the nothing of the finite, it is what the latter is *in itself*, what it *ought to be*, but this ought-to-be is at the same time reflected into itself, is *realized*; it is a purely self-related, wholly affirmative being. In infinity we have the satisfaction that all determinateness, alteration, all limitation and with it the ought itself, are posited as vanished, as sublated, that the nothing of the finite is posited.[28]

Consciousness is faced with a problem. If the infinite is *not this thing*, it has only negative being. It is being that is not. If infinity is the essence of all being—what all being is not—infinity overcomes its merely negative character in relation to a particular finite thing, but, instead, infinity becomes a void. It is a whole in absentia. Hegel suggests a movement between these two grasps of infinity. The notion of the infinite as not this particular thing leads to the idea of the infinite as what all particular things are not. The particular is overcome, a totality is grasped—for Hegel, always the goal of thought—but this totality is not a true infinity, a true totality. It is a spurious or bad infinity, a *Schlecht-Unendliche*. The bad infinite has no end; it is always just one thing more, or that which all things are not.

Hegel writes:

> It is only the spurious infinite [*Schlecht-Unendliche*] *which is the beyond*, because it is *only* the negation of the finite posited as *real*—as such it is the abstract, first negation; determined *only* as negative, the affirmation of *determinate* being is lacking in it; the spurious infinite, held fast as only negative, is even *supposed to be not there*, is supposed to be unattainable. However, to be thus unattainable is not its grandeur but its defect, which is at bottom the result of holding fast to the finite as such as a *merely affirmative being*. It is what is untrue that is unattainable, and such an infinite must be seen as a falsity. The image of the progress to infinity is the *straight line*, at the two limits of which alone the infinite is, and always only is where the line—which is determinate being—is not, and which goes *out beyond* to this negation of its determinate being, that is, to the indeterminate; the image of true infinity, bent back into itself, becomes the *circle*, the line which has reached itself, which is closed and wholly present, without *beginning* and *end*.[29]

The bad infinity is imaged as the limits of a line without end. Consciousness extends outward, held to the particular and trying to find the infinite in the negation of each particular. But, there is no end to particularity. Consciousness, Hegel believes, has to come back to itself, to understand that the finite or the infinite are relations it has established, although not merely this. Consciousness does not create the world, for Hegel, but without consciousness, the world would have no meaning. Meaning is acquired in consciousness's determinations. The finite and the infinite are basic determinations. Consciousness must discover that the infinite and the finite are codetermined, not merely as negatives but also as moments in relation. They need each other.

Hegel writes:

What is required in order to see into the nature of the infinite is nothing difficult: it is to be aware that the infinite progress, the developed infinite of the understanding, is so constituted as to be the *alternation* of the two determinations, of the *unity* and the *separation* of both moments and also to be aware that this unity and this separation are themselves inseparable.[30]

The key to Hegel's dialectic is the notion that consciousness never fully escapes itself nor does it ever fully encompass itself, or whatever object it attempts to comprehend. Consciousness knows itself in the act of knowing, in the process of making determinations. It seeks the absolute as a unity of subject and object, but, in my reading of Hegel, consciousness always fails partially, though never absolutely. Absolute failure would be as impossible as absolute success.

Hegel, at the end of the *Phenomenology of Spirit*, articulates the goal of his phenomenology—the science of knowing appearance—which applies his dialectical method, wherein the object is grasped not merely as it appears in itself but also as it appears for consciousness: one cannot appear without the other. He writes:

> The *goal*, Absolute Knowing, or Spirit that knows itself as Spirit, has for its path the recollection [*Errinerung*] of the Spirits as they are in themselves and as they accomplish the organization of their realm. Their preservation, regarded from the side of their free existence appearing in the form of contingency, is History; but regarded from the side of their [philosophically] comprehended organization, it is the Science of Knowing in the sphere of appearance: the two together, comprehended History, form alike the inwardizing [*Errinerung*] and the Calvary of absolute Spirit, the actuality, truth, and certainty of his throne, without which he would be lifeless and alone. Only
>> from the chalice of this realm of spirits
>> foams forth for Him his own infinitude.[31]

On my reading of this—and here I am aided by Donald Phillip Verene's valuable book, *Hegel's Recollection: A Study of Images in the Phenomenology of Spirit* (1985)—Hegel does not claim to present absolute knowledge as it would be in-and-for-itself.[32] Absolute knowledge appears as a form of recollection, as knowledge recollects itself in the history of its knowing. Appearance is known as a history and as a totality. The totality is not known as a completed object, however. The object itself does not appear as independent of spirit's grasp and determination. The infinitude that is grasped is not lifeless inasmuch as spirit is led always in two directions: outward toward the object as an in-itself and back toward itself as a for-itself. For spirit to be lodged either in itself or in its object would be the death of the spirit, understood as the canceling of the dialectic. The Calvary of absolute spirit, referred to above, is a place of death and rebirth. Spirit is transformed by the process of inwardizing—recollection—and externalizing, such that all moments are understood as a totality. The true is the whole and not any one of its parts. The bad infinity, for Hegel, is a stopping of the dialectic as the infinite is grounded either in the negativity of the particular or in the negativity of the totality of particulars. The true infinite is both outside and inside the totality at the same time.

Ellul, from a different direction but with a similar purpose, understands his God to be a true infinite and not a bad infinity. Ellul understands technique to be consciousness's attempt to reside in an object that it has reified; consciousness does not move beyond the object. But the technical object, the technical phenomenon, does not have the otherness to pull consciousness from itself. For technique, nothing exists outside the technical system to save consciousness from itself. Technique aims at a totality but a merely negative totality. Technique is led from one particular moment to the next, seeking efficiency as an absolute that is always acquired by some form of measurement or is revealed in the Cartesian clear and distinct. A real totality that includes the real negative is not achieved. Moreover, consciousness does not recollect its activity, does not understand that the object before it in the shape of the technical phenomenon is the object that it has made. Further, Ellul understands a necessity to the process of sacralization, such that a totality is always needed. Culture does not proceed without some notion of origins, meaningful ritual, and transcendence. Technique, which abolishes the sacred in nature and religion, becomes the sacred itself. A bad infinity, likely, leads to a failed transcendence.

Donald Phillip Verene connects Hegel's notion of a bad infinity with Hegel's philosophical portrait of "the unhappy consciousness."[33] This connection is significant. The unhappy consciousness feels estranged and alienated from the world. It looks to another world for comfort. It needs an infinity and a sense of the unchangeable, and so understood, the unhappy consciousness is often seen as related to stoicism or medieval piety. Of the unhappy consciousness, Hegel writes:

> Its thinking as such is no more than the chaotic jingling of bells, or a mist of warm incense, a musical thinking that does not get as far as the Notion, which would be the sole, immanent objective mode of thought.

This infinite, pure inner feeling does indeed come into possession of its object; but this does not make its appearance in conceptual form, not as something [speculatively] comprehended, and appears therefore as something alien. What we have here, then, is the inward movement of the pure heart which *feels* itself, but itself as agonizingly self-divided, the movement of an infinite yearning which is certain that its essence is such a pure heart, a pure *thinking* which *thinks* of itself as a *particular individuality*, certain of being known and recognized by this object, precisely because the latter thinks of itself as an individuality. At the same time, however, this essence is the unattainable *beyond* which, in being laid hold of, flees, or rather has already flown. It has already flown; for it is in part the Unchangeable which thinks of itself as an individuality, and consciousness therefore directly attains in its own self—*its own self*, but as the antithesis of the Unchangeable; instead of laying hold of the essence, it only *feels* it and has fallen back into itself.[34]

Thought has become a music, a chaotic jingling of bells and a burning of incense, a ritual. Medieval piety is suggested. But the object for this thinking—and such it is—is not conceptual, ultimately. Thought has somehow become feeling. The concept is lost, however much it was once present. The infinite appears to a divided self as a yearning. The finite world has lost its savor. The self flies from the world to the unchangeable, to that abstract infinity outside of space and time. Hegel suggests, ironically, that this infinity is another self—the self's own projection, from which the self has become estranged. Hegel writes:

In the struggle of the heart and emotions the individual consciousness is only a musical abstract moment. In work and enjoyment which make this unsubstantial existence a reality, it can directly forget *itself*, and the consciousness of its *own particular role* in this realization is cancelled out by the act of thankful acknowledgement. But this cancelling-out is in truth a return of consciousness into itself, and, moreover, into itself as the actuality which it knows to be true. . . . Work and enjoyment thus lose all *universal content* and *significance*, for if they had any, they would have an absolute being of their own. Both withdraw into their mere particularity, which consciousness is set upon reducing to nothingness.[35]

Consciousness loses contact with the other, to the particular, which is reduced to nothingness. The infinite becomes merely a particular *other* that has been reified. The work of consciousness, once present, is lost. Consciousness is trapped in an individuality that lacks objectivity and, concomitantly, lacks a true subjectivity as well.

The unhappy consciousness appears in the *Phenomenology* at the end of the discussion of self-consciousness. Consciousness has done battle in the famous master-slave relationship. Consciousness achieves a sense of itself as it does battle with the *other*: it becomes either a master or a slave, whose identities are dialectically joined. The slave achieves final mastery over the master who does not realize the slave's servitude is contingent upon the slave's self-perception as a slave and upon the master's demeaning gaze. Freed from its condition of dependency, the self is now an enlightened slave or master and may drift into stoicism or skepticism. This is the path Hegel's phenomenology seems to chart—although as Verene points out, the direct progression is not deductively or necessarily determined.[36] It is quite useful to remember that Marcus Aurelias and Epictetus, master and slave, respectively, were both stoics, however. Consciousness as self-consciousness, an unhappy consciousness, is exhausted from its work in the world and loses itself in an abstract infinity, a bad infinity.

For Ellul, technical consciousness, separated from the world and moving back toward the world with the symbolizing force of technique, loses touch with its own conceptualizing powers that distanced itself from the world in the first place. Technique, no longer a specific form of desire, becomes desire itself, yearning after absolute efficiency that has become a disembodied abstraction, endlessly embodied—an infinity of one more technique, one more device. Ultimately, as Ellul understands, technique becomes the sacred, a form of mysticism that worships the finite infinite—the technician's own gaze in the computer screen.

My reading of Hegel is not necessarily Ellul's reading, although it is clear that Ellul appreciates Hegel's dialectical genius, however much he fears that Hegel's absolute is a finished conceptual structure. Ellul requires a notion of the infinite that is never finished by consciousness's labors but that appears in symbolic form. Ellul requires, further, a goal beyond consciousness, which Hegel would distrust, perhaps as another type of bad infinity. However much Hegel and Ellul might agree or disagree, they both understand the importance that a bad infinity holds for the freedom of consciousness. Hegel, unlike Ellul, is concerned with the many forms of reason. Ellul's analysis focuses only on reason as technical application. Ellul, however, seeks an angle on reason, a level beyond reason in the symbolizing powers of consciousness that produce more than conceptual structures. Hegel, too, is interested in the symbol, in the imagination, and certainly in memory, but of course he lacks Ellul's purpose. Ellul is an evangelist of freedom, out to destroy the false gods, the bad infinities, on which humanity currently wagers. And his analysis never drifts far from the life world into the purely conceptual, from which Hegel's analysis rarely emerges. Hegel and Ellul are *others* to each other. Hegel has worked out with great subtlety and care the various traps that befall reason as it attempts to construct and to remember the Absolute; Ellul reminds us of the existential and moral dimension that accompanies reason's labors with the negative and reminds us, as well, of reason's own limitations.

The Dialectical Structure of Ellul's Work

I have argued that Ellul's readers have not penetrated to the inner workings of his thought, to his dialectic, which engages a theory of the symbol, a notion of technique as a form of consciousness, an understanding of God as the Wholly Other, and a theory of culture and history. Apparently, Ellul agrees. In a remarkable epilogue to *Jacques Ellul: Interpretive Essays*, Ellul was asked to respond to the critical essays in the volume. Instead, he offers the epilogue "On Dialectic," which addresses the lack of attention his dialectic has received. He writes:

> If, however, dialectic is at issue, the whole must not be made up of two unrelated parts: there has to be correlation. The negative exists only in relation to a positive; the positive exists only in relation to a negative. The two play their parts reciprocally as in musical counterpoint. Hence it is perfectly possible to think of a correspondence between apparently unrelated books. There is counterpoint, for example, between *The Political Illusion* and *The Politics of God and the Politics of Man*, or *The Ethics of Freedom* and the exact dialectical counterpart of the two books on technology (*The Technological Society* and *The Technical System*). I have at once provided both an instrument of knowledge and the possibility of progression through a crisis. This crisis may actually be seen in our society, in the political and economic sphere as well as in the Christian and ecclesiastical. But it cannot have a positive outcome, and avoid sinking into incoherence and nonsense, unless there is a clear recognition of the two factors present. This is what I have tried to offer. In truth, however, my attempt seems to have failed: no one is using my studies in correlation with one another, so as to get at the heart of our crisis in a conscious manner, based on a Christian understanding of it; instead, they continue reacting unconsciously, using reflex not reflexion, and adopting Christian positions on which no reflection has been done.[37]

Note that Ellul understands his theological and his social works to be in musical counterpoint. Two parts are played simultaneously.

God's ways are *others* to the world, and yet, negatively, God's ways appear in the world and show the world what it is not. Conversely, the ways of the world are not God's ways, although God may use them to show what He is not. This is the counterpoint to which Ellul alludes. Ellul regards this as an instrument of knowing, which is no mere form of Faith. Ellul wars continually against any conception of Christian faith that reduces God to image or dogma.

In *The Subversion of Christianity* Ellul argues that after the fourth century A.D. Christianity becomes a form of technique. Ellul writes:

> The Christian God makes himself known in Jesus Christ and not elsewhere. (I refer to what was affirmed in the first century, in the first three or four Christian generations: primitive Christianity.) Outside Jesus Christ God is totally unknowable and inaccessible. As I have said above, the only possible theology relative to God is what much later (from the twelfth to the fifteenth century) will be called negative theology, that is, declaring what God is not. There is no possibility of saying positively what he is. This means that the condemnation of the visible in the religious domain receives emphasis. There can be no demonstration of either the divine mystery or God's revelation. The Christian God is a *hidden* God. Nor can any image of Jesus be preserved or imagined. We have here a religion of the Word alone, and Jesus is himself the totality of the Word, living and not ritualized.[38]

Ellul's Christian God is not the God most Christians know. Ellul continually berates Christians for not doing their homework, for not engaging in social analysis to encounter God as the Wholly Other in their times, and for not reading the Bible dialectically. Ellul's social and theological analyses show the importance of the dialectic between the image and the word and the appearance of God as a bad infinity. This I take to be the philosophical importance of both Ellul's social and theological studies. Ellul's studies as an instrument of knowledge involve learning the difference between the image and the word, between truth as a clear and distinct manifestation and truth as a metaphor embracing contradictions and engaging both similarities and differences.

Ellul, here, seems to be an unusually doctrinaire Christian until a careful reading shows his rejection of doctrine. Ellul's version of Christianity is unique because it refuses a doctrinal and imagistic account of God. His Christianity also disallows a remote and disinterested God outside of space and time. Ellul's Christianity affirms the impossible: that God once appeared as a man and was crucified and died as a man. Only God can do the impossible, which humanity continually tries to copy, with God's blessings and punishments. Thus, Ellul as social and theological critic is both in and out of the world he encounters dialectically.

To think of dialectic is to think of both Marx and Hegel, by whom Ellul is influenced. Ellul, as stated above, values Hegel's negativity although he avoids, in his reading of Hegel, the promise of syntheses, the overcoming of dialectical tension. In the world there are only conflicts, Ellul understands. Only provisional resolutions to conflicts are found in the symbols humanity creates. For Marx, there is a dialectic between humanity and society, grounded in a political-economic substratum. Conflict thus occurs between the haves and have nots. Work becomes the method of mediation. But, for Ellul, work provides no mediation, having been made over by technique. Humanity no longer works, no longer projects intentions and abilities on the world to create products that reveal those intentions. Humanity's work now is the impersonal extension of the technical system itself.

For Ellul the dialectic is a confrontation with *otherness*, whether finite or infinite. Humanity challenges God with temples honoring itself. The challenge retains dialectical tension as long as God remains as *other*. Opposition occurs on finite levels, as between the worker and the world in the working of technical operations. Wherever humanity encounters *otherness*, there is the dialectic. When the *other* is not encountered, the dialectic collapses, as it does in the technical phenomenon. Ellul's faith in Christianity is a faith in a perspective that promises continual dialectical renewal that is expressed in an *Urtext* of symbols. The symbol requires *otherness* and is an expression of *otherness*. Meaning is possible only in relation to consciousness's awareness and grasp of *what is not*, which is then taken up simultaneously in language and society. Ellul's readers, put off by his Christianity, can instead come to terms with what he means by the symbol, which focuses his faith in *otherness*.

As noted above, from his reading of Genesis, Ellul observes that the other's *otherness* is provisionally canceled in the name. Humanity names the objects in the world after it has alienated itself from that world. Naming and symbolizing the world are humanity's challenges to God, challenges that nonetheless establish humanity's place in a region between nature and God. Without the symbol, Ellul observes, humanity would be crushed by "raw physical contact" alone, by wild being in its pure otherness. God allows humanity's challenge because He does not want humanity to break fully away from its contact with the Wholly Other and with the natural object, a more particular form of *otherness*. Humanity is thus saved from its failures to become God, by living in the symbolic world and being content to be God-like. In being God-like, humanity must learn God's medium, the word and the Word. Language is a common world, a *sensus communis*. Whatever the content of the world, for consciousness, that content will be, in part, symbolically expressed and produced in conjunction with *otherness* and paradox. The symbol expresses what the world is and what the world is not, simultaneously. The symbol is the expression, in my view, of divine ignorance and the recognition that symbolizing flows from a sense of lack. If one's knowledge were adequate to the object expressed, the expression would be pointless. The symbol, tacitly, is the admission that the object is not known and that the knower requires the expression of the known as much as the knower the known itself. Like God, we make in order to know; knowing and making are one. But unlike God's, our making is never equal to the task. We require the symbol and the social witnessing of this act of creating meaning. We symbolize so that we can know what we think we mean and so that others may join us in meaning and knowing, in reaching for the *other* that continually hides, that alternately refuses and allows itself to be named. Absolute knowing would be surrounded by silence.

Ellul's implicit philosophy of culture—one that fits quite well with that more explicitly worked out by Ernst Cassirer, as noted above— is based on the power of the symbol to mediate a subject-object bifurcation that is an epistemological given. The symbol also has epistemological power, but it requires an understanding that few of Ellul's sociological readers share. Those of a materialist or behaviorist persuasion are hardly convinced by Ellul's sociohistorical analysis, which they continually find too vague and general. These readers do not follow Ellul's argument that the belief in facts and in data gathering is tied to the technical phenomenon. Ellul clearly states:

> It is never a fact in itself (the exact quantity or date) that counts, because a mere fact is at once insignificant and destructive. It is significant only from the moment when it is re-endowed with a meaning, that is, when it has entered the world of symbols where man is master and is secure in his dominion. Consequently, that which will be retained in the collective memory is not the materiality of a fact, but its significance—its position in relation to the ensemble of symbols by which the group lives and the possibility of mastery over fact which is thus given to man. Hence the collective memory assures the transmission of this universe of meanings, constantly enriched by new symbolic acquisitions which permit new symbolic possibilities that can only be constituted because they can be inserted into a previously existing system of symbolization.[39]

To make cultural sense, the mere fact must be taken in a cultural context that moves in, around, and through the fact. The fact, on one level, is the image that seeks the word. Ellul notes that the fact is taken up by memory and is moved to the level of that which is not, and back, by the collective memory. The symbol is this labor of memory. The symbol, the fact, and memory move together. With memory, that which is not is placed in relation to that which is. Memory is made possible by symbols, which, in turn, makes other symbols possible. As Ellul states: "Thus the symbolic universe is constantly produced at the same time as it is acquired."[40] The technological society, however, forgets the past in a present it creates. And then it forgets its own creation. This forgetting takes place as the symbol and the word are humiliated in their reduction to the fact.

Ellul lives in the Skinnerian age— in the age when the symbol is disguised as the fact. Ellul's social analyses recount this humiliation and directly parallel his historical studies. Ancient Rome provides the modern world with its own origins and a sense of *otherness*, Ellul realizes. In the Roman world *otherness* is transformed by the symbol to found Roman society. Ellul wishes us to recall this time prior to a world silenced by the image and the fact. He writes:

I have demonstrated that the aristocracy in primitive Rome could not have emerged except by the process of symbolization. Formerly, it was claimed that the aristocracy arose from physical force, or the courage of a war chief, or from riches, and so on. Such simplistic, positivistic expressions completely contradict the facts. In reality, when one intimately analyzes the patrician families and goes back, generation through generation, to the historical conditions of their origins, one perceives that all patrician families are connected to some primordial ancestral hero celebrated for his excellence. The important term is celebrated. That is to say, his great deeds were collected, transformed into an epic *account*, and then reconstructed in such a fashion as to become symbolic. At this moment, a double movement is produced: one moves towards the heights, further from the origins, as the eponymous ancester becomes the concentration point of symbols and is attached to a higher symbolic origin. This results in a god—goddess or demigod— who is established symbolically as the true origin and as the explanation of the progenitive power of the ancestor.[41]

Ellul's reading of history requires a double movement of con- sciousness like that witnessed in Roman society. The present has to be seen in relation to the symbols that construct it. The Roman present, our past, was constructed by the symbol, by that which surrounded their present. Our own present is explained only by the fact. Nothing surrounds the fact. Thus, we assume that all societies are so constituted. Ellul's Roman society is not available to the social historian who only understands the fact. These are the historians with materialistic and behavioristic assumptions who find technology always to be present, who view the past as only another version of the present, and who cannot see the past as truly *other*.

Ellul's history of ancient Rome involves understanding society as a narrative act—emmeshed and embellished in the symbol. In this past stories of heroes and gods are the basis for institutions and values. Value is no mere fact, no mere given, apart from its construction in these stories. Thus, the historical fact points in two directions at once—toward the physical—to that which is—and toward that which it expresses—to that which the physical is not, that is, toward the transcendent and the symbolic. The transcendent in pretechnological societies is not expressed in some arcane and obscure metaphysics but appears in the story. Social meaning and coherence are possible with a sense of community established by symbols, stories, and their remembrance.

Ellul's historical studies proceed with the notion that each society has its own sacred—the motive force of all symbologies. The sacred provides a society with origins, a sense of time and place, with meaningful rituals, with notions of transgression, and with a feeling of destiny. Of the sacred in Roman society, in his *L'Histoire des institutions*, Ellul writes: "The Roman sacred is at the same time both religious and magical. It is religious in that it worships the transcendental powers and it is magical in that it utilizes these powers which are immanent."[42] The triad of Jupiter, Mars, and Quirinus thus provide the locus for Roman institutions and values. These gods and godesses are found in nature as well. Jupiter is the god of light and the god of trees, as well as the god of Roman law. Mars is the god of war and strife, establishing the military. Quirinus, the god of all fecundity, the god of earth, water, and plants, brings about agriculture. The heroes were transformations of these gods, giving roles and types to humanity. In Ellul's understanding, these gods are true symbols, having double and triple significance. Law is not established through rational social contract, through a clear and distinct understanding, but through a story, through metaphors and not concepts, and through a logic prior to and now inaccessible to, technical understanding.

In the sacral world, all is of a piece. No thing is just a thing. Everything is alive with powers, full of significance, having a name and calling to be named. Everything is symbolically connected. In societies more primitive than the Romans, lightning is not simply lightning. Lightning is a presence that points beyond itself. Ellul writes:

> It is not because there is thunder and lightning that man invents the sacred. Man made the thunder the source of meaning and of limitation because the world has to have an order, because action has to be justified. With a spontaneity, an "instinct," as inescapable as those he could have for hunting and fishing, man "knew" that he could not justify himself, that he could not tell himself that he was right . . . neither can he can he say to himself that it is he who establishes an order in the world whereby he can locate himself.[43]

The true is present in that which surrounds; the finite weaves the infinite from a symbolic cloth, from a presence that overflows, and requires the word. The true is made out of an *otherness* that is named—the thundering sky. Only the name—the word—is equal to the task.

The world of the ancients instructs Ellul and provides him with a sense of what the present is not and explains how the present came to be. Ellul's grasp is dialectical and narratival. History, he understands, is impossible and beyond comprehension, beyond the productive and constructive symbols of the imagination.[44] History is an act of imagination and memory, about which Ellul provides no special theories. Nonetheless, he places this understanding of history alongside of the notion of history as fact gathering, to which feelings for origins and destiny are not available. Caught in a bad infinity, the past and the future are simply more of the present, more of that-which-is. Consequently, modernity is without a sense of the past by being cut off from the symbolic powers that formed ancient societies and that are needed to understand those societies.

Ellul writes:

> Here is man in his new milieu, in our modern society, feeling alone all over again, and without a respondent. He directs at the empty sky a discourse without dialogue. He embraces things, which are never anything but objects. He is living anew the horror of silence and incompleteness.[45]

Nature no longer speaks. The gods are silent. The object does not gesture beyond itself. The object simply points, a one-dimensional, clear, and distinct sign. This is the world that Skinner can understand because it is the world the Skinners have constructed, although they could not know *the world* to be *their world* in this way. Knowledge attained by symbolizing powers requires distance and *otherness*. The Skinnerian world "... reveals an alarming speculative poverty,"[46] Ellul writes. Ellul explains:

> He [Skinner] has not situated himself beyond freedom and dignity, but is, on the contrary, prior to them. Therefore this order of reflection, which is pseudo-scientific and explains nothing, is, regarding the specificity of man, totally devoid of philosophic interest. Rather, the theories of Skinner and his followers reflect all too eloquently the situation in which man now finds himself: they do not present a true scientific theory but only a formalization of the particular reality created by their own methodology. If we consider their doctrines as expressing our situation, that means in effect that the process of symbolization is in fact excluded and that symbols become stripped of sense.[47]

Freedom and dignity are possible by virtue of symbolic powers. Language provides the trap door out of the merely given world, the world of necessity, constructed by the Skinnerian consciousness, by technical consciousness itself. Technical consciousness does not consider how the meaningful object appears or how the meaningful can appear as an object. The object is there before the mind, a *tabula rasa*, that must await instruction from the outside world.

The behaviorist assumes that the mind can know the value or truth of these instructions. But it is unclear, beyond these assumptions, how the object can know the language of mind or how the mind can know the language of the object; or how any knowledge of the object could accumulate, how a sense of significance could be obtained. If the object is merely *there*, a *that-which-is*, *what-it-is-not* cannot be. It is an object with no past and no destiny, as is the subject viewing that object, asleep to the symbolic dimensions of the world.

Ellul's books do not provide arguments so much as sustained narratives on at least three levels—historical, sociological, and theological [epistemological-metaphysical]—where ideas, like notes in counterpoint, move with and against each other. As in counterpoint, there are no final resolutions. Patterns appear as a result of this movement, but there are no final endings and no one pattern emerges as the truth, although the search for the true as a Wholly Other persists. Ellul's histories are stories that recount dialectical and physical opposition as humanity moves in relation to notions of the absolute. His biblical studies reveal, for example, humanity's attempts to put the city, money, and power before God, to worship images rather than to hear the true word; his sociological works assemble details of the erection of the city and its various desires. The city's wills to power—money, propaganda, and technique—are dialectically motivated but founder in the dissipating powers of the image and the concept, which starve it of the domain that surrounds, the medium of the word.

Ellul's historical accounts divide history into three milieus, characterized by specific symbologies—nature (*la nature*), society (*la société*), technique (*la technique*)—and that point to spiritual dimensions in the life world. From 3000 B.C. to the eighteenth century, society emerges.[48] Tools proliferate and machines appear, along with banking, the printing press, and the nation state. The human body and the body that is nature are dissected through a variety of scientific theories, means and methods. Humanity begins to speak of the book of the world. Humanity's gaze, instructed by Italian Renaissance painting and power politics, stands at a distance from a world desired that is to be conquered. From the eighteenth century to the present, *la technique* predominates, characterized by a flood of machines and methodologies, by the state as a propaganda mill—both the extender and the extension of the mass media, which manufactures the modern environment—a decor of images. The world becomes a text of a text, systemic but nonreferential. Images and humiliated symbols in the modern world do not point beyond themselves.

Within each of these areas—the theological, the sociological, and the historical—there is an independent drama: the sense of attempt and failure, a *hamartia*, a missing of the mark. These failures establish the human perspective as finite. On a secular level, the sense of tragedy reminds us of the provisionality of all accounts that claim to reach the infinite, which become a bad infinity in the consciousness of technique. Each of Ellul's studies can and should be read separately, with the appreciation of the dialectical tension within and between each one. Each study recounts humanity's engagement with *otherness*, an encounter found within and between each study. Ellul's biblical studies resonate with his social studies, not as cause to effect, but as proscenium arch to a stage or as an obligato to a melody. Ellul's studies provide a humanistic instrument of knowledge that is in opposition to technique itself, which requires clear and distinct analyses that further the mentality that produces them, that makes them possible. Ellul asks us to try a different perspective founded on the literary and philosophical power of the word that confronts the concept.

Ellul's reading of the Bible is instructive, regardless of the reader's religious affiliation or interest. His reading shows us how symbols work and reminds us that facts and things acquire meaning in relation to symbols and stories; Ellul, further, reminds us of the need to remember and that memory is a key to understanding. As we remember we establish significances that are embedded in stories, although often the original stories and sensibilities are forgotten. It is amazing that the Bible still informs our culture with its stories, which Ellul explains in relation to his understanding of the technical phenomenon. The technical phenomenon attempts to silence the traditional story with the image, which Ellul hopes to challenge with the word. Ellul wants to make the image speak.

Ellul understands that we build radio and television stations, babbling towers, in which faint echoes of stories somehow can still be heard. These stories—top-40 songs or daily news items—merely repeat what can barely be remembered. Memory is supplanted by repetition. Metaphors are reduced to clichés. On the news and in these songs, if the ear is tuned, we can still hear fascinations with the prodigal son, with the slaying of Abel by Cain, with the force of the flood, with the apocalyptic nuclear disaster. These stories are so secularized, so routinized, however that it takes a literary critic like Northrop Frye to decode them. Ellul understands that the logic of the story, the drama of history, and the tragedy of technique has to be told, that *la technique* must be engaged, not merely replicated.

Ellul believes that our technical phenomena—our modern symbologies—have lost their dialectical character. We no longer recognize the need of things to speak, of information coming from the uncertain, which is reduced to the image and to the mathematical formula. He understands the need for us to separate from our technical constructions and to engage the *other* in whatever form it might appear. We need to realize that the technical world is one of our making, for which we must take responsibility, which ultimately means that we must destory the power of the modern sacred in a free act of symbolization. Ellul writes: "New acts of freedom are constantly required. There is no such thing as a state or acquisition in this matter. Reality encircles me. The sacred hems me in. I have to respond afresh to the summons of thunder."[49] Ellul offers an ancient image of the thundering sky, which the ancient Italians understood as an image and metaphor necessitating a symbolic response with social and philosophical import. The image needs the word; *that-which-is* requires *that-which-is-not*. The present as present will appear significantly only in relation to a past and a future that confront it and not merely repeat it.

Ellul's thunder has largely been lost on critics who seek arguments and clear and distinct accounts regarding the so-called technical nemesis. The critics who regard technique as too encompassing call for a more manageable accounting. I regard this attitude not as

wrong but as a form of technical *hamartia*, a missing of the mark.
Ellul brings into the limelight the *form of technique*, a kind of
metaphor that makes sense, as the ancient stories do, of the
oppositions and symbols, which inform the technological society but
which are not known as symbolic. The technological society requires
that symbols must give way to facts. These facts, Ellul suggests, hide
an unacknowledged symbolic level. Ellul's analyses take us to these
levels, to these presuppositions, which require a bit of imagination
and memory on our parts.

For example, the tragedy of the 1986 space shuttle *Challenger*
incident will likely never be known until we can penetrate the news
story to the level of the real—not simply the apparent, but real,
tragedy. The technical *hamartia* is found in the announcement of the
tragedy as a "major malfunction." It surfaced in the need to classify
the event with fact, logic, and media simulation, a feature of
technique to be discussed in chapter 5. The tragedy *should* appear
in the extraordinary loss of memory that surrounded the
event, and that now is likely completely forgotten in the "Success"
of the 1988 launch of the shuttle *Discovery*. Consider President
Reagan's remarkable epitaph for the ill-fated *Challenger* crew: "We
will never forget them nor the last time we saw them this morning
as they prepared for their journey and waved goodby and slipped the
surly bonds of earth to touch the face of God."[50] Reagan invokes,
in ill-fitting and stagey poetic prose, the need to remember what he
had in fact forgotten. When the "tragedy"—a media event—was
initially announced, he was reported to have asked: "Is that the one
the schoolteacher was on?"[51] Reagan had in fact decided that a
teacher should be the first civilian so launched. We, like Reagan,
were enjoined to remember what we could never have known—these
media figures as real people, something more than the inevitable
decor that establishes their significance. Their celebrity, as Andy
Warhol knew, was to last for only fifteen minutes.

The tragedy, on one level, was a failure of technique, which
surfaced in the epitaph "major malfunction," though even the
technicians knew this was not enough. Reagan's speechwriters had to
haul out poetry. The media had to eulogize these victims of
technological mishap as heroes, which in ancient, pretechnological
tradition refers to semidivines who express nobility of purpose. But
what was their purpose beyond the goals of technique? What great
goals of humankind were invoked, beyond doing what was
technically possible and, therefore, inevitable? Tip O'Neil, in trying
to get a handle on this heroism, states: "We salute those who died
performing exploits that people my age grew up reading about in

comic books."[52] The tragedy, on another level, is the expression of an impoverished literary, philosophical, historical tradition in which the infinite—in whatever transcendent form it might appear—is reduced to a bad infinity, a simpering version of present-mindedness, no matter how sincere.

What is needed, on Ellul's account, is a critique of the present-mindedness that has become technical intention, for which the past as recollected tradition holds no importance. The present seemingly has no drama: facts are gathered, lists are made, and method is maintained. Work, seriousness, and a fixed attention are virtues. And, like puppets, we hang from the device.

4

Historical, Social, and Intellectual
Dimensions of Ellul's Thought

Ellul is a dialectical thinker who views the present-mindedness of contemporary society as, in part, a dialectical construction. Ellul's dialectic is at once conceptual and perceptual. Ellul's dialectic is based on the recognition that the true is never what is perceived and that what is thought is equally at a distance from what is experienced. One is always at a remove from the reality in which one lives, from the milieu in which one lives, from the milieu in which one finds oneself; yet, one also finds that milieu in oneself. One is both a part of and apart from that milieu. The environment that one constructs must first be found in oneself. The idea of an objective observer in the social sciences is both a dream, reinforced by computers and other such technological wish devices, and a mistake. Social understanding for Ellul is understandable only through the filter of the personality. He states:

> If he (the observer) does not examine himself in and for himself the meaning of such and such a social movement, if he does not take himself as the first object of his observation, he is neglecting a major part of his work. He is not an independent observer; he is not a man watching an avalanche. He is a man observing human phenomena, in which he is involved willy-nilly.[1]

Ellul's critique is familiar. The intellectual must live in relation to his or her ideas, which are then turned back on the intellectual to become part of the observation. One does not live in a world in which significance is simply given. Significance is made and apprehended at the same time. The given always has a symbolic nature: meaning points to the object of meaning as well as back to whom that object has meaning. Meaning is the *result* of experience with an object. It is not simply outside or inside the observer. Meaning is in the conjunction of innerness and outerness.

As stated in the preceding chapter, memory gives force and meaning to symbolic construction. Because of memory, the given is not really given. Finding means finding again, discovering the inner element of experience in the outer element that makes possible experience as remembered. For example, the primitive finds the natural object sacred because it was previously given as sacred. Ellul understands that the Roman citizen finds his own heroism or the heroism of his father by finding it again within his cultural tradition. Thus, the individual connects with a sense of personal and collective memory to construct and to understand the present. The symbol is what gives shape to this present, joining it to the past—to what the present is not—and giving movement and dimension to the present. Continuity is provided for the individual and for the society. That is, the fullness of the present is made possible by seeing it in terms of what it is not, in relation to what it lacks. Again, this lack—this absence that is present—is not negative but constitutive. Without it politics and history are impossible. The modern age has adopted the science of forgetting, what Orion called *lethotechny*, an idea Ellul applauds.[2] He states:

> The most important kind of forgetfulness is political. Our recent experience of this runs deep. . . . How prophetic were Nietzsche's words in *Beyond Good and Evil*, "Blessed are the forgetful, for they shall recover even from their own stupid mistakes." This is most certainly true, but people who live submerged in forgetfulness cannot help being beset by fears about the present, which seem incomparable, unheard of, insurmountable, because they have lost all their memories of war, famine, errors, obstacles, lies, wandering in the desert, persecution, all the things that past generations in their obstinate will to live managed to overcome.[3]

Technique is *lethotechny*, opting for a life in the future, in mere possibility. Technique is the art of the possible. Typically, when nuclear scientists are asked about the dangers of nuclear waste material, they *remind* us that methods for safe storage are just over the horizon, an interesting sense of "remind" that promises a "return to the future." Outside the physics building at Emory University is a monument erected by the Gravity Research Foundation for the following purpose: "It is to remind students of the blessings forthcoming when science determines what gravity is, how it works, and how it may be controlled."

The real dangers that confronted the past are replaced with false dangers created by technique itself—mere possibility—the new necessity. Ellul states:

With no more future or past or frame of reference or meaningful connections, contemporary people confront the solitude in time and space that gives rise to their unconditional fear. But over this deep structure of fear a complex superstructure is erected, whose elements are the (real) facts previously alluded to, which are recognized but blown out of proportion in the universe of fear. Every item in the news feeds our anxiety (oil shortages, muggings in the subway, etc.). People often accuse the media of creating such anxiety, but radio and TV reports are simply responding to what the public wants to hear. The whole business of the news has become part and parcel of the climate of fear we live in.[4]

Mugging is a real danger; muggings on the news are not. Reported news is taken as real news, a real event. Oil shortages are caused by the economy having become technique and by technique tying together the whole economy. The fear generated by the mass media is more accurately anxiety, attached not to a real object over and against which we work, but to a climate created out of the media decor.

Real fear before a real object brings about symbolic activity. *Real fear* can only be experienced within a frame of reference by a subject that is distant from an object. The thundering sky provided this for the ancients, showing them with its immensity their limitations—what they were not. This absolute reference allowed them to become objects for themselves, creating opposition, taken up but not canceled, in the symbol. Anxiety is fear without object, an ill-defined and therefore more troubling malaise, the cause of the above condition. Ellul states:

... to prompt the transformation called for by the terrible conditions of our time, by the frightful complexity of the problems and tragedies overwhelming us, we need nothing less than an absolute frame of reference, a qualitative critical distance, a differential index, an outside "viewpoint," an epistemology that is not connected to our sociocultural mechanisms.[5]

Within sociopolitical mechanisms there is tension and conflict, but not all tensions are dialectical, for which the truly negative is needed. Most conflicts in a technological society produce more technique, when a nontechnical approach might be needed. Ellul observes:

Hegel in a well-known formula spoke of the positivity of negativity. This is essential, for if the positive remains alone, it remains unchanged: stable and inert. A positive—for example, an uncontested society, a force without counterforce, a man without dialogue, an unchallenged teacher, a church with no heretics, a single party with no rivals—will be shut up in the indefinite repetition of its own image. It will live in satisfaction at what was produced once, and will see no reason to change. Facts, circumstances, and events that might be contrary will be no more than annoying embarrassments for it.[6]

Thus, technique produces Hegel's "bad infinity," where the particular is produced indefinitely, masquerading as an infinity, but where there are no real differences between the false identities. This is the logic of mass production, where difference is only appearance, a matter of packaging. Problems within the system are indefinitely reproduced as it becomes impossible to get outside the system.

The individual feels increasingly powerless in a society whose institutions make decisions in which the individual seemingly has no part. Decisions are increasingly made by experts, and are purported to derive inexorably, from the system. Recently, for example, technical disasters like Bhopal, the space shuttle *Challenger* explosion—a "major malfunction"—and the Soviet Union's Chernobyl "accident" are met with a parade of experts, a flood of media coverage, and a decision to produce "safer technologies." This is the logic that hastened the development of nuclear power in the face of the atom bomb, namely the need to develop a "peaceful" use of the atom. Thus, technique grows regardless of the individual's role. As a result, or perhaps because of this, the world loses its capacity for dialectical inspiration.

The parade of technical innovation reveals a curious transformation of the relationship between the individual and the world. To court paradox, the individual, as mass man, *becomes* the world, but as an individual, he is alienated. Ellul states: "There results, then, an increasing distance between the situation of fact and the organization (or individual) in question. The only thing that can produce change or evolution is contradiction, contestation, the appearance of the negative, negativity. This implies a transformation of the situation."[7] An individual who remembers, a person committed to the vision "outside," is required. The computer has become the society's memory. Ellul states:

> In the human condition it is not enough that this contradiction be that of facts, events. There usually has to be an express and explicit contradiction put in words by someone who contradicts, who bears the negation. In this way the negativity induces and provokes innovation, and consequently the history, of the group or individual. One can see, then, that negativity has a wholly positive side. If there is transition from one state to another, we can thank negativity alone.[8]

The individual must appear speaking words, adopting a position wholly outside the technical society.

Ellul claims that the individual must reassert a dialectical relation with the world that is both similar to and different from that world. Within this important gap arises the symbol, language, and memory, which provide the basis for Ellul's methodology of non method. Because one is not the world; one speaks, writes, and remembers.

Ellul is an embodiment of his own method, finding in himself and in his distance from his place and time the force that he understands as technique. The dialectical distance Ellul commends is the one he finds in himself and in his encounter with his age. I am interested in narrating that encounter. I will discuss Ellul's dialectic by using his autobiographical works *A temps et à contretemps* (1981) [*In Season, Out of Season* (1982)][9] and *Perspectives on Our Age* (1981)[10] as springboards, placing them in relation to *L'Illusion politique* (1963) [*The Political Illusion* (1965)], the most personal of his theoretical works. *The Political Illusion* arose out of the gaps he found in his own time. He states: "Some of my books, for instance *The Political Illusion*, derive in part from my experiences in the political milieu— from the politician's inability to really change the world they live in, the enormous influence of administrative bodies. The politician is powerless against government bureaucracy; society cannot be changed through political action."[11] To abandon political action, for Ellul, was to recognize that there was no longer politics apart from technique—the recognition of the political illusion. This theory Ellul finds in his own life at the same time he finds his life caught up in technique.

Ellul, as an intellectual, constantly engages his theories in relation to his life. Therefore an intellectual biography is more appropriate than with most thinkers and is not merely a formality, a filling of space in the absence of real investigation. My purpose is not to do a "true" biography but to take Ellul's words and place them in relation to each other, to show how his social, political, theological, and existential reflections and recollections reveal his notion of *la technique*. I do not intend to reduce Ellul to any of his works or to a set of facts. I am interested in the shape that *la technique* reveals as it is placed in relation to the narration of a life—my narration of Ellul's account of his life and times.

Ellul's Intellectual Development

Jacques Ellul's life, like his thought, is a tapestry of extraordinary conflict and tension, taken up in his writing as it was and is lived. He is currently Emeritus Professor of the History and Sociology of Institutions in the faculty of law and economic science of the University of Bordeaux. He is known in France as an important interpreter of the Bible, for a time active with the Reformed Church of France. He is a social critic and intellectual, the author of at least forty books and eight hundred articles,[12] the editor of *Foi et Vie*, and the recipient of the Académie Française's Prize for History. He was, further, a respected member of the French Resistance during World War II, an officer of the Legion of Honor and Order of Merit, and ex-deputy mayor of Bordeaux. He has been a social worker with juvenile delinquents and he is an ardent environmentalist.

Ellul understands his studies and his life to be of a piece, its apparently various elements in dialectical relation with one another; he lives and understands his time in relation to technique as an absolute force, seeking to establish the goal of absolute efficiency in all domains and rigorously applying to all domains a mathematics-like methodology. This force establishes contradictions that can only be lived out, not allowing abstract intellectual solutions. Moreover, this force, not external to humanity but a feature of human intentionality, has shaped religion, law, history, politics, in fact, all the institutions of modern society. Technique has become the new sacred, a new religion, in direct conflict with Christianity. For Ellul, these two domains are in absolute conflict *and* they are the poles around which his life and his thought move. God functions as the Wholly Other, the completely transcendent. As transcendent, He moves against the finite, which has established its own hegemony, masquerading as the Wholly Other. The Christian speaks for the truly transcendent, thus setting up a conflict with the society. Ellul states: "In the realm of human history and in our society, Technique actually becomes the positive factor in the dialectical process; the role of mankind bearing the transcendent will necessarily be the negative. But, let us remember that the negative is the truly determinant element in the dialectical process, since it forces changes."[13]

In the last chapter I noted that Ellul believes that the dialectic has stopped. His mission is to keep the dialectic moving, for the sake of freedom. Ellul states:

> . . . dialectics is a procedure that does not exclude contraries, but includes them. We can't describe this too simplistically by saying that the positive and the negative combine; or that the thesis and the antithesis fuse into

a synthesis; dialectics is something infinitely more supple and more profound.[14]

Ellul's dialectic is not the simplistic reading of the Hegelian dialectic where thought and culture move hand in hand to more rational perfect harmony. There is, instead, always dramatic tension.

Ellul was born 6 January 1912 in Bordeaux, France. His father, Joseph, was of Italian-Serbian origin. His mother, Martha Mendes, was a native of Bordeaux, a mixture of Portuguese and French, with perhaps some Jewish ancestry.[15] The name Ellul is Jewish, the name of a month in the Hebrew calendar. Ellul is forever fascinated with the Jews as chosen people who nonetheless challenged God; who, though having challenged Him, could never really break with Him; who, in spite of all of their political and social problems, could never give up their quest for a New Jerusalem.

Ellul's father, Joseph, was a stern, severe man, who apparently never felt at home in Bordeaux. His grandfather was a ship owner in Trieste, and his grandmother a Serbian from the Obrenoviche line, a dynasty founded in 1817. Joseph Ellul was a great believer in honor, losing his job when he demanded an apology from his boss who had insulted him. Ellul states:

> I'll tell you about an event that had a great effect on my childhood. My father had a gift for languages—a gift that I don't have—and he spoke five languages fluently. He was a senior executive in a very large commercial company whose director was an extremely overbearing and quick-tempered man. It was an excellent position for my father. One day, the boss became terribly angry at my father in front of strangers. My father stood up and said to him, "Now you will apologize to me." The boss replied, "If you demand an apology, I'll fire you." "That is perfectly alright with me," said my father, "But I demand an apology." And he was fired. That is when the hard times began, because he had a horrible time finding another job.[16]

Ellul's relation to authority and his search for origins, his feeling for honor, and his embrace of language are motivating forces within his life and thought.

Ellul makes much of his feeling a foreigner in Bordeaux. He feels that neither he nor his family ever quite fit in. His grandfather committed suicide in the 1920s after he went bankrupt, and Ellul reminisces: "My father always held him up to me as an example: 'This is what an honorable man is like.' My grandmother was still young when my grandfather went bankrupt and killed himself. She dressed in black, shut herself up in an apartment, and never left it again."[17] In *La Foi au prix du doute* (1980) in [*Living Faith and Doubt in a Perilous World* (1980)] he states:

> It's worthwhile to die for honor. My grandfather committed suicide because he had gone bankrupt. Nowadays people don't do that anymore, nor do they know what they're talking about when they pronounce the word "honor." I admire my grandfather, and I have always been imbued with the value of honor. But I know that it's relative and changes with time, which is something that belief will not tolerate.[18]

This sense of honor feeds Ellul's sense of being "foreign." His grandfather's honor seemed out of place in a materialistic world.

Ellul's father, though raised in the Greek Orthodox, tradition was what Ellul called a Voltairean liberal: "(The bust of Voltaire sat enthroned on the mantle—he was the authority), [and Joseph was] an epicurean (even in practice, at least during his youth when he had a good position), but very liberal."[19] His mother, on the other hand, was a devout Protestant, although Ellul feels that there was "... some sort of agreement between him and my mother that she would never go to church. ... I only recall seeing my mother kneel at times and perform this mysterious act she called prayer, but I had no idea with it meant."[20] Religious training was not a part of Ellul's early home life, present more as an absence, present as his mother's private ritual in opposition to his father. Later, there was some training:

> At the age of fourteen, I did have a year of catechism, which I did not find the least bit interesting. No, there was something—the pastor who taught us the catechism had us read a text from Pascal's *Pensées*, and it struck me. (At the same time in school we were studying *les Provinciales* of which only the reasoning interested me because we quite naturally understood nothing of the crux of the argument.) There again, a phrase became true. Surprisingly, I never found it again exactly as I had remembered having read it. It was a text by Pascal in which he indicts those who try to walk two different paths: "*Vae ingredientibus in duabus viis.*" Another text which, *a posteriori*, I consider prophetic for me. It is the only thing I got out of this catechism.[21]

Ellul remembers Pascal's phrase, possibly altering it as he remembers it, warning of the dangers of pursuing two paths, prophetic for a dialectical thinker.

Ellul had a happy childhood, although plagued by poverty. He writes:

All of my childhood I lived the life you read of in novels about working class families in the depression ... [although] I was perfectly happy. I have wonderful memories of my childhood. Every facet of it brought me happiness: the ice and snow, spring flowers in the public park, the quays and docks that I knew inside and out; the arrivals of transatlantic steamers and the departures of cod-fishing boats; the storms (I loved to go to the park when there was a storm). At home, my playmate was a marvelous cat. Everything was an opportunity for happiness. I didn't need toys. And though I was an only child, I never suffered from loneliness (I enjoyed the silence and solitude) nor from lack of conversation.[22]

Solitude, silence, and nature seem to be the sources of his childhood happiness, as he was left to his own devices while his parents worked away from home.

By the time he was sixteen, and after his father's run-in with authority, he and his mother supported the family, she by teaching art lessons and he by giving lessons in Latin, Greek, German, and French, three to four hours a day. Although claiming no abilities with language, he continued teaching upon entering the university. He shopped and cooked for the family, as well. He states: "Since I had to do everything (and pass my exams), I very quickly organized myself so that I knew exactly how much time I required for each activity, each errand, each reading assignment. I had to become efficient at all costs. I used the Taylor system on myself."[23] *La technique* in its most subtle and sophisticated form was demystified for Ellul at an early age.

Ellul received his youthful passion for the visual arts from his mother. He says: "I believe she was a very good painter. If she had had the chance to exibit her work, she would certainly have been successful. So, I lived in a certain artistic atmosphere—though exclusively one of visual art, which is also significant. I never heard music. I must have been twenty-three or twenty-four the first time I attended a concert."[24] The absence of music, as the presence of many absences, becomes a feature of the dialectic later for Ellul, who finds sound to represent the domain of the all-encompassing, while the visual points to the sensual and to the certain. The word, *la parole*, the other of the image, is tied to music.

In school, Ellul showed great gifts for literature and history, digesting much classical literature. He states:

I knew by heart miles of Latin, Greek, and French poetry—classical poetry. But modern poetry did not exist for me. In 1931 I had never heard of Gide. And when I suddenly realized that since 1880, fifty years had passed, I was seized with an intellectual panic, saying to myself that I would never be able to read all of Proust, that I could never absorb all of that. And I was overcome by an insatiable appetite for reading.[25]

Literature and memory were closely aligned. His knowledge of history was mostly a collection of detail, stimulating another appetite, the desire for a key, for deep connections.[26] Reading and knowing carried very profound existential weight for Ellul, who states: "I have sometimes been captivated by a line of poetry or by an expression from a novel. There is a mysterious instant. Suddenly a phrase becomes a personal utterance. It penetrates your life."[27] Ellul's aesthetic education provides him a place to which he frequently returns. The word connects memory with desire; desire inhabits the evanescent space of the word, both music and image.

The decision to study law was not Ellul's own: "... when I graduated from high school, my father told me, 'Now, you are going to study law.' I went through some rebellion, but when my father said something, there was no question of putting up an argument."[28] He states further: "My father had spoken, and I accepted, but after a few weeks I affirmed, 'Then I will go all the way with it.'"[29] His decision to go all the way takes him to the study of Roman law from an unusual angle, with a characteristic irony: "I thought, 'Isn't it extraordinary? Here I am going to become a professor of Roman Law and be very well paid by a society that I will not be serving in any way. Because it is quite clear that Roman Law is of no use to anything or anyone.' I was taking a little personal revenge on society; I thought my joke was quite good."[30] As if to answer his father's authority, he writes his doctoral thesis on the *mancipium*, a Roman institution that allowed a father to sell his son.[31]

Behind Ellul's joke—his irony—there is comedy, a move toward a reconciliation of tensions in his life and society, uniting his literary and historical studies and answering the political-economic tragedies that accompany much of his early life. The study of Roman law provided direction for this move:

> Roman law speaks of things that people have lived and invented; it has this historical dimension to it that I liked. And then, I had always enjoyed reading the Latin writers, much more than the Greeks; I felt in harmony with the Roman mind. They were not philosophers, either. Roman law attracted me even by its structure: a pragmatism proceeding by analysis of reality, and then reconstruction of this reality by applying precise categories, finally arriving at the resolution of concrete human problems.

It was never a matter of abstract deductions nor even of arbitrary regulations. Moreover, up until the classical period, it was a system of law developed outside of the political powers; it took experience very much into account, to the point that it seemed to me to fulfill the role of a barrier against abuses of power. And certainly, even at that time, I didn't like the state. This took place during the thirties, when fascisms and ideologies of the state sprang up everywhere.[32]

Literature, history, and politics are yoked together, pointing toward a pragmatism not merely material but founded on a *sensus communis*, a politics grounded in literature and common sense. These realizations occurred when politics, grounded in technique, science, and propaganda, was on the march. The engines of facism and modern politics were plowing up the ancient fields sown by Roman tradition, to which Ellul returns to understand his own time. The Romans were aware, he leads us to believe, of their makings, their symbolic constructions, which were down to earth and not metaphysical, while not being wholly materialistic either. It is at this point that he discovered Marx.

After the financial crash of 1929, Ellul first read *Das Kapital*, in 1930. He says:

I felt that at last I knew why my father was out of work, at last I knew why we were destitute. For a boy of seventeen, perhaps eighteen, it was an astonishing revelation about the society he lived in. It also illuminated the working-class condition I had plunged into. ... Thus, for me, Marx was an astonishing discovery of the reality of this world, which, at that time, few people condemned as the "capitalist" world. I plunged into Marx's thinking with an incredible joy; I had finally found *the* explanation. ... It was a total vision of the human race, society, and history. And since I did not follow any creed, religion, or philosophy— for I am very unphilosophical—I was bound to find something extremely satisfying in Marx.[33]

Marx provided Ellul with that necessary key, that vision of totality. Marx explained the need for social change and the need for revolution, the need for historical analysis that is also social analysis, and the need to understand the poor as those whom the society excludes.[34]

Marxism was not without problems, however. A consistently dialectical thinker, Ellul disagreed with Marx's undialectical belief in the reality of progress and in the so-called liberating capacities of work. He also took issue with Marx's criticisms of the transcendental arts:

... I rejected something that Marx said: "There are an infrastructure, seriousness, solidity, economy, technology, and then there are imagination, philosophy, theology, which are not important." For me, the two elements were to be kept together and it was necessary to progress stage by stage and with this permanent contradiction. That was ultimately the key to all my later thinking.[35]

Ellul understands that Marx's thought was rooted in a bourgeois faith in technique as having its own status as an ultimate value, as a transcendent phenomenon.

In 1932, Ellul underwent a radical conversion to Christianity. He states: "I was converted—not by someone, nor can I say I converted myself. It is a very personal story, but I will say that it was a very brutal and very sudden conversion. I became a Christian and I was obliged to profess myself a Christian in 1932."[36] About this event, Ellul says little, adding:

And then there was an event in my life that could be called a conversion and that I don't wish to relate. We have heard too many conversion stories. ... I will mention just two things on this subject. First, it was as violent as the most violent conversion you have heard of; second, I started to run for my life from the One who had revealed himself to me. It wasn't the kind of positive conversion that pushes you to read the Bible or go to church. It was the opposite. No, not exactly the opposite; I realized that God had spoken, but I didn't want him to have me. I fled. This struggle lasted for ten years.[37]

In whatever form, Ellul encountered the *mysterium tremendum*. What is important is that God spoke and that Ellul was afraid. Around twenty-two, Ellul had a second conversion:

... [it] came in reading chapter eight of the Epistle to the Romans; it was an awesome experience for me. It is often said that the Epistle to the Romans is the Protestant epistle. It is the chapter where "nature suffers and groans in the pains of childbirth." It gave me a response both on the individual level and on the collective level. I saw a perspective beyond history, one that is definitive.[38]

From this point on Ellul had two masters—Christianity and Marxism—and he was unable to give up either. With Marx he had a ground in the world and with Christianity he obtained a transcendental sense.

The tension between Marx and Christianity is fundamental, fulfilling Pascal's warning. Ellul writes:

I realized that Christianity was a totality implying an ethic in all areas, and that Marx too claimed to be a totality. I was sometimes torn between the two extremes, and sometimes reconciled; but I absolutely refused to abandon either one. I lived my entire intellectual life in this manner. It was thus that I was progressively led to develop a mode of dialectical thinking which I constantly made my foundation. In my own life, I confronted the demands of Marx and the demands of the Bible and put them together.[39]

Although these two domains cannot be reconciled intellectually, Ellul realized that their contradictions could be lived out.

Marx altered Ellul's reading of the Bible, forcing his thought to become contextual, sensitive to the milieu in which it occured. He was, further, led to read and reread the Bible in relation to this contextualization. His Christianity forced him to examine every finite claim to a totality. Both perspectives move in creative opposition to one another. He states: "I have come more and more to consider that we all have a certain interpretation of the same revealed truth, but no one possesses it completely. We all ought to come together in such a way that we may recognize in others what we lack in ourselves."[40]

Never a conventional Christian, Ellul tried Catholicism briefly in 1932, but he found Protestantism closer to his understanding of the Bible, concerned more with a reading and interpreting of the text.[41] He then joined the Reformed Church of France, which was tending toward Calvin. Ellul states, ". . . [Calvinism] beguiled me with its rigor, intransigence, and total use of the Scriptures."[42] Calvinism, however, failed to meet Ellul's dialectical requirements in matters such as grace. Calvin's theory of predestination worked against the notion of a forgiving God. With his friend Jean Bosc, later a theologian in the Reformed church, Ellul turned to Barth, a dialectician who enabled him to deal with such problems as grace. Ellul writes:

There is, however, another type of dialectical thinking, which inspired Hegel. This is Biblical thinking, both in the Old Testament and in Saint Paul. Here, we constantly see two contradictory, apparently irreconcilable things affirmed, and we are told that they always meet to wind up in a new situation. One example is Saint Paul's assertion: "You are saved by grace; *therefore* work for your salvation by your works." This sounds perfectly contradictory. Either one is saved already and saved by the grace of God; in that case, one need not bother working. Or one is called upon to work toward salvation with works, which means that one is not already saved and that one is not saved by the grace of God. Now Saint Paul says both things in the same sentence. This is dialectical thinking: once you are saved, you are integrated into history, into a process leading to your salvation, which is given to you in advance, but which you have to implement, which you have to achieve, which you have to somehow take in hand and utilize. But this cannot be done on an intellectual and schematic level. It will be done in the course of your life. That is why we are dealing with something contradictory, yet it is not contradictory when we live it.[43]

Salvation is a process in which one becomes what one is not, a limitation that is not experienced as such unless it is both fulfilled and unfulfilled. It is this sense of dialectic that Ellul feels inspired Hegel, a sense of the movement of consciousness out of itself toward what it lacks. The Absolute is given in advance as a lack, an absence that is a present toward which one must work. This was the dialectic Barth also championed, showing that God's concept of Grace was liberating in its embrace of opposition, opening possibilities rather than forcing closures. The Barthian is not to conform to absolute limits.[44] These limits must be viewed and achieved through conflict with existing orders, always related back to biblical exegesis.

Barth enabled Ellul to connect Christianity with his classical training, to integrate "... the myth as a means of comprehending the biblical text. Now, at this time the myth was considered to be equivalent to legend or even fabrication. Myths were stories that should be ignored. ... This was a significant discovery for me."[45] The myth, like the biblical story, embodies contradiction as a mode of telling, of narrating, and of understanding, opening up a sense of history. The Roman myths, impossible stories about gods who were somehow men, particular beings, although eternal and universal, provided a foundation for Roman society. The gods provided humanity with a sense of what they were and were not, a knowledge based on contrast and opposition. The Roman religion and the Christian religion, although distinct cultures embodying distinct sensibilities, are both based on this sense of lack and opposition.

Ellul shared with Barth his mission to examine God's word from the standpoint of man's finite actions, actions that allowed the Absolute, the Wholly Other, to appear in dialectical relief. Ellul also shared in Barth's attack on a subjective liberalism prevailing in Protestant theology, opting instead for the primacy of the biblical text. Ellul and Barth refused to identify human action and word with the Word of God, fearing in part that the church would come to be identified too closely with the social condition, rather than to stand in opposition to it, agreeing that salvation came only from God, and emphasizing the relativity of earthly religion, forcing it always to return to biblical revelation. They conceived of it more as a book of questions than as a book of answers. The Bible perpetually asks the fundamental questions: Who am I? Who are you? Who is your brother? Whom do you seek?[46]

In the end, however, Barth was too systematic for Ellul. Ellul states: "I have never adhered to a system. In regard to Barth himself, I have always taken a critical distance. My relation to Kierkegaard is not comparable. Here, I am only to listen."[47] Kierkegaard becomes a mirror and Ellul finds himself in his reflection in Kierkegaard.

With Barth, dialectical themes move toward the Wholly Other; with Kierkegaard, these themes, flow back to the self. Ellul turns to Kierkegaard seeking guidance for the Christian's proper response to contemporary life. He states:

> When I speak of the individual as the source of hope I mean the individual who does not lend himself to society's game, who disputes what we accept as self-evident ... who questions even the movement of this society. ... This radical subjectivity will inform also three human passions which seem to be the essential ones—the passion to create, to love, to play. But these mighty drives of the human heart must find a particular expression in each person. It is in the building of a new daily life, in the discovery of things, acts, situations utterly different from those that society would fasten on us, that this subjectivity can express itself. ... I am convinced that Christians are the only ones who can attempt it—but here on the condition that they start from zero. Kierkegaard, it seems to me, alone can show us how to start. ... If we are to question our society in so radical a fashion we must adopt a point of view essentially different from that of society's—one that we cannot arrive at by starting from our human wisdom. It is precisely because (the Bible) speaks of a Wholly Other that the revelation provides us with a point of view and a point of departure that are essentially different.[48]

Kierkegaard's subjectivity is radical because it leads of necessity outside of itself and back to itself, at once distanced and yet individual—ironic, in a word. It is finding the Wholly Other in one's self that enables one to create, to love, and to play—passions that lead backward to the mythopoetic responses of the first societies, and forward to those technical societies wishing to retain their humanity. It is a passion to create that is a form of knowing and remembering together, a return as Ellul puts it, to zero.

In summary, Ellul's approach to theology develops out of these influences. From Kierkegaard, he takes the importance of the self, the radical faith in the presence of despair and anxiety, the need to follow Abraham's example in his "teleological suspension of the ethical,"[49] and the importance of love and hope as a Christian response. From Barth and Calvin, Ellul adopts a radical attention to scriptural exegesis, emphasizing Barth's dialectical concerns. These dialectical studies occurred while Fascism was in power in Italy, and Nazism was transforming Germany. The *Section Française de l'Internationale Ouvrière* (SFIO) begins to gain political acceptance along with the Communist party. Ellul states:

> Of course, my approach to the Bible has been influenced by several factors in our society. For example, I developed a dialectical approach to the Bible not because I am a genius but because Hegel's and Marx's dialectics had been revived and because Barth himself was essentially a dialectical theologian. All of this was furnished me by the cultural milieu in which I developed. My cultural setting also gave me the critical method I applied to the Bible.[50]

Thus, Ellul is well aware of the relativity of his own approach, moving from his analysis and its relation to his environment back to himself.

In this period of great political conflict, Ellul became actively involved in the fight against Fascism, and he participated in the Paris riots on 10 February 1934.[51] Then, with his lifelong friend Bernard Charbonneau, he joined Emmanuel Mounier's anti-Fascist *Esprit* movement, in 1934. Mounier, a devout the dedicated Catholic, espoused the philosophical movement called Personalism, which rejected the modern social tendencies toward individualism and collectivism, to which Ellul and Charbonneau also found much affinity. Ellul states: "We were able to assume the perspectives of Personalism ... which advocated a return to man's basic dimensions, insisting upon the human being as a totality, as embodied, and as engaged as a result of a free choice, politically motivated. ..."[52] They were in agreement that modern society was depersonalizing and that it robbed man of his sense of political and bodily involvement in the world. Man was being turned into an abstraction. Consequently, they participated in the founding of the journal *Esprit* and in the founding of the *Nouveau Ordre*, an activist group to engage the ideas espoused in the journal.[53]

Both Ellul and Charbonneau were upset, however, by Mounier's militant Catholicism, by the propensity of the Paris group to dominate over more regional concerns, which ignored, for example, the groups in the provinces, and by the intellectualist tendencies of the group. Ellul and Charbonneau were more concerned with beginning local activist groups, more consistent with *Esprit*'s stated commitment to decentralization. In a later reflection, "Pourquoi Je me suis separé de Mounier" (1950), Ellul argues that it was the obsessions for unity that ultimately broke the *Esprit* movement, and that his Barthism allowed him to keep a critical distance on all political movements at that time. He writes:

> If "pluralism" remained a necessity, we experienced that it was not possible to work in common when there were different and even opposed theological presuppositions. I believe that communal action is possible between people who have divergent political opinions. But when these opinions are based on a spiritual judgment [*jugement spirituel*] (like, for example, the Communist judgment) then the collaboration quickly breaks up. This experience of engaging the facts forced us to confront our own spiritual positions which was dishonest for pretending that we could bring everybody together.[54]

The "spiritual judgment" is the belief that each person contains a special, pregiven nature, making absolute unity possible. On Ellul's view, after the Fall, all breaks up and humanity begins to babble; unity is only achieved at the price of a labor with the negative, the labor of dialectic, which never abates.

Moreover, Mounier and his group ignored Ellul's and Charbonneau's warnings that technique and science were the main disruptive forces of the time, an idea Ellul often credits to Charbonneau who was at the time, he says, more advanced than he.[55] Ellul writes:

> He [Mounier] rejected the idea that man was really able to be put in danger by the powers of the world and the forces in action today, of which man could be aware. Above all, since 1933, he repeatedly came to the idea that, "It is not the state, it is not technique, nor is it money that is the danger; it is the use man makes of them."[56]

Power, money, and technique, the spiritual triumvirate, were not understood by Mounier as forms of intentionality, but this is the sense Ellul adopts from this moment on. Mounier believed in the efficacy of the human spirit and reason to triumph over the alienation and malaise caused by technique. He did not follow Ellul and Charbonneau, that technique had become reason itself. By 1939 the movement had disbanded, leaving Mounier as the editior of *Esprit*, which remained only as an intellectual's journal, standing apart from the currents of politics and everyday life.

Ellul's political consciousness took shape, as it did for many Europeans, against the rise of Fascism, against Hitler's coming to power, against the socialist-Communist controveries, and finally,

against the Second World War. Having received his *Doctorat* in law
in 1939, he became a lecturer at Montpelier and at the University of
Strasbourg from 1937 to 1940. In 1940 the Vichy government,
headed by Marshal Petain, was installed in Paris, and Ellul
denounced it. He further advised a group of Alsation students
against returning to Germany. He writes:

> ... I gave a small political talk, telling them not to believe anything that
> Marshal Petain said and, above all, absolutely not to return to Alsace,
> where they would obviously be drafted into the German army. I told
> them that the Germans would use any means to get them back to Alsace,
> which turned out to be true. ... I gave this speech to some fifty or sixty
> students, and one of them reported my statements to the police. (His
> fellow students told me who it was, and I later found out that the
> unfortunate boy was indeed conscripted into the German army and died
> on the Russian front.)[57]

Ellul was summoned by the police commissioner, who was a
reluctant supporter of the Vichy government. Ellul was told by the
commissioner that his speech was irresponsible, that he should have
been arrested, and that he should calm down. Ellul states:

> Nevertheless, the report reached the ministry, and they also discovered in
> my file that my father was foreign-born. So, according to the laws of
> Vichy, there was a double reason to dismiss me: for being the son of a
> foreigner and for having made hostile statements.[58]

Ellul was fired and he recalls the drama of the event—the betrayal,
the retribution—and reiterates his position as foreigner and as
speaker of the word. Events were taking on the character of
necessity, requiring action. He says, "At the beginning ... the events
had control over us."[59] A sense of destiny pervades Ellul's life: he
realizes that violence, propaganda, technique, and the state are all
tied together.

Three weeks later, Ellul's father was summoned to appear before
the German police and then sent to a detention camp. Knowing how
the Nazis had behaved in the past, Ellul attempted to persuade him
not to go. Ellul recalls, perhaps ironically: "My father replied, 'No,
I have nothing to worry about. I'm over seventy years old, and the
international agreements prohibit the arrest of people over seventy.'
My father had always trusted in laws."[60] Having studied them Ellul
knew better. Learning of his Dutch-born wife's imminent arrest,
Ellul moved to the little town of Martes, forty kilometers from
Bordeaux, and joined the resistance.

Ellul's resistance activities were basically nonviolent, providing help and hospice for escaping Jews. Ellul insists, however, that these activities began without political aim.[61] The National Council of Resistance was formed, and talked of revolution, and for a time Ellul hoped that a new state would arise from the rubble of wartime France. Charbonneau, however, remained a skeptic.[62]

In 1943, Ellul was given a small, anonymous teaching assignment at the school of law at Bordeaux, for fear of Nazi retribution.[63] He and his wife also farmed to support themselves. In 1944 he participated in the liberation council and was assistant to the mayor until 1946. Of this period he writes:

> And since it was obviously impossible for me, even working hard, to seriously study thirty issues during one day, I had to rely on departmental heads. Now, by probing I found out several times that the reports were complete fabrications. They gave me files that were not based on serious technical studies, or they asked for my signature, just my signature, and that meant committing myself to things that I didn't agree with at all. I finally said to myself: if that's what it is like for a city concilman, what must it be like for a cabinet member who receives not thirty files but three or four hundred? He finds himself totally dependent upon the departments.[64]

Ellul begins to encounter the new political necessity, *la technique*. Politics takes on an abstract and anonymous character, removed from the lives it serves. Most important, Ellul finds himself reduced to a signature, to a sign devoid of reference.

Ellul was asked to continue in the Bordeaux government after the liberation, but Charbonneau and his wife advised against it. Ellul left politics. He writes:

> I had seen the failure of the Popular Front in 1936; the failure of the personalist movement, which we intended to be revolutionary and which we tried to start on a modest scale; the failure of the Spanish revolution, which had great importance for Charbonneau and me; and the failure of the liberation. All of this formed an accumulation of ruined revolutionary possibilities. After this, I never believed anything could be changed by this route.[65]

Ellul transformed these failures in a writing and teaching career, exposing what he understood to be the forces at work in the modern age.

From 1947 on, he taught at the Institute of Political Studies, while teaching on the law faculty at the University of Bordeaux. It was at the Institute that he lectured on Marx and developed his theory of technique.

The Political Illusion

Between 1942 and 1943, Ellul planned his writing in two directions: the theological and the sociological, with works in history providing connections between the many themes he developed. His first study after his dissertation was *Le fondement theologique du droit* (1946) [*The Theological Foundation of Law* (1960)] which argues that all law exhibits a transcendental character: (1) all societies have laws that bind them together in a desire to found limits; (2) laws fundamentally serve of protect property, family, and life; (3) laws themselves may be arbitrary, but the desire for law is not.[66] Law arises, however, in a mythological-theological context but later comes under rational contemplation. Then, theories of natural law appear, and the law becomes an abstract, philosophical object. Ellul writes:

> The affinity between man and law is gone, except for the fact that certain people take advantage of the law. Reason remains, but it hardens law into an object so that it strikes no truly responsive chord in man. The fact that the average human being is no longer either at home in the world of law nor deeply attached to it has a most serious result. Man no longer sees why he should obey this law. Law is molded according to economic and political necessities and becomes absurd in relation to man.[67]

The origins of law are lost, forgotten; and law becomes a manipulation of reason, a kind of technique. The Romans recognized this in their phrase *summa ius, summa injuria*, meaning that when law becomes a mathematical function, a rule, it serves as justice for no one.[68] For Ellul, the true origins of law are outside the natural order. Ellul writes this study at a time when laws in the modern state move by the demands of technique, serving the new sacred. The decadence of law, however, begins when it is turned into an absolute.[69]

In his next book, *Présence au monde moderne* (1948) [*Presence of the Kingdom* (1951)], Ellul enunciates his opposition to technology as the new sacred, maintaining the importance of a God who is a Wholly Other.[70] It is such a God who keeps man's actions from becoming closed, from having an absolute character. Freedom can only be defined as a perpetual becoming of that which is moving in relation to that which it is not. This involves the powers of the individual always sensitive to a context that is spatial and temporal and dialectical.[71] Freedom is possible only under a law which is not worshiped. The current law has become technique.

The sociological situation Ellul spelled out in a trilogy—*La Technique ou l'enjeu du siècle* (1954); *Propagandes* (1962) [*Propaganda: The Formation of Men's Attitudes* (1965)]; *L'Illusion politique* (1965) [The Political Illusion (1972)].[72] *La technique* shows the extent of technology's power, its penetration into the heights and depths of modern daily life. *Propagandes* shows the power of technique to exist in relation to the reduction of daily life to the ephemeral—abstractions created by the machinery of the state for the purpose of effecting unified action. *L'Illusion politique* explains how the state is reduced to the ephemeral with the cooption of each person's sense of self, memory, and otherness.

The Political Illusion, dedicated to Charbonneau, begins with an epigraph from Saint-Just: "The people will fancy an appearance of freedom: illusion will be their native land."[73] Ellul proceeds with a discourse about absence. He indicates that the loss of true political freedom may be measured by the amount of discourse on a subject. He states:

> Everyday, scientific, polemical, didactic, philosophic studies on politics and democracy are appearing. Every one of these studies—my own above all—testifies to our attachment to these works of man—politics and democracy—and the fear that haunts us because we know well at the bottom of our souls that nothing is left of them but words.[74]

What we possess, we do not talk about. So much discourse about freedom fills the air in the presence of its absence. In this, little is new. Symbols are the attempts of the within-that-is-without to make a fullness of the world. The poem about love in the absence of love is an expression of love. True symbolic expression, as discussed in the preceding chapter, points in two ways: toward the object and back toward the self that expresses the object. But the current words about freedom are just words, as Ellul says above. He means that they have become signs and not symbols. They have become puffs of wind devoid of qualities of universality: they are simply expressions of thereness. Our current freedoms, he argues, are just words, like his own signature on the forms, that he signed as deputy mayor. The poet is aware of the absence of his love, the reason he writes poetry; the modern citizen is unaware of politics as absence, but feels the absence nonetheless and speaks strings of meaningless words—clichés about freedom as politics.

Since the French Revolution, Ellul states, freedom has been conceived in political terms.[75] All know, all believe, that politics is the most important discipline of study and practice. Women, for example, had not been thought free until they had achieved the right to vote. Voting is freedom, and abuses of human rights in underdeveloped countries can be tolerated as long as the freedom to vote can be brought to those lands. Democracy has come to mean the freedom to vote. This freedom is even thought to be necessary. If one does not vote, one is not doing one's duty. Nonvoting cannot be tolerated. A country's progress is measured by the achievement of these voting rights. As a result, paradoxically, the state has grown in power as reality has come to be defined in terms of laws, expressions of voting rights. Moreover, if people are to vote intelligently, they must be informed: the media and the news are thus fundamental political tools. People must learn to read reports and to interpret facts and statistics to become rational and good citizens. Since the French Revolution, then, two political characteristics have surfaced: statism and rationalism.[76] Either as a result of or in spite of revolutions, the state has increased in power, and power is managed in terms of reason, in terms of science and technology.[77] The irrational is not tolerated. As Foucault has observed: the irrational was locked up, dissected, punished, and perpetually observed. Political freedom has necessitated the prison, the asylum, the clinic where disease, unreason, and recalcitrance can come under the technician's gaze.[78] Freedom has become a serious business.

Politics becomes a necessity, an absolute, when no one is free not to participate in it. Reason is confined to science and technology, to the fact and to empirical evidence, to the image. Political values thus are denied any transcendental quality by being located exclusively in the here and now. As Ellul says, " . . . the decisive trait of today's politics is the fusion of two contradictory elements: the necessary and the ephemeral."[79] While eternal truths are claimed to exist no longer, science and politics establish themselves as absolutes. From these standpoints, it is held that true knowledge of a fixed reality cannot be obtained. Reality changes ceaselessly; all, it is believed, is contingent. Nonetheless, the technical demands for consistency and efficiency persist, in spite of the above claims. If true reality cannot be known truly, then this truth could not be known. Nor could it be known that consistency was a test for truth or that efficiency amounted to anything more than reinforcement of the demands of an existing system.

The full irony of Ellul's claim may be put simply: politics becomes necessary just at the moment it no longer exists. Authentic politics requires two qualities: (1) dialectical reason, as opposed to technical reason; and (2) a wide ranging vision of the future. Considering the first, following Hegel, necessity and contingency must be held in dialectical tension.[80] The necessary is, by definition, that which is considered so. True political freedom of choice maintains a consideration and discourse between real alternatives such that possible choice between alternatives remains open. For example, the mere presence of the Communist party in America is not clearly an expression of political choice until it becomes a possible option. Similarly, a political decision requires a view of the possible made out of a grasp of the past and the willingness to risk failure in projecting and acting on a future envisioned from the sense of continuity thus obtained.[81] Most modern political decisions are made merely out of a consideration of the possible. What *can* be done usually *is* done, if it can be sanctioned by technology, science, and other concerns for efficient ordering. As Ellul understands it:

> Thus the role of politics is not to "freeze" society into a certain shape, but to introduce into it factors of continuity without which the coherence and continuity of the group would become too much a matter of chance. Finally, permanent arrangements always lead rapidly to an exhaustion of human and social substance.[82]

A society needs a sense of destiny, a feeling of continuity with a past, or the society falls apart in the exigencies of an eternal present, leaving a belief in progress that borders on the mythological and reveals that no society can break free of its myths.

Ellul draws on an etymological distinction in French between *la politique* and *le politique*.[83] The latter refers to politics as the general interest of the public, to their common good, their common concern. *La politique* refers to the machinery, to the institutions for implementing notions and goods to benefit the common good. Thus, *la politique* and *la technique* are reflective of each other. *La politique* is to serve *le politique*. But, in a technical society, eventually means become ends. Ellul is drawing upon his own experience as well, and upon the theories that gave them form, that is, upon his past experiences with the liberation government, with the *Esprit* movement, with his father's reverence for law, which made him its victim. Further, his recent experiences under de Gaulle's Fifth Republic confirmed these notions and allowed him to conclude that conservative de Gaulle and socialist Pierre Mendes-France really did not disagree on the fundamental goal of government: the movement of France into the future under the auspices of more technical development and a more planned economy.[84] Moreover, this development seemed to take place regardless of traditional political or economic concerns.

The Pierrelatte atomic energy installation project, begun in 1953, clearly reveals the autonomy of technical development. Originally opposed on the grounds that it was too militaristic, the development of atomic energy for "peaceful uses" was carried forth under all succeeding governments, indicating that peaceful and military uses of technique are indistinguishable, no matter how liberal or conservative the regime.[85] The *unicité*, the monism, of the technical phenomenon, that is, the tendency of technique to become a world, as I discuss in detail in the next chapter, is here apparent: what is technically possible will become actual. All other ends and goals— political, philosophical, religious, artistic—are subordinate to it.

Ellul's Marxist sympathies are strained during this period when technique becomes for him the necessary, as had politics earlier. Marx's insistence on the need for dialectical movement in history took a bizarre turn during the Stalin regime, as Stalin's *techniques* of force and terror were interpretable as a dialectic return. This point, Ellul remarks, is missed by Maurice Merleau-Ponty in *Humanisme et Terreur* (1947) [*Humanism and Terror* (1969)].[86] Merleau-Ponty understands that "... the dialectic is effectively replaced by the scientific rationalism of the last generation apparently because the dialectic leaves too great a margin for ambiguity and too much scope for divergences."[87] But he does not question the necessity of instituting force by technical means. Merleau-Ponty correctly notes the disappearance of choice in modern politics but then sanctions a violence only possible by technique to bring about the dialectic's return. He states: "For, by hiding violence one grows accustomed to it and makes an institution of it. On the other hand, if one gives violence its name and if one uses it, as the revolution always did, without pleasure, there remains a chance of driving it out of history."[88] Reason is given a priority, a power, tied to naming. It is assumed that one will not get used to naming; that naming is naming. Technique, according to Ellul, humiliates the symbolic order. Naming becomes an act of propaganda, of unreason and obfuscation through apparent clarification. This is all a function of technique to which the modern Marxist has subordinated the dialectic, Marx, and history.

As technique becomes a reality, the only realistic approach becomes technique, obeying its own logic, eschewing a transcendental perspective. Ellul writes:

Because of external competition and internal pressure, efficiency must become the primary aim. But this means that one must adopt the system of the enemy, and that those we hate will still win in the end. We have known for a long time that only a dictatorial regime can oppose a dictatorial movement on the rise (Romania between 1935 and 1939, for example); that only propaganda can oppose propaganda; that only a rationalized—a planned economy—can withstand the competition of another planned economy. All of which means that ultimately Hitler really won the war.[89]

Arms buildups may only be met by arms buildups. Defensive systems will engender offensive systems, and *vice versa*. Defensive systems require coordination by computers, by those who can run them, and by a society that can afford them. Society must build, educate, and budget for these concerns. The military uses of technique will spill over into other areas of society as they did when high-rise apartments were inspired by army barracks and when fast food appeared, modeled after the K-ration.[90]

Technical rationality entails organization, and organization entails rationality. *La technique* becomes a circle, a concentration camp where suffering has been minimized and even air-conditioned. This desire to coordinate all areas of state life follows Hitler's ideas. In "Victoire d'Hitler" (1945), for the journal *Réforme*, Ellul prophesies that Hitler's way would become the ways of all modern states in using propaganda and technique to gain total control, the goal of any planned economy.[91] The goals of each state might differ, but the means, which become the ends, are ultimately the same. Ironically, the greatest control is gained in regimes that consider themselves the most free. Much of Hitler's propaganda was overt, inflammatory, and hence ineffective. Ellul's genius was to see, as early as 1946, that *The Reader's Digest* was propaganda of the most insidious sort. He states:

It [the *Digest*] is concerned not only to inform but also to form public thought. Under the guise of anecdotes, facile presentations (no matter how complicated the issue, all must be immediately understood by a .high school student of medium intelligence, says the editor), the *Digest* has a clear dogmatic goal: of making the thought of men adapt to certain criteria, of forming a common thought. And, most important . . . is the reduction of all sensibility to a common denominator.

The hero of M. Wallace, editor of the *Reader's Digest*, is Henry Ford. He wants to succeed in publishing like Henry Ford did in the automobile industry. He wants to reach each reader on his own level. Like Ford, the move is toward mass production. Wallace has declared: "As Ford has standardized machines, Wallace will standardize ideas.'' Thus, people will think everywhere in an identical manner.[92]

Ellul does not mean that all will think the same thoughts but only that their perspectives will all be the same. That is, they will live in a world constructed by the media, receptive to its projections and to the institutions that support it. Receptivity comes in two forms: either people believe the messages they receive, finding in them basic measures of truth or they become media-induced skeptics, believing nothing they see or read.[93] In both cases, the individual's own perspective is lost. In appealing to the lowest common denominator —the statistical average—one appeals to what does not exist, to an abstraction. The individual, on whatever level, is held in contempt by being reduced to a level. What is often not acknowledged is the elitism of the newspaper editor demanding that all copy be written to a reader of the sixth- to eighth-grade level. Few see in this an authoritarian determination—afterall, the masses must be educated. But while they are being educated, they are also being formed.

Ellul is also aware that the *Reader's Digest* is simply part of a massive system. While the technological imperative becomes the new necessity, the life-world—the technological society—becomes the ephemeral (*l'éphémère*). It is in this way that technology truly becomes a system in which values do not exist apart from the system. Ellul states:

> If was are placed in a period of history and in a society in which necessity becomes ever more exacting [*ou la Necessité se fait toujours plus exacte*], then nothing is truly continuous or durable. Our entire civilization is ephemeral. When one glorifies increased consumption, one must discard machine-made objects in the course of rapid usage. We no longer repair things: we throw them away. Plastic, nylons, are made to be used for an infinitesimal period of time and, as they cost nothing, are destroyed as soon as the gloss of newness is gone. Houses are constructed for the duration of their mortgage; automobiles must be replaced every year. And in the world of art we no longer build cathedrals, but we make moving pictures, which—though real works of art in which man has fully committed himself and expressed his most profound message—are forgotten after a few weeks and disappear into movie libraries where only a few connoisseurs can find them again.[94]

Ellul begins with a paradox, the idea that when necessity becomes more exacting—or, to be more precise, when there is no longer any continuity—at this point nothing is truly durable. The paradox derives from the notion of necessity (*la Necessité*), which initially suggests permanence. The idea that eating is a necessity is clear. People need to eat. But, in the idea of eating as a necessity, the notion of exactness is foreign. In traditional societies, eating is necessary to keep alive. The value of eating is measured by the success of fulfilling this goal. Ancient societies have successful cuisines. Exactness, now, has become a new necessity. We must be clear, however, that exactness is not a fixed idea but is part of a never-ending process. It is a goal not outside, but very much within, the process. It is simply another step in the process. For example, in a technological society, the aim of eating is not the health of the body. The goal is to produce "new" food, to work the technological process.

Thus, a simple food like potatoes becomes Tater-Tots, something that is not clearly food at all, and that contains elements of no clearly known nutritional value. What is clear is that each piece is made to look like the other piece, identities which are also different, new. McDonald's markets and produces sameness. A French fry in Dallas will be exactly like the one in Chicago; computer-controlled fryers assure this uniformity. Nutrition is typically a question, if raised at all, coming from elements outside the system by consumer interest groups (but not wholly outside, for if protesters are to be effective, they must organize, advertise, etc.), but rarely by the consumers themselves. To understand fast food, a purely technological phenomenon, one must look to the walls and notice the pictures of the food. One buys the picture, which will never nourish, but which will always keep the customer coming back for more, the ever-perfect, indeed, the same, hamburger, designed in the laboratory and cooked by computers.

The natural object, appearing as the not-made, resists the viewer's gaze, having its own world, and inviting a dialectical adventure. Totem animals, as Lévi-Strauss points out, "are chosen not because they are 'good to eat' but because they are 'good to think.'"[95] With them, we not only satisfy our body's needs but we also unify elements in opposition. This unification is not fixed, but must actively perpetuate itself. Opposition is kept alive, providing a sense of the past and present and a place of origin that leads to a feeling of and for destiny. With the eating of the totem animal, the primitive finds a place in nature, as both in nature and above it. Nature is transformed by and in the symbol before it is cognized through rational laws. The totem animal in the form of the bear may eat the Eskimo, who is thereby returned quite directly to the natural order, to the whole always beyond the particular. This cultural system is no bad infinity but is a true infinity with a transcendental realm very much beyond the control of the people. The totem animal is wild being, unpredictable and valuable in its otherness, instructive of our finitude by its power and its wildness.

The ephemeral object of technique loses its wildness, its independence, through domestication or through creation in the laboratory. Today's totem foods, if such they are, are created in the laboratory, in the food pen, or like the Big Mac, are created *ad hoc*. The danger in these animals, these creations, lies in what we have put into them and in what we have then conveniently forgotten. Most of the food additives, microbiologist Michael Jacobson has pointed out in *The Eater's Digest*, are present for cosmetic purposes, to make them appear like the food in pictures.[96] The fascination of the totemic value of food still survives in food such as children's cereal, for example, through the invocation of Tony the Tiger. The humiliation of citizens begins early, preparing them as adults to order, in all seriousness, food like "Whoppers," "momma-burgers," or "poppa-burgers." The political effects of such humiliation are altogether unexamined, not suitable, not serious enough for sociological analysis. Brillat-Savarin, however, in his *Physiology of Taste* (1826), understood that food had a political dimension, that "... the destiny of nations depends on how they nourish themselves."[97] Ironically, the depoliticalization of food occurs at the same time food is becoming a matter for technique, toward which Brillat-Savarin's own book contributed. Cuisine moves one step further towards the Cartesian rationality and hence to the technological dimension with the introduction of proper rules and understandings for the regulation of eating. The political dimension of food is clarified with Ellul's analysis of the ephemeral.

In the ephemeral, both the natural object and the awareness of that object are transformed: Being becomes being-there, a state detached from the existential life-world. The object becomes a two-dimensional image of technique. The individual's being is projected out-there, losing itself among the objects it can no longer distinguish in terms of the made and the not-made. It takes a careful eye in the grocery store to pick the dairy cream out from among the other genuine imitations.

Modern politics is made possible by the *fact*, an immediacy transformed by the media or by the system of propaganda available to all modern states, no longer residing in the bodily dimension but now in the realm of technique. Ellul states:

> ... in traditional society, facts transformed into images by some collective mechanism were rare and secondary. Troubadours brought

their fellow men songs on historical themes, merchants brought news from a faraway world; but they did not really concern the listener, who remained aloof from these stories—such things were only distractions, not part of the setting in which he lived. Conversely, as a result of the mass media, these verbal or visual images constitute the total world in which modern man lives. He now spans the entire globe, but experiences it only indirectly. He lives in a retranslated, edited universe; he no longer has any direct relation to any fact.[98]

The pretechnological human lives in an oral-aural world, whereas technological humanity lives in a world of images. The image encourages the feeling of certainty, although it is only two dimensional; moreover, the image tends to silence discourse while the word opens it up. Pictures do tend to replace thousands of words. Hitler understood this when he contracted Leni Riefenstahl to film the National Socialist Party Congress of 1934 in the famous *Triumph des Willens* in which, according to her, "... the preparations for the Party Convention were made in connection with the preparations for the camera work."[99] The event was constructed for the sole purpose of filming it. It is immediately apparent today that when an image is not available for a TV news story, a simulation is used, covering, for example, moon walks and terrorist hostage rescues. Sometimes the certainty of the image causes embarrassment, as when ABC showed a film supposedly taken of the 9 April 1986 Chernobyl power disaster that was actually a film taken of a scene in Trieste. The error was caught by an anonymous sharp-eyed Italian.

The statistic and the fact, in part verbal and related to the word, really function in the form of an image, and so are unable to convey the ambiguity and the dialectical dimension of the word, the realm of discourse. Without discourse, the statistic, the mere fact, conjuring up only powers of belief and not knowledge (knowledge being dialectical), leads to curious situations. Ellul observes:

A case in point is the famous poll undertaken by *Tide* in 1947 on the subject of the "Metallic Metals Act." Americans were polled on this "act." Seventy percent of those polled gave an opinion, 30 percent did not. Of those having an opinion, 21.4 percent thought the act was of benefit to the United States; 58.6 percent felt the matter should be determined from case to case; 15.7 percent believed that such arrangements were possibly of benefit abroad, but not in the U.S; and 4.3 percent said the act had no value. But the most remarkable thing was that there had never been such a thing as the Metallic Metals Act. Yet, there was public opinion on the subject.[100]

This is a clear example of the kind of exactness technical necessity has come to mean. Once the facts are given, more facts are appropriate, but there usually is no dialogue. For example, when ABC admitted that the Chernobyl films were fake, Peter Jennings apologized, and said that all efforts would be made not to let this kind of thing happen again. There was no consideration of how this deception had been possible or of why everyone assumed the newsreel footage to be true. Once educated to see the media image as true or certain, its falsity must be proved.

The news has come to be the modern citizen's duty. And yet, a simple test calls into question the meaningfulness of this duty. Ellul states:

> The man who lives in the news ... is a man without memory. Experimentally this can be verified a thousand times over. The news that excited his passion and agitated the deepest corner of his soul, simply disappears. He is ready for some other agitation, and what excited him yesterday does not stay with him. This means that the man living in the news no longer has freedom, no longer has the capacity of foresight, no longer has any reference to truth. Lequier has said that "memory is free man's action when he turns to his past acts in order to retrieve them." Memory in a personality is the function that attests to the capacity of acting voluntarily and creatively; personality is built on memory, and conversely memory lends authority to personality. "One only remembers oneself, which means that one must already be self, capable of creating oneself in order to remember." And, still from this personal perspective, one can also say that only memory permits us to turn to the future—that there is a relationship between imagination and memory.[101]

It is a common experience that fewer than five news stories may be remembered at the end of a half-hour news program. One can find this forgetting in oneself. The television image is not created to be remembered, but to be consumed. We are then to wait for the next image, and the next image. News images are spliced together with commercials, blending with the news items and suggesting that respite from the world's problems is available through consumption.

What news items are remembered are those which tie into popular stereotypes. Few will forget that Ronald Reagan, after seeing the popular movie about vigilante justice, *Rambo*, declared that he now knew how to handle foreign policy in regard to terrorists, that during the capture of the terrorists that had taken hostages on the cruise ship the *Achille Lauro*, Reagan had adopted the code name "Rawhide," or that originally he had starred in a film early in his Hollywood career—*Bedtime For Bonzo*. What he claimed during his debate with Jimmy Carter in regard to lowering the cost of government, in relation to decreasing the federal defecit, has been long forgotten; that Reagan, while governor of California, signed the bill that made abortion legal and created one of the most costly state governments on record, is even more forgotten, ancient, history, not coinciding with the public's perception. Ellul states:

> To become "true" in the eyes of the crowd, fact must be social—registered and localized in society—not necessarily collective, but social in the sense that everyone can recognize himself in it. The most individual fact, taken from what is most typical, such as, for example, the death of a well-known young hero, is a collective fact if everyone recognizes himself in the act of heroism: the suffering, the combat with death, the dead hero's feeling. The same social identification accounts for the success of melodrama and of the radio and TV serial. The mass media can deal only with this type of fact; and where it is social, but simultaneously takes its seeming reality from being individual, it leads to confusion between the individual fact experienced by the reader or listener and the massive fact transmitted to him by his paper or radio. He can no longer differentiate between what is his own life and what is not.[102]

Whereas technique officially adopts the logic of efficiency and noncontradiction, beneath it is the logic of myth, the logic of the story; the search for the hero, the need to find the hero, is what gives the fact its significance. The *Challenger* tragedy will be remembered because its participants were heroes. More importantly, however, modern stereotypes are produced from the media itself and not from the activity of culture or from personal experience. These are myths created anonymously and collectively, at once. Modern symbols, however, are out of control. They have become part of the logic of technique itself, a logic that denies the very efficacy of the symbol, making its use, through denial, even more insidious. The fact is invoked, all the while it is manufactured in the laboratory of technique, a process immediately forgotten.

The media experience is presented as organized and complete in the sense that it is a package. The audience is directed through the experience with commentaries and analyses of what is pertinent, tying up and wrapping the package; and what is important will be repeated, for what is important is the next, the "new," the "now." Repeating has become a substitute for remembering. The instant replay, for instance, has likely transformed the watching of a sports event, where, before this technique, each moment had to be attended to as if each moment would be the last. The continuity, what the viewer brought to the game, is now taken up by the commentary and the replay. Each moment is complete in that it is a perfect package, but incomplete in that what is needed is the next, an endless stage in a bad infinity.

Collecting the past has become a full-time occupation. The current rage for cameras, VCRs, tape recorders, and the like attest to the emptiness of a present that we are afraid to lose—perhaps because *we* never have it—but that we endlessly and trivially reclaim. What we no longer can do, namely remember, we entrust to machines and devices. In this sense, technique is *lethotechny*. Movies are taped so that they do not have to be watched, studied, considered, and remembered. Once shown in the theaters and then forgotten with a discarding of the popcorn box, they are now forgotten in the tape libraries of individuals who accumulate as many tapes as possible. Tourists often have little time to vacation, as they are busy taking snapshots and collecting souvenirs; what *they* do not experience, the recording device will, in the process bringing the unfamiliar back to the safety of their homes.[103] Modern humanity has become a recorder of life, which is given to consuming and watching.

Memory, like knowledge, is not stored, a mistake perpetuated by libraries and computers. It is a commonplace to understand a library as stored knowledge. However, a book is not knowledge until it is read. A photograph is only a photograph, which may or may not have a memory attached. A memory involves an individual's relationship to an experience which is given form and shape and to which he or she may return.

Ellul's Life as Dialectic

Ellul's life, as I have shown, is a life of tension in relation to otherness in the variety of forms he is able to grasp. He studies law under the influence of a distant but forceful father; he resists institutionalized wisdom with what he understands to be divine guidance—under the influence of the Wholly Other, and he insists that all views are relative to this Other which focuses his social perspectives. Ellul is indeed of his time, while also standing as *Other* to it. He lives when propaganda and technique direct a wartorn Europe, and he remembers this direction which he sees from his own transcendental perspective. He lives according to an understanding he has fashioned for himself out of an experience of a world often foreign to him. *The Political Illusion* is a book of Ellul's own memories during the war and during de Gaulle's rule of the Fifth

Republic. It is a view of the entire modern period shaped from what he understood of the Roman Republic, where law was seen as arising spontaneously and, to a degree, self-consciously, out of a *sensus communis*. Unable to return to this past, Ellul's interest is in making his own age aware of the degree to which its world is symbolic, fashioned, made—and hence relative. In this sense, Ellul's own Christian beliefs need not become the issue. The issue is philosophical and epistemological, rising out of a theory of the symbol and a notion of nonresolvable, perpetual dialectic that is abstract and concrete, particular and universal at once.

Ellul's goal is like Plato's in *The Republic*, a work to which John Wilkinson likens Ellul's *La Technique*, although the comparison in never explained. In an important way Ellul and Plato have the same goals. Plato's goal in this complicated work is to instruct the Athenian citizen that life takes place in a cave where appearances have become reality. These appearances to be meaningful must point to the transcendental realm of Forms, which make the appearances possible. Further, Plato holds that Athenian life has been dressed up and confounded by Homeric myths, which must be denuded. Humanity must become responsible for the world, which must be governed by reason. For Plato, reason is tied to the earthly realm, to the body, and to the myth. Thus, more rational myths are needed for a true *Republic*. *The Republic* is such a myth. Ellul, too, understands his age to be a construct of myths, but of rational myths, dressed in commonplaces constructed by the media. The modern cave is outfitted by technique. The fires that illuminate it are electric. The shadows on the wall are images on television screens. They are all appearances that we have come to confuse with reality of the most absolute kind.

Plato wrote *The Republic* in what he thought to be Athens's collapse. *The Republic* was a project of restoration, a task for the dialectic, begun in oral form by his teacher Socrates. Ellul's restorative project, too, is one of language and dialogue, asking the reader to engage in discourse with the world and himself. Like Plato, Ellul understands his age as decadent. The Second World War is barely over and the superpowers begin to destory the environment and to engage in a nuclear arms race. What is needed, Ellul believes, is a critical distance between the subject and object, a distance taken up on language. He writes:

> For example, language reminds us of the necessity of tension at two levels: tension or contradiction is based on a similarity between the signifier and the things signified (when that tension disappears, there is no

more language—that is why, whatever one may think, imagined reproduction of reality is not language); the other aspect is the tension between two interlocutors; if a difference does not exist, if they are identical, there would be no language because it would have no content; if a common measure did not exist, there would be no language because it would have no form.[104]

This is the logic of the symbol, enunciated in chapter 2. Symbolic reference requires difference and distance. What I mean is thus always what I mean *and* what I do not mean. The success of language and knowledge is always partial. The object and my idea of the object are always at odds with one another. The language I use to refer to that object is at further odds with the object; object and idea and are skewed. What is required is perpetual discourse in the search for the object—for the truth in whatever form that search might take. In such discourse, the tension between the signifier and the signified must never collapse. Held in tension, discourse can continue and spill over into the social realm, which is sustained in and by dialectical tension. The search for the Good is an individual and communal concern, where the limits of thought and language are at once strained and strengthened.

In political terms, there are many visions of the good life. Political value, in the sense of *le politique*, is obtained in discussion about these visions held by unique individuals. Not living in the City of God, humanity will have to be content with relative absolutes, which are recognized as relative. The epistemological and political value of tension is affirmed. Ellul continues:

> ... tension makes sense only between two elements that are part of the same system, of a whole that does not destroy itself, that does not disintegrate because its elements are in opposition (and we are not describing here a static whole in the state of equilibrium); tension presupposes a progression of both factors by a suppression of the conflict which entails the creation of a new tension, situated normally at a higher, more enriched level, but also one that is more demanding for both partners.[105]

Humanity never escapes the condition of bifurcation. Attempts to move closer to the world through symbols both fail and succeed. Life is tension; only death would be the unbroken calm. Yet, technique seeks calm, unification, identities without differences on the one hand; while on the other, it creates a world in which no one is at home or in peace. Violence and force are the typical methods of the modern states. To eliminate murder, murderers are destroyed; to combat terrorism, counterterrorism is used; to eradicate crime, criminals are abused.

Typically, the source of crime is sought either in the institution or in the individual. Rarely is the dialectical relation between the two considered. In his work with the delinquents of Pesac in the 1960s, Ellul noted that the usual social goal was to make the individual adapt or to make the laws stronger. Ellul's goal was to help the individual become more responsible and to find a more exciting life within a repressive and excluding society. Both the society and the delinquent, he realized, had much to learn from one another. Ellul felt that helping the individual to come to terms with his own life was "... taking a moral stand against technique."[106]

Like Plato's prisoner of the cave, we must discover the chains that enslave us. Although attempting to transcend the cave, our bodily condition, we will always be held back by our language and our symbols. In our age, the symbolic chains have been technologically forged. In breaking one set, we find others. A failure of memory risks worse enslavement. Our failures must remain ours. Technique, like Plato's River Lethe, is our *lethotechny*, a source of forgetting the past and the actual in a flood of technical possibilites. New symbols require a break *and* a transformation of the past. The dialectic requires memory. The mere possible apart from the past is impossible. Symbols depend upon dialectical nourishment, upon the powers of memory and imagination. The technical phenomenon is a symbol, a project taking place in history, but is in danger of collapse, which neglects its own symbolic dimensions. Creation requires memory. *Le politique* depends upon it. The future to the technical phenomenon depends upon it as well.

La technique is Ellul's symbolic construction of the shape of the modern age, offered to be destroyed and to be seen for the symbolic construction that it is. Like Plato, Ellul offers a philosophical myth to energize the dialectic. Thought and imagination have tired of making sense. Society is a series of interconnected wholes, fragile and needing attention. In Ellul's view, the technological society is in danger of breaking down under its own weight.

5

The Technological Phenomenon and the Technical System

Ellul's theory of technology rests on the following four points: (1) *la technique* (as the sum-total, the ensemble of means, rationally arrived at by a mathematics-like method and seeking the goal of efficiency) is a mentality, an intentionality, a way of symbolizing the world. More, it *is* a world. Technology is a way of life, one of the reasons that efficiency always begs the question. What is efficient is always systemically defined and never has any absolute meaning. Thus, child labor laws, in nineteenth-century England, are greatly efficient. Children are quite small, do not eat very much, and generally do what they are told to do; further, they do not require great sums of money. From the standpoint of saving manufacturer's money and of providing the work place with the docile body, child labor is ideal. Technology is, however, a mentality seeking the "one best way in all things,"[1] at the same time assuring that no one way will be the best way. Progress, meaning a move toward the next moment, toward the "new," is always a given. As a way of life, it is a life that changes and that *is* change. Related to the tools and the machines of the past, *la technique* is the mentality that gives those tools its force and power. Tools existed long before technology became a world. From the standpoint of *la technique*, a child work force is inefficient, lacking in sufficient rationality, and so it is legislated out of existence as "immoral."

(2) The technical phenomenon (*le phénomènon technique*) is the result of technological rationality, technological consciousness. It is the objectification of technical mentality and only related to the tool mentality in a distant way. The technical phenomenon is unique in the history of civilizations in allowing technical consciousness to take on substance. The point of coincidence between the tool mentality and the technical mentality is the technical operation. The tool is an extension of the body. It requires the use of an operation, a bodily movement. The technical phenomenon is not such an extension. The

flying shuttle, the space shuttle *Challenger*, and guidance counseling are all technical phenomena. For the technical phenomenon, the body is usually *the* problem. Early machine manufacturers had difficulty designing machines that the body could use.[2] The first astronaut, Alan Shepard, was on the launch pad for four hours before he discovered that no provisions had been made for him to urinate; following some discussion with technicians over whether or not the suit's delicate circuitry would be damaged as a result, he urinated in his suit.[3]

(3) The technical phenomenon does not exist by itself. Alone it has no meaning. It forms a system, a series of internal relations such that meaning is purely an internal affair. A pretechnological society would have no use for guidance counseling or for a space shuttle. Needed is the development of a textile industry, which soon necessitates a planned economy. Once the space-shuttle stage is reached everything becomes possible: ball-point pens that write under water, Tang, razor blades from nose-cone metal, and the microwave oven. This path could be traveled from a number of directions. It is perhaps only historical coincidence that Italy developed the textile industry and banking at nearly the same time. What is important, however, is the systemic nature of the technical phenomenon, making it tend toward a way of life.

(4) The technical order becomes the sacred order, autonomous, nearly having the power to generate itself. Man, at this point, hangs from the device, becoming an extension of technique. Technique moves solidly to the symbolic order, leaving behind the material world to which technique often seems quite attached. At this stage, the material world, the natural world before the proliferation of technique, is coopted; the natural object no longer appears to the viewer as an *other* but as something waiting to become a technical phenomenon. Thus, to the technical mind, children playing seren-dipitously on a corner lot are a Little League Organization waiting to be born; a forest becomes a nicely manicured retirement village; a redwood tree becomes a stack of memos. Humanity's sense of space, time, and order is altered, leaving the bodily realm, the seat of the irrational, and taking up residence in compelling and convincing abstractions. The social effects of MTV, video TV, are likely positive, lending a touch of reality to the child's otherwise surreal surroundings.

The previous four points presuppose a dialectical theory of consciousness that is always an embodied consciousness. For Ellul, there is no pure thought. Thought is always *of* something. One never thinks purely empty thoughts, which, if possible, could never be remembered. The symbol is evidence of this lack of purity of thought, as discussed in chapter 1. Thought is never far from a "real world," from an institution, as Marx realized. For this reason, one may see institutions as the extensions of thought. It is this rationalist model that provokes Ellul's critics to argue for more rational uses of technology. Ellul's point is that technical thought, although once dialectical, has lost tension with its object. The object no longer has the critical quality of otherness. The technical phenomenon is a symbol that has lost its symbolic dimension and has thus become the sacred.

The sacred, for Ellul, is not the religious, although it may establish the religious. In the sacral realm, consciousness is not separated from the object, whereas in the religious domain it is. In the sacral world, all is of a piece. Nothing is in principle separated from anything else; the primitive world is made of whole cloth, as I will show. The totem animal, mentioned in the last chapter, ties primitive man into the world with its connection to powers and forces that run throughout the world. The totem animal is good to eat because that animal, no mere object, brings man closer to that world. Thus, from modern man's standpoint, the primitive projects his mentality upon that world, which is to that extent irrational. Sacral consciousness, our current common sense has it, is part of the primitive, pre-technological world. True consciousness, scientific consciousness, must separate itself from the world. Science teaches, for example, that we need to eat a certain amount of vitamins, proteins, carbohydrates, minerals, etc., and that totem animals have little to do with our physical health, supposedly the purpose of eating. Ellul's contention is that this sacral consciousness returns to the world after its initial separation from the world in early technological development. Myth provides what science cannot, what science presupposes: an overarching sense of significance, a grasp of purpose, destiny, and fatality.

Lévi-Strauss's distinction between the scientist and the *bricoleur La Pensée Sauvage* (1962) [*The Savage Mind* (1966)] is useful in understanding Ellul's point: "We have already distinguished the scientist and the 'bricoleur' [mythmaker] by the inverse functions which they assign to events and structures as ends and means, the scientist creating events (changing the world) by means of structure and the 'bricoleur' creating structures by means of the events."[4] For sacral consciousness, events provide the means for creating structures, while for the scientist, structures are the means for creating events. This is further clarified as we consider the structure of games in relation to the structure of rituals:

... the game produces events by means of a structure; and we can therefore understand why competitive games should flourish in our industrial society. Rites, and myths, on the other hand, like 'bricolage' (which these same societies only tolerate as a hobby or pastime), take to pieces and reconstruct sets of events (on a psychical, socio-historical or technical plane) and use them as so many indestructible pieces for structural patterns in which they serve alternatively as ends or means.[5]

The unity and reality of the event are presupposed by mythical consciousness, which further provides unity for any other seemingly divergent events. For example, according to Lévi-Strauss, when football was introduced to the Gahuku-Gama of New Guinea, the game was played for several days running so that each side could reach the same score, showing that an original balance or harmony preexisted between both sides. The game for the technical mentality, is produced by analysis or by the work of reason. What is forgotten is an original unity that had made the analysis possible. The scientist, for example, presupposes that the world is or will be receptive to his manipulations.

It is Ellul's contention that myth is always around the corner of consciousness, that beneath the most rational structures is the tendency of consciousness to lose itself in the object. In seeing myth as a support for structures of rationality, Ellul is in good company. Lévi-Strauss sees myths as providing the ground for classifying activity, leading ultimately to scientific classification, however much myth and science differ in fundamental direction. Mircea Eliade and C. G. Jung both understand primitive consciousness as providing modern man with certain all-pervading structures of consciousness that differentiate modern man from the primitive, yet at the same time provide a sense of continuity. Jung argues, for example, in "Flying Saucers: A Modern Myth" (1958), that flying saucers may be interpreted as archetypal mandala figures, which in primitive cultures served as expressions of unity and harmony, as messages from the gods. In modern skies, these objects still appear, reminding us of man's need for harmony and symbols of unification. However, there is a fundamental difference: "It is characteristic of our time that the archetype... should now take the form of an object, a technological construction, in order to avoid the odiousness of mythological personification. Anything that looks technological goes down without difficulty with modern man."[6] The gods currently ride technological chariots.

Eliade, in *Myths, Dreams and Mysteries* (1967), states:

In many religions, and even in the folklore of European peoples, we have found a belief that, at the moment of death, man remembers all his past life down to the minutest details, and that he cannot die before having remembered and relived the whole of his personal history. Upon the screen of memory, the dying man once more reviews his past. Considered from this point of view, the passion for historiography in modern culture would be a sign portending his imminent death.[7]

The recent concern for memory has other implications. Science acts as if memory is of no importance, much beyond the incanting of the formula and the review of the experiment. We may determine what foods are nutritionally sound through food analysis, but this analysis will not yield the wisdom behind, for example, the Chinese or the northern Italian cuisines that kept civilizations healthy for centuries prior to the science of nutrition. Nutrition may analyze foods down to their parts, but not tell what value they might have when put into a whole, into a traditional dinner. Beyond what science tells us, there is a different knowledge gained in and by tradition.

According to Ellul, tradition is originally formed by poetic acts, to which one can never exactly return but from which societies can never fully escape in their attempts to obtain a sense of origins, a sense of significance, and a feeling for meaningful behavior. This is the locus of myth, not the locus of science, although science too is not far from this domain. Some years ago in the *Chicago Tribune* it was reported that Northwestern University's psychology department was experimenting with rats swimming in a tank of water. One group of rats was fed all the food they wanted, while the other group was nearly starved. The animals in the well-fed group, when placed in the tank, swam for quite some time before they drowned, while the poorly fed rats gave up almost immediately. It was concluded by the psychologists that the starved rats who drowned without much fuss were the more realistic. Even the scientist brings to the experiment his own sense of the tragic, *hamartia*. The well-fed rats had missed the modern mark. They could not accept the inevitable, the drowning tank, the tank of technique.

This story is not offered as fact but as metaphor. It suggests that science and technique, while trying to ascertain fact, assume plot and structure. Usually, the plot, as above, is not consciously or artistically held; it instead reflects or succumbs to the commonplaces of the age, common places in which this story is particularly rich. We can imagine that the reporter of the event recognized the old familiar story of the cold, calculating scientist sacrificing animals for science. We can imagine the scientists who saw in the rats their own conditions—beasts of the burdens of science and logic, where contingent facts are the mothers of their necessities. Following Ellul's analysis, we are drowning in our own tanks of contingencies, in which the transcendental has been reduced to the particular or where the particular has been reified. The effects are nearly the same. The objects in our so-called immediate worlds have been made over by technical manipulation. The rats are not necessarily behaving "naturally." They are behaving like creatures stuck in a laboratory—perhaps they are really our totem animals, which we think we have banished to the world of the primitive, to the museums of natural history, or to the pages of *National Geographic*. This experiment may speak to us, revealing our own commonplaces formed in the world of the technical phenomenon. This chapter, then, will discuss the structure of the technical phenomenon, the nature of the system in which it exists, and the character of the new sacred that it forms, as well as the logic of technique, building on my previous study: "Jacques Ellul and the Logic of Technology" (1977).[8]

The Technical Phenomenon

Ellul's study of technique in *The Technological Society* begins with the commonplace that technique is a part of the natural history of all cultures. This is true to the extent that "technique" refers to any method used to attain a particular end.[9] However, breaking from this tradition, Ellul announces that in a technical civilization, a unique form of culture and society, ends become means and means become ends. Behind this cliché is a dilemma. Ellul draws on two senses of "technique": (1) technique generically as reference to the totality of methods used to attain an end; (2) technique as a method of rational efficient ordering refers to one species of techniques in the technological society. It is important for Ellul's case that "technique" refer to the totality of methods rationally employed, seeking the end of absolute efficiency. In this way he does not restrict "technique" to a specific application. It is this concern that leads Ellul to state:

> When I use the French word *technique*, normally translated into English as *technology*, I do not mean exactly the same thing as the French word *technologie*, which is also translated into English as *technology*. We have to be meticulous about this simple point of vocabulary. I know that the two are habitually confused. Etymologically, of course, *technologie* means a discourse on *technique*. That is the true meaning of *technologie*.

> Now when I speak of *technique* [English *technology*], I am speaking of the technological phenomenon, the reality of the technological. When I view an automobile, the engine of the automobile is in the category of *technique*, i.e. the technical. It is not what the French call *technologie*, even though English usage tends toward *technology* in this point. The study of the engine and the discourse on the engine is *technologie*. But the phenomenon itself must be viewed as part of *technique*. . . . But for me, *la technique* is a far wider concept, referring to efficient methods applicable in all areas (monetary, economic, aesthetic, etc.). I would prefer that English retain the word *technique*. Thus, in this sense, it is *technique*.[10]

Although I mentioned this issue in the first chapter, its importance requires reiteration. It is the point to which Ellul most frequently returns. It recurs often because people are not used to thinking of technique as a form of intentionality. Typically, they only view it in terms of application, for example, as a machine. Technique, for Ellul, is the totality of discourse about the ensemble of objects used for the purpose of establishing an absolute methodology in all areas; in addition to the discourse, it refers to the phenomena themselves and to the system in which they are found. Thus, the totality points to a mentality. When I speak about technology or technique, I mean it in Ellul's sense. I have avoided current attempts in Ellul scholarship, also mentioned in the first chapter, to capitalize "technique." I find that this artificiality vitiates the need to think about the subject. There are no techniques, in short, with which to clarify this phenomenon.

The machine is, of course, symptomatic of technique. No discussion of technology can avoid machines. Ellul's concern, however, is to contextualize the machine. Technique, as he shows, appears just as fully in the form of labor management in industry, in the role of urban planning in city politics, in the guise of the "scientific method" in the laboratory, as it does in the machine. Ellul remarks: "The machine is, solely, exclusively technique; it is pure technique, one might say. For wherever a technical factor exists, it results, almost inevitably, in mechanization: technique transforms everything it touches into a machine."[11] Technique is the consciousness that gives the machine force, that sees everything else as machine-like or as needing to serve the machine-like, the ideal toward which technique strives. The machine is the technical phenomenon, *par excellence*.

For Ellul the technical phenomenon has at least seven characteristics: (1) rationality (*la rationalité*), (2) artificiality (*l'artificialité*), (3) automatism (*l'automatisme*), (4) self-augmentation (*l'autoaccroissement*), (5) monism (*l'insecabilité* or *unicité*), (6) universalism (*l'universalism*), (7) autonomy (*l'autonomie*).[12] These terms are as specialized as Ellul's discussion ever becomes, although they are quite common French words that connote a discussion about *la technique* and/or *la technologie*. Ellul refers to this list, drawn from *The Technological Society*, in all of his later discussions, although the list is clearly not to be regarded as categorical, fixed, closed, or logically necessary. For example, in *The Technological System* he speaks of the characteristics of the technical phenomenon in terms of autonomy, unity (*unicité*), universality, and adds totalization (*la totalisation*), which simply affirms the capacity of technique to be open-ended in the sense of being all inclusive.[13] I should add that translator Joachim Neugroshel departs from Wilkinson's rendering of *unicité* as "monism," opting instead for "unity." This shift, however, loses the sense of technique as a "world." I will, therefore, retain Wilkinson's choice when discussing this term.

Further, in *The Technological System*, Ellul refers to the characteristics of technological progress in terms of self-augmentation, automatism, causal progression and absence of finality (*la progression causale et l'absence de finalité*), and the problems of acceleration (*le problème de l'accélération*).[14] In adding the section on causal progression and the absence of finality, and the problems of acceleration, Ellul emphasizes the systemic nature of the technical phenomenon, how it moves always in causal ways but never toward closure—thus, a bad infinity—even though it tolerates no perspective outside of its own sphere. Further, its moves accelerate with each development, such that speed increases with geometrical progression: twice as many items appear twice as rapidly. Thus the importance of Ellul's original list remains. I choose not to divide or to separate my discussion of the technical phenomenon from the process or the progress it engenders. Although it is little noted, we should remember, that Ellul, clearly an accomplished scholar, begins his bibliography to *The Technological Society* with the following warning: "And since books are made to be read and not consulted, I have rejected the scholarly tradition of specifying pages in footnotes."[15] This warning to read and not to consult applies to Ellul's other books as well.

In *The Technological Society*, the categories of rationality and artificiality overlap significantly. I consider rationality first. Note, however, that in brackets I have added a clause that was left out in Wilkinson's translation. Ellul states:

In technique, whatever its aspect or the domain in which it is applied, a rational process is present which tends to bring mechanics to bear on all that is spontaneous or irrational. This rationality, best exemplified in systematization, division of labor, creation of standards, production norms, and the like, involves two distinct phases: first, the use of "discourse" in every operation [under the two aspects this term can take (on the one hand, the intervention of intentional reflection, and, on the other hand, the intervention of means from one term to the other.)]; this excludes spontaneity and personal creativity. Second, there is the reduction of method to its logical dimension alone. Every intervention of technique is, in effect, a reduction of facts, forces, phenomena, means, and instruments to the schema of logic.[16]

Ellul uses "rationality" in a restricted and exclusive way. It is being used to refer to the logical and to the methodological, insofar as method can be reduced to logic, understood in its mathematical—its most restrictive—sense. Thought, for example, is reduced to the laws of identity, contradiction, and exclusion. A thing, thus, is what it is, is not both what it is and something else, and is either what it is or not what it is. Technique's dictum, then, is that for all things there must be a method that is reducible to an abstract, logical schema. Thus technique is always artificial in that it is reductive and abstractive.

The relationship between reason and artificiality is understood best in the important relationship between the technical operation and the technical phenomenon. "Technical operation" refers to all activities carried out in accordance with a specific method for the implementation of determined ends.[17] Characterized by method, these activities provide the continuity for all technical experiences from the rather simple task of chopping out a log canoe to the more complex programming of a computer. Such restricted logic makes us believe that primitive techniques differ from modern techniques only in degree as a result of scientific refinements, and hide from us the fact that modern techniques are also different in kind, entailing a completely different orientation toward the world.[18] Technical operations concern the worker's immediate and bodily relation to the task at hand, which requires, at least in its initial phases, the use of hands, muscles, etc. in order to accomplish the task. A technical operation may require concentrated effort while it is being learned, but soon it becomes a spontaneous and natural routine, and it is from this point that we may speak of technical operations.

"Technical phenomena" appear when consciousness surveys and rationalizes what was once a spontaneous technical operation, seeking the "one best means" and the fixed but indeterminate end of efficiency.[19] Thus, at this stage a dialectical distance is supposed between subject and object. Considering a simple task at hand, like the chopping of wood, a technical operation involving a tool like an ax, the worker begins before the object: a piece of wood, a log. The ax becomes a mediary to that log, a resistance that must be overcome. The ax is an attempt to close that dialectical distance. The chopping of the wood puts the worker in touch with other resistances, like the ground on which the log rests, the solidity of the handle of the ax, and the limitations of strength that may soon become apparent in the arms of the worker. The natural environment, too, plays a part in the worker's awareness; the coolness of the day may prompt more vigorous work to stay warm, or the appearance of a strange bird might slow the progress to a halt. Suppose, however, the worker decides to become efficient, to introduce concerns of technical reason to attempt to cut the tree or the log according to the one best way. Here, the dialectic shifts from the long and the natural world, the not-made, to the ax, the made. The technical phenomenon is the result of this shift.

A chain saw is a basic example of a technical phenomenon, the result of a concern to cut wood in a better way. The worker's awareness is altered. The chain saw is the result of applying mathematics and logic to the more primitive technical operation with the concern for eliminating the often inefficient motions of the body. It is an objectification of technical intention. With its use, the tree is no longer the goal. The focus shifts to the saw itself: one must guide it, support it, keep it from cutting more than it is supposed to, wary lest one harm oneself. Mistakes are not so easy to catch, typically, with the technical phenomenon, which is no longer an extension of the body. Phenomenologically, *I* become an extension of *it*. Further, my awareness of the natural world is altered. Filled with the fumes and the noise of the saw, I no longer hear and smell nature as I once did. A quieter saw could, of course, return this aspect of attention, but the relation to the resistance of the *other* would still be altered. Of this relationship Ellul notes:

> This formula is true of the tool which puts man squarely in contact with a reality which will bear no excuses, in contact with matter to be mastered, and the only way to use it is to obey it. Obedience to the plow and the plane was indeed the only means of dominating earth and wood. But the formula is not true for our techniques. He who serves these techniques enters another realm of necessity. This new necessity is not natural necessity; natural necessity in fact, no longer exists.[20]

The natural necessity is in the domain of the not-made. This is the shift that has been effected. The bulldozer as an example of the technical phenomenon would be more dramatic, but my point requires not drama but thought. The technical phenomenon could, in principle, be any object. What is important is that it is the result of scientific calculation, seeking the one best way, that it tends to vitiate the mind-body relationship, and that it alters the distinction between the made and the not-made to the degree that a dialectic between it is lost.

The second aspect of the technical phenomenon—consciousness —appears when the one best way is sought in all fields of endeavor. Ellul states: "It is no longer the best relative means which counts, as compared to other means also in use. The choice is less and less a subjective one among several means which are potentially applicable. It is really a question of finding the best means in the absolute sense, on the basis of numerical calculation."[21] At this stage humanity's decision to master nature takes a definite path, resulting in a union of spiritual and material techniques. Technique becomes a decision to objectify reason itself; it is now, ". . . a means of apprehending reality, of action on the world, which allows us to neglect all individual differences, all subjectivity. . . . Today humanity lives by virtue of participation in a truth become objective. Technique is no more than a neutral bridge between reality and the abstract man."[22] This is a crucial point in the logic of technique. Technique cancels individual subjectivity by objectifying that subjectivity and by turning the object for which it is a subject into an abstraction.

I wish to develop here a phenomenological point. While the logic of technique proceeds according to an abstract logic, it cannot be understood in those terms. Or, rather, it cannot understand itself in those terms. One must return to an embodied logic, to how the world fundamentally appears to an embodied subjectivity, to matters I considered above in regard to the use of the tool. It is in this sense that I speak phenomenologically, concerned simply with how the phenomena appear, appealing to my own senses, to my experiences of others and of their experiences, and to my recollections of these things. Husserl's more specialized concerns will not be mine. Further, I will not be appealing to scientific proof.

Most simply, my idea of the world is never of the world as it is—as an absolute necessity—but is always of the world as I see it as a body located in a certain space at a specific time. My perspective is thus partial and fragmented to a degree, confined to what Aristotle once called "the oval of vision." Anything I see, I can see more fully, needing only to walk about, to turn my head, to ask others. The same is true for my other senses. Thus, my *idea* of the world, *A*, is never the same as *A*. This is a truth of existential logic, a logic confined to appearances. A strict identity, as in the law of identity, is possible only for disembodied thought. The *A'* that I apprehend is always an *A'* over there, while I am here. I apprehend *A'* now, not later and not in the future. Thus, my body, once regarded as an object, of which, as an awareness, I am both a part and not a part, is an obstacle to the world. Try as I might, I can never get beyond my body's experience of the world.

The natural body, as the not-made, is the enemy of technique, the body keeping the world from appearing as it truly is. The fate of the body in the technical process is the fate of all natural objects, the dialectical *others*. The natural object is to be taken up in a conceptual relationship, reduced to an abstraction, and projected upon the world. Thus, the goal of technique, understood in this way, is to deny the body, the natural object, to deny anything that makes the individual different from the world. Difference for the individual starts with the embodied experience. The idea of fashion in which "one size fits all" is an important clue to technical logic; recent trends, supposedly for purposes of health, to make all individuals measure up to Cartesian "coordinates," from which one reads the correct weight and measurements for an individual of a certain body-type, a certain age, etc., are more than significant.

Siegfried Giedion traces the history of the natural object as obstacle to technique in his study, *Mechanization Takes Command* (1948), a work that Ellul holds in high regard. The assembly line, Giedion announces, owes its origins to the meat packing industry. Many designs for automation, ". . . did not work; in the slaughtering process the material to be handled is a complex, irregularly shaped object: the hog. Even when dead, the hog largely refuses to submit to the machine."[23] This is more than metaphor. The body is not only the obstacle between the mind and the world, a fact that deeply troubled Descartes, not so much the father of modern philosophy as the father of the logic of technology, a point to which I will return. The body is the obstacle technique faces in pursuing its total integration into society. The technical system is, by definition, at least from a dialectical point of view, abstract. *The Technological Society* is Ellul's warning in 1954 about the dangers of technique, about the ubiquity and insidiousness of technical logic; *The Technological System* (1977) speaks some years later from the standpoint of hope:

> But there is always something unpredictable, incoherent, and irreducible in the social body. A society is made up of multiple systems, multiple types, multiple patterns, on different levels. Saying that technology is the determining factor of this society does not mean it is the only factor! Above all, society is made up of people, and the system, in its abstraction, seems to ignore that.[24]

The body is one important element in that social body, a dialectical element, which keeps reasserting itself like the dead hog in early industrialization, like Alan Shepard's need to urinate on the launch pad.

From the standpoint of technical logic, however, with bodily processes turned into abstractions and with abstract thought processes treated as concrete realities, a new subjectivity, a new being in the world appears. The technical mind no longer lives in a traditional world of natural objects to be manipulated bodily, but it lives among embodied conceptions that it does not distinguish from natural objects. At this point, technique becomes automatic, self-augmenting, monistic, universal, and autonomous—the elements of the technical system.

For the technical mind exhibiting the characteristic of automatism, all choices are made automatically; this mentality "... can only decide on the basis of maximum efficiency."[25] All things must be used to their ultimate capacity as use—a perpetual process—becomes the ultimate value, the result of natural objects losing their "objectivity," their value as *other*. Now, no object is valuable or valueless, because "value" is conceived solely in terms of "usefulness." For example, machines that help to pursue destructive ends—machines that, say, produce weapons—become good by becoming useful. In other words, a machine that simply produces, no matter what the product, constructive or destructive, is deemed good if it produces with maximum efficiency. Any other value judgment is irrelevant. Thus, an irony: the universally useful object is, by definition, an abstract object. That is, that which is useful in all ways becomes useful in no way. It ties itself to *the process*. The object that technical consciousness posits is relieved of its particularity with the universal objectivity of method and with the logic of calculation. The technical mind thereby becomes "... a device for recording effects and results obtained by various techniques."[26] The universal object of technique, determinable by mathematical measurement, is not universal in the sense that it transcends and therefore explains a given order, and yet it is no longer merely a particular object either, having its reality in the system, the process. Thus, the individual differences between objects, defining their particularity, are reduced to mathematical abstractions as "reality" is determined by the process of continual measurement.

The transcendental perspectives are transformed. Religion, aesthetics, and philosophy, are present in modern society as ornaments, ". . . like the ruffled sunshade of McCormick's first reaper."[27] The transcendental object is the functional object. In regard to philosophy, Ellul remarks: "The principles established by Descartes were applied and resulted not only in a philosophy but in an intellectual technique."[28] Descartes's method does indeed afford a clue to the technical mind. Descartes, in the *Discourse on Method*, suggests that in the intellectual process one should: (1) consider only that which is evidently true; (2) divide initial difficulties into parts; (3) move from simplified parts to complexities; and (4) achieve completeness through a process of continual review and enumeration.[29] Descartes believed that this method would lead to certainty, to identities without differences, to clear and distinct ideas achieved through reflection and introspection. This method led Descartes, through a further sundering of mind and body, to conclude that nothing could be known as certainly as thought itself.[30] The Cartesian intellectual technique is no longer confined to scientific and philosophical activities, but is now the guide for nearly all activities in the technological life world. The body that provided Descartes with so much trouble has now been eliminated as a locus of being, with the result that individual and relative choices are now made on the basis of mathematical calculation or abstractive reasoning. The leisure world, the industrial world, and the academic world all embody the Cartesian method: even the history of "Deconstructionism" is an intellectual version of the assembly line, a mania for analysis, reducing problems to their parts, which are then assigned only a "systemic reality" that have no meaning in and of themselves. Deconstructionism is simply another place on the academic assembly line; the "text" becomes a technical phenomenon. Ellul sees structuralism and many versions of the hermeneutical movement as aligned with technique, in search of an abiding, abstract, mathematics-like structure for meaning.

Mathematical analysis is important to technique because it provides a purely formal truth that may be indifferently applied to any content. One is not burdened with the necessity of making value judgments, even though the value judgment that technique alone is suited for solving all problems, is presupposed. This viciously circular, amoral method of calculation is aptly exemplified for Ellul by Adolph Hitler in *Mein Kampf* (1940), when he writes: "Unless the enemy learns to combat poison gas with poison gas, this tactic which is based on an accurate evaluation of human weakness, must lead almost mathematically to success."[31] Only technical phenomena can compete with technical phenomena when traditionally conceived objects are transformed into abstract processes. Warfare, for example, has been traditionally limited to a bodily combat among warriors whose ultimate success depended upon individual strength, courage, and abilities with weapons that were extensions of their bodies. Modern warfare, however, has become a battle of almost purely technical phenomena: people, combatants and non-combatants, die indirectly as they happen to get in the way of mathematically conceived and aimed devices.

Technical phenomena become self-augmenting such that (1) growth is irreversible and (2) growth assumes geometric rather than arithmetic proportions. As society becomes more and more infused with technical processes, it exhibits the qualities of a collective unconscious, encouraging the anonymous but steadfast involvement and submersion of the individual in the technical process. As Ellul states, "The worker is asked not only to use the machine he operates, but also to find remedies against... faults in the machine, and in addition to determine how its productivity might be improved. The result is the 'suggestion box' by means of which the workers may indicate their ideas and plans for improvement."[32] The worker is in danger of losing his distance from the object, and identifying too greatly with the machine's functions. His world, soon, is no longer his own as he joins the factory bowling team or becomes, in the fast-food world, "Griddleman of the Month." Technology, telling humans that they are more important than ever before, fails to reveal that their importance is seen only in relation to technical performance. Further, Ellul reminds: "Human beings are, indeed, always necessary. But, literally, anyone can do the job provided he is trained to do it. Henceforth, men will be able to act only in virtue of their commonest and lowest nature and not in virtue of what they possess of superiority and individuality."[33] By working at a job anyone can do, the worker becomes *anyone*, an abstract element in the overall means of production, a wholly replaceable part.

From the standpoint of self-augmentation, the world takes on the character of a single process, albeit infinitely divisible. Ellul understands that technical development in one area assigns a necessary direction for all areas and thereby increases the proliferation and the complexity of technical development. He states: "Thus, a purely mechanical discovery may have repercussions in the domain of social technique or in that of organizational technique. For example, machines that use perforated cards affect statistics and the organization of certain business enterprises."[34] It is, then, to be expected that a metal developed by the space program also will also be used in razor blades, that the techniques of the assembly line will be employed by the university to make professors more "accountable," as the computer grades their performances, and that the scientific method will be employed at McDonald's as hamburgers and french fries are cooked uniformly with the aid of a computer. It was not the cunning of reason that lead McDonald's to name their training school in Chicago "Hamburger U.," only the necessity that is technique. Technical consciousness is irreversible precisely because it is not conscious growth; paradoxically, it is a result of technological consciousness, which has lost self-consciousness and has taken on a life of its own. Mind has thus begun to fall to the object, to become indistinguishable from it; the made is the not-made and the not-made is the made.

Technical growth is geometric rather than arithmetic, to consider the second aspect of self-augmentation, because technique produces results that are neither calculable nor completely predictable even though technique itself depends upon calculation and prediction. Rather, technical devices proliferate *ad infinitum*, having their own necessity for being, following the "law" that that which can be made will be made and that that which is possible is necessary. But the number of devices that will be made and their effects on the task to be performed, their effects on the performer, and the effects on those outside the process, are largely unknown. In 1954, Ellul wrote:

> Since the scientist must use the materials he has at hand; and since almost nothing is known about the relationship of man to the automobile, the telephone, or the radio, and absolutely nothing about the relationship of man to the *Apparat* or about the sociological effects of other aspects of technique, the scientist moves unconsciously toward the sphere of what is known scientifically, and tries to limit whole question to that.[35]

And in 1986 we can observe that in the wake of the Chernobyl power plant "incident," acceptable levels of radiation are being measured for adults without even knowing what such levels are. Danger is being assessed by what we know of the life of radioactive elements and their rate of decay without knowing to what degree exposure to them has detrimental cumulative effects. To predict means to be able to control. By confusing "technique" with tools that are extensions of our bodies and intentions, the pernicious quality of the technical phenomenon escapes us. Tools are adaptable because their meaning transcends their use. They can only be used for directed purposes. With the technical process, each use must be objectified, increasing the unpredictable nature of the objects now defined in and by the system. The meaning of the object is lost within the system and the meaning of the system can only be defined in terms of the elements, in terms of whether they are used or not. The useful object becomes use itself. Thus, the decision to use or not to use rarely comes up. In this we see the triumph of hope over reason.

The clock and the technical phenomena of the mass media are particularly important in the process of self-augmentation and in the cooption of the individual's self-consciousness as it is revealed in and against bodily activity. The privately owned clock, first appearing in the sixteenth century, displaces psychological, lived time.[36] Personal time is objectified and with it an abstract social time is created, completely apart from the individual needs of the human. Needs no longer determine time, but time determines needs, Before we know whether it is time to get up, we, like Gulliver, must consult our oracles, the clock. As I mentioned in the last chapter, the camera and the tape recorder have made personal memory and experience suspect, if not irrelevant; the world is captured and thereby made rational with ontologically superior copies. Humanity then, loses touch with immediate reality as that reality becomes a media event—a world of images.[37] Good citizens watch the news to figure out what happened in the world that day, as if what happened in *their world* was of no consequence. As the individual loses a distance on the world, self-augmentation increases and opens the way to monism.

The closed world of technique illustrates what Ellul calls the characteristic of monism. All the elements of this world, the various techniques and the relations they form, "... are ontologically tied together; in it, use is inseparable from being."[38] This can be understood in a number of ways: that which can be conceived will be applied, as evident in the self-augmenting character of technique, in which theory is inevitably tied to practice. Further, only that which can be applied will be conceived. Government grants, in the main, are only awarded to scientists who are working on theories with immediately practical results. Theory is no longer restricted by morality or by aesthetics, nor by any transcendental perspective. Instead, use has become a moral command. It is, therefore, useless to condemn a technique because of its immoral uses or to suggest that it should be used in a more moral fashion. Ellul states: "To say of such a technical means that a bad use has been made of it is to say that no use has been made of it, that it has not been made to yield what it could have yielded and ought to have yielded."[39] A car may be a means for transportation or a murder weapon. If we use it as a murder weapon, we are using it badly because it was not designed to kill people. This may be why an auto accident resulting in the death of a pedestrian is assumed to be, at worst, reckless homicide, although it is likely to be adjudicated as manslaughter. To sustain a murder charge requires intent to kill, which would be difficult to prove because a means would have been used improperly. On the other hand, if one person shoots another, murder would be the assumed charge unless it could be proved that it was a crime of passion and that there was no premeditated intent to kill—all because a gun is designed to kill and because judgment is inherent in the technique. Similarly, if a nuclear power plant explodes, the resulting deaths would be considered accidents, for clearly it was not "designed" to explode.[40]

The characteristic of monism also refers to technique's capacity to form a world, to provide systems that link up in unusual and surprising ways. During the first New York televised showing of *Love Story*, it was reported that New York City was at one point almost out of water; apparently a significant number of TV viewers had waited until the first commercial to go to the bathroom, and the immediate drain on the system had deleterious effects on system pressure. This points to the strength of the technical system and to its fragility, with each part depending on other parts. Ellul states:

> The technological system, in which all the technologies are related and coordinated, should be compared to the electric network on which everything depends. A broken line has far-reaching human and economic consequences because of the technological solidarity of the entire network: an interruption in the mass transit of workers, work stoppage in the factories involved, a delay in the arrival of raw materials, a loss of working time, with repercussions—e.g., in Paris, for the 260,000 suburban workers arriving at Gare du Nord, or the 300,000 at Gare Saint-Lazare. The collectivity has to pay dearly for the tiniest snag. The more unity in the system, the more fragile it becomes.[41]

This point, made in *The Technological System*, marks his advance over *The Technological Society*; it is his prognostication of the breakdown of the system under its own complexity. Coherence and internal linkages, two major features of the system, have their price. I will make more of this later, with a discussion of the ramifications of the loss of dialectic in the system.

Technical universalism is the tendency of technique to be universally adopted wherever it is introduced. Productivity with technique is highly compelling, as it promises the human a world that is better than the natural world because it is made. The irony here is that the human world is as mysterious as the natural world. Technique has obscured but not disposed of this essential mystery. In traditional societies techniques are just another part of life and are subject to the ends determined by that culture—to tradition, philosophy, aesthetics, or religion, for example. The family, the church, the intellectual, and the individual have to efface their authorities. At this stage technique becomes rigorously objective: "It effaces all individual, and even all collective modes of expression. Today man lives by virtue of his participation in a truth become objective."[42] Technique is a culture as well as a society.

Technique becomes universal on a national and international scale in that all nations adopt essentially technical ends. Japan is an example of this phenomenon. The traditional Japanese society has all but disappeared—relegated to museums or shrines that present Japanese culture as exotic curiosities to the Japanese themselves—in favor of Western technique. Technique has reduced the East-West cultural dichotomy to myth. Consider Mao Tse Tung's remarks:

> This process, the practice of changing the world, which is determined in accordance with scientific knowledge has already reached a historic moment in the world of China, a great moment unprecedented in human history, that is, the moment for completely banishing darkness from the world and from China and for changing the world into a world of light such as never previously existed.[43]

The scientific way of understanding the world takes precedence over other traditional methods. Techniques may vary from culture to culture, relative to climate and natural resources, for example, but the goal of technique will be the same.[44] And ". . . what differences there are will result from the cold calculation of some technician, instead of being the result of the profound spiritual and material effort of generations of human beings. Instead of being the expression of man's essence, they will be the accidents of what is essential: technique."[45] Humanity's essence, however, cannot be regarded as something set over against the cultural milieu in which it finds itself, as a thing-in-itself unaltered by the relations in which it appears; instead, humanity's essence is that which appears as necessity is confronted.[46] That essence is thwarted when humanity succumbs to necessity. For Ellul, humanity's essence must remain importantly problematic.

The human essence is worked out as symbol systems in cultures. The varieties of traditional cultures marked the diversity of approaches, testaments to the finitude of humanity's knowledge of itself. The technological society is a symbol system, although it is not self-consciously perceived as such. Ellul states:

> The technological system is a real universe, which constitutes *itself* as a symbolic system. With respect to nature, the symbolic universe was an imaginary universe, a superordinated reflection, entirely instituted by man in relation to this natural world. It enabled him to *distanciate* himself and *differentiate* himself from that reality, and at the same time to master reality through the mediation of the symbolic, which attributed an otherwise undifferentiated meaning to the world.[47]

We have heard this before. The natural object as the not-made allowed consciousness to confront itself in relation to an *other* and to respond to that *other* within symbolic structures. This, we remember, was a relation of consciousness to its object, to what it is not. The technical phenomenon, lacks this quality of otherness and appears instead as the objectification of technical consciousness. Ellul's case here is not a metaphysical case, arguing on the basis of what the object really is; this is a case made from appearance. What is important is how the object appears. Technical consciousness does not have a distance on itself, on its objects, which it confuses with itself. This accounts, on the one hand, for universalism. It also explains technology as a sacred order, while also appearing as the enemy of the sacred. Ellul continues:

> In the technological system, there is no more possibility of symbolizing. ... First of all, this possibility is not present because the reality is produced by man, who does not feel mystery and strangeness. He still claims to be the direct master. Furthermore, it is not present because, if symbolizing is a process of distanciation, then the whole technological process is, on the contrary, a mechanism for integrating man; and finally, because now, it is no longer man who symbolizes nature, but technology which symbolizes itself. The mechanism of symbolization *is* technology, the means of this symbolization are the mass media of communication. The object to be consumed is an offered symbol.[48]

Here, there are important ironies. Technique is a symbol that is not a symbol, a kind of intentionality that is nonintentional, and is a form of inclusion that excludes man from the process. Moreover, it destroys a sacred order, while becoming one. These ironies can only be explained by considering technique as autonomous, as the new sacred order.

Technique becomes autonomous when all goals become subservient to it, when all that is transcendent becomes immanent, and when "mystery" is reduced to the light of day. A sense of mystery is essential to humanity's spiritual well-being, to his symbolizing powers. Ellul states:

> Jung has shown that it is catastrophic to make superficially clear what is hidden in man's innermost depths. Man must make allowance for a background, a great deep above which lie his reason and his clear consciousness. The mystery of man perhaps creates the mystery of the world he inhabits. Or perhaps this mystery is a reality in itself. There is no way to decide between these two alternatives. But, one way or the other, mystery is a necessity of human life.[49]

The first otherness, perhaps in the form of the thundering sky, provides a primal sense of otherness, as I stated in the first chapter. This encounter with mystery is the basis of humanity's creative urges, the attempt to find a place and to establish a sense of meaning and a feeling for purpose and destiny, for a transcendent that frames the daily world and gives it context. That which is truly mysterious—the sacred—is that which humanity decides to respect. Technique, however, denies mystery *a priori*. The mysterious is simply that which is not yet the technical. Technique is now the only mystery, that which is ultimately deserving of respect.

One central irony behind Ellul's discussion of technology is that, on the one hand, technology appears tied to reason and science, supported by logic and the scientific method. What is not practical, it would seem, would be abandoned; what is logically inconsistent would not be attempted. And, yet, it is well known that the military, with the aid of science and technology, builds weapons that are obsolete, and sinks millions of dollars into research for developing things like the Frisbee as a possible antipersonnel weapon, perhaps on the grounds that what is useful as a toy should be useful in all ways. Currently, science is working to implement President Reagan's dream of a "Star Wars" defense system, the name inspired by the popular George Lucas science-fiction film, with apparently little actual scientific knowledge as to how such a system would be possible. One could conclude that the military and the scientific communities are in principle separate and that these absurdities are the result of the ineptitudes of military and bureaucratic minds. But in this argument there is an interesting level of idealism at work. The current reality in most modern countries is that science and the military are not separate. To see them as logically separate and to take that abstract separation as significant is to speak of logical possibility devoid of content, a ploy of technique. The fact is that modern bureaucracy and science do need each other, that they have much in common in the rage for order. The central irony appears as the absurdity to which such rage leads. Science, dependent on reason and experiment, also finds need of myth and power. Further, it is useless to argue that the real problem is politics, inasmuch as politics is inherently tied to the military, to technology, and to science.

The further ploy to separate science from technology on the grounds of a great epistemological gap is not satisfying. It is a commonplace to say that science seeks the truth no matter what and that it is to the scientists' dismay that the technician-bureaucrat enters, riding roughshod over these sensitive individuals. Remember that these sensitive scientists were led to warrant the exploding of the first atomic bomb while scientific opinion was divided as to whether the world would be destroyed as a result. That the earth did not explode is not necessarily a credit to these sensibilities. It is possible to put ex-Nazi luminaries of the American space program on the stand to testify as to their complicity in building rockets during World War II, but we might as well try to derive morality from arithmetic, to argue that two opposites equal zero and that this has moral ramification.

Instead, it is Ellul's view that the separation between science and technology after Galileo and the telescope is simply wishful thinking. He writes:

> All science, having become experimental, depends on technology, which alone permits reproducing phenomena technologically. Now, technology abstractly reproduces nature to permit scientific experimenting. Hence, the temptation to make nature conform to theoretical models, to reduce nature to techno-scientific artificiality. "Nature is what I produce in my laboratory," says a modern physicist.[50]

Reality is made over to conform to scientific expectation. Atomic research requires, of necessity, an atom smasher or some other such device for putting nature on the rack to extract truth. Technique creates the objects with which science can work, either by reducing them to mathematical abstractions or by creating the context in which they are to function. True scientific objectivity is a myth.

In Ellul's eyes, science has become a will to power, furthering the autonomy of technique, pulling it to the dimension of the sacred, and giving up the dialectic necessary to epistemic claims, which are currently reduced to the methodological. He states:

> ... science becomes violence (in regard to everything it bears upon), and the technology expressing the scientific violence becomes power exclusively. Thus, we have a new correlation, which I consider fundamental, between science and technology. The scientific method itself determines technology's calling to be a technology of power. And technology, by the means it makes available to science, induces science into the process of violence (against the ecology, for instance).[51]

Despite claims to the contrary, the scientific method, the Cartesian method, or one of its versions, becomes an act of violence, in which things are reduced to abstractions and to procedural constraints, to continual enumerations simply from the standpoint of logic. Ellul states:

> ... technique desacralizes because it demonstrates (by evidence and not by reason, through use and not through books) that mystery does not exist. Science brings to the light of day everything man had believed sacred. Technique takes possession of it and enslaves it. The sacred cannot resist. Science penetrates to the great depths of the sea to photograph the unknown fish of the deep. Technique captures them, hauls them up to see if they are edible—but before they arrive on deck they burst.[52]

Technique takes the notion of truth and reduces it to a mere fact, to evidence. Reason in its dialectical form is abandoned, and the turn toward the sacred is complete. Truth that can be measured and reduced to method is the truth sought. The natural object is cast into the rat tank, mentioned earlier, and then observed for puposes of determining its "natural behavior." The natural object has become a technical phenomenon, however, curiously resulting in a loss of objectivity that initially was of so much importance.

It is now important to review the stages of the logic of technique. To desacralize the natural object, the objects must be taken up in technical processes. For example, from the primitive's perspective, the decision to turn to the soil amounts to a penetration of the Earth Mother. This involves a separation from the earth, disarming her of her powers or considering whether she wants to be penetrated. In either case, a will to power has been effected. For example, as Mircea Eliade understands it:

> It is not our technical discoveries in themselves, it is the magico-religious acceptation of them which has altered the perspective and the content of the religious life of the traditional societies. Nor must it be supposed that agriculture itself, as a technical innovation, could have had such repercussions upon the spiritual ambience of archaic humanity. Within

their horizons there was no separation between the tool—the real, concrete object—and the symbol which gave it value: between a technique and the magico-religious operation which it implied. Let us not forget that the primitive spade symbolized the phallus and the soil the telluric matrix; the agricultural action was assimilated to the generative act: in many Austro-Asiatic languages the spade still has the same name as the phallus.[53]

Thus, for the primitive, the will to power is taken carefully, accepting the power of the dangerous but yet powerful, nourishing other. The tool is, further, the extension of the body. Thus, in primitive societies technique located beneath the sacred is subject to time, habit, and religious-aesthetic determination. With the aid of science and technology and a seeking of the one best way, the whole cloth of the primitive world suffers a cosmic tear. It is well known in the study of cargo cults that the introduction of a technological object in primitive societies often disrupts the entire society; during World War II, for example, it was not uncommon in places like New Guinea to find religions developing around such things as a flier's jacket, with the natives creating mock airports to call in their savior.[54]

With the development of technical rationality, techniques become self-augmenting, with a spade becoming a bulldozer, leading to the development of CB radios, high-rises, life insurance, and Coca-Cola, "the real thing." As Umberto Eco has observed: the concoction of the real thing, the genuine imitation, leads to a desire for "more," objects from the cornucopia of technique; the copy, Eco also observes, in *Travels in Hyperreality* (1986), leads to the realization that the original pales before it.[55] Thus, choice for technique is made automatically. No one can resist the fascination of technical performance, which explains why the entire society is geared to watching football, ballet, a car chase on a TV detective show, and the electric can opener in the kitchen, as it twirls the can around, and lift in a grand finale, the lid with its magnetic arm. The fascination for performance, for technique, is seemingly inexhaustible, as after each sports event, announcers query athletes about what techniques they used to perform a specific task, as the instant replay goes over a particularly successful kick or an especially bad fumble.

Nothing is too important or too trivial to inspect with endless technical attention: the space shuttle *Challenger* disaster is shown for an entire day, nearly every hour. Walking into a video store, one may notice tapes of it playing to no one in particular, alongside a new music video by Michael Jackson. Each tape may play for hours, and the shopper or consumer watches whatever is before them. Thus technique is a world in which the natural landscape becomes a media decor. Whatever virtues are permitted, appear in relation to technical activity itself: " . . . (precision, exactness, seriousness, a realistic attitude, and, over everything else, the virtue of work) and a certain outlook on life (modesty, devotion, cooperation)."[56] Value is based on what is serious and what is not, on what is efficient and what is not.

These values located around the technical phenomenon, embedded in the logic that accounts for technique's proliferation, spread nationally and internationally. In pretechnological cultures, culture was determined by geographical location and the amount of natural resources, and by the political, religious, aesthetic, and philosophical attitudes of its people. Because of this, cultures lacked uniformity, but in the modern world all cultures are either technological cultures, developing technological cultures, or problems for other technological cultures. Just as technique assumes its most rational and monolithic proportions, Ellul notes, technique, in the form of mystery itself, appears. That is, the function of the sacred in a culture is to determine a direction and a meaning, a locus in time, a sense of beginnings and endings. All temporal events flow from the sacred. I now therefore consider technique in greater detail.

Technology as the Sacred Order

Ellul's discussion of technology as the sacred appears throughout his work, more like musical composition than argument. His most developed account, however, occurs in *Les Nouveaux Possédés* (1973) [*The New Demons* (1975)]. The sacred, he reminds us, is the ultimate mystery, which is at once threatening and comforting, a *mysterium tremendum*, as Rudolf Otto considered in his masterpiece, *Das Heilige* (1917). Ellul states: "The sacred is an organization of action in space and at the same time it is the establishment of a geography of that space in which the action can be undertaken. It is a veritable general topography of the world, involving all aspects of the latter, material and spiritual, trans-cendent and close at hand."[57] Although for the primitive the sacred was in the natural world, it may lie anywhere. Wherever it appears, it serves as a point of order but also as a locus of disorder, as the extraordinary, as that which is somehow beyond temporal ordering: sacred time is the time of ecstasy, of the festival of transgression and, hence, of disorder. Ellul states: "It is a time between the times, a silence between words, a plunge into the absolute origins, which one must *come out of* in order to begin. It is a plunge into chaos which one must come out of if the order is to have force, virtue and validity. It is a delimitation of the time during which the dark powers can act, an opening into that which man distrusts but cannot eliminate."[58] The sacred serves an integrating function and a disjunctive function as well. It is the ultimately transcendent that is at the same time wholly immanent, the tie that runs throughout the social collectivity, making its unity possible. It is a unity based on disjunction and disunity. Sacral consciousness, appearing as the mind collapses to the object, cannot, however, apprehend itself as the sacred.

These functions of the sacred, typically, appear within specific forms: as unpredictable, dark and destructive, as a concentration of all that threatens man, but yet as that which saves man, as that which provides a sense of absolute meaning and justification; the sacred and the absolute values and rites of commitment attendant to the sacred are always incarnate in a person or in some object, and in this sense provide a transcendent that is immanent. Finally, the sacred is the unity between antitheses, between such opposites as the "... pure/impure, holy/blemished, cohesion/dissolution, profane/sacred, respect/violation, life/death."[59] These opposites are held in a tension of contradiction; there is no synthesis, although an identity is formed between them. Ellul states: "In the world of the sacred, man is related to the world directly. There is a lack of distinction of subject and object, an immediacy of relation, an experience of totality."[60] It is a totality, however, with two opposing sides. The symbologies of the sacred take up the implicit disjunction between consciousness and its object, forgetting that bifurcation in the process of constructing the symbol. This symbolic unity is not a conscious unity, not known to be a symbol, an identification of subject with object. As I suggested above, once the symbol is known to be a symbol, it loses its power and is no longer able to vivify the sacred.

For Ellul, the sacred must be distinguished from the myths that vivify it. The logic of the sacred is a logic of identity between subject and object, between the world and a particular account of it. Myths, are projections of this mentality. Ellul adds, however, that "Henceforth the myth is seen both as the subconscious stand taken by the human collectivity toward the structures, and as the meaning which it attributes to them."[61] Thus, myth is an expression of the sacred and not, as the structuralist Roland Barthes understands it, a form of rationalization. Barthes is aware of the vitalizing force of myth as a power of joining, for example, joining the subject and predicate in the metaphor; but his analysis of language presupposes a language where such a split has already occurred.[62] Thus Barthes is able to speak of modern myths, but not of myth as a direct expression of the sacred or of myth as a form of sacralizing consciousness. For Ellul, myths appear as unauthored sacred symbols, losing their power only as they become detached from mythical consciousness.[63] Myths as vivifications of the sacred are neither revolutionary nor conservative, inasmuch as they are tied to the sacred.[64] From these facts one may infer that "The organization of the sacral world is an organization of the actual world in which man lives. Myth, on the other hand, is a fictive statement about a reality in connection with a given portion of that world. Hence, the sacred keeps man constantly at the level of the real, whereas myth leads him into a fictive universe."[65] That is, the sacred is an immediate experience, while myth is mediated experience. Myths are not fictive in that they are false. They simply point in another direction, away from the object, back to the subject and to the subject's grasp of the object. We thereby remember that experience, or our grasp of it, is never total, always having three components: the subject, the object, and our mediation of it. The mediation pulls us in two directions: toward the object or back to the subject. Synthesis does not occur while consciousness obtains.

Understanding technology as sacred involves being clear about the essential irony that it is a form of consciousness that has become unconscious. It is also important to remember that technical development in the form of industrialization was taken on with great foreboding, that initially the worker's attitude toward the machine could have been described as admiration mingled with terror, that the train and the automobile were looked upon with great suspicion and fear. It was soon a fear overtaken by a sense of necessity. Ellul remarks that it is not uncommon to hear modern man deprecate his technological life and its evils of pollution, overcrowding, depersonalization, and global extinction, while at the same time shaking his head and saying: "What can one do? It's the way things must be." This attitude suggests the way the primitive faces the absolute, the *mysterium tremendum*.[66] The gods are fearful, the gods are harsh, and their demands are exacting; but without them the universe would have no meaning. According to Soviet Marxist interpretations, technology is viewed as the proletariat's salvation, indicating an almost Messianic respect for this force. Thus, today, all political forces, from radical to conservative, see their economic and political futures in terms of technical innovation, which thus becomes a true ground of being.

The mass media reinforce technique as the sacred. With television, the miracles of technology are rendered visible, while they retain their essential mystery. The world of immediate reality pales before the image from Pakistan or New York; the faraway is produced here and now—a denial of space and time itself—but in this denial the mystery is preserved as the transcendent is made immanent. Any time, any space may be produced at the technician's will, resulting in a true eternal moment. But in this way the mysterious also becomes the familiar:

> This somewhat mysterious, yet completely scientific power, which covers the earth with its radio waves, wires and paper, is to the technician an abstract idol which gives him a reason for living, and even joy. One indication, among others, of man's sense of the sacred in technology is the care he takes to treat it with familiarity. It is well-known that laughter and humor are frequently a person's reaction in the presence of the sacred. That is true of primitive peoples, but it is also the reason why the first A-bomb was called "Gilda," that the giant cyclotron at Los Alamos was named "Clementine," ... and that radioactive contamination is called a "burn." The technicians at Los Alamos rigorously banned the word "atom" from their vocabulary. All that is significant.[67]

The technician's laughter, like his reality, is canned, based not on an orginal and transcendental grasp of something that is stood on its head and taken in an original way. As Donald Verene has shown, the technician is a great punster, the genius of what Freud knew as the *Kalauer*, the old chestnut; the technician knows the power of the laugh, fearing it.[68] Calling a reactor Gilda and a cyclotron Clementine warrants the horselaugh, howlers of radical insignificance. Verene, quoting poet Lawrence Ferlinghetti, would conclude, "The thinkpad makes homeboys of us all."[69] Ellul's point, however, is that technique is a new sacred, one that is manufactured, but that nonetheless reveals ancient roots. That, too, is significant. The modern familiar is no longer the sensory immediate of an individual with his own past, present, and future; it is the eternal present of transformed massman. Media as pure technical phenomena serve an integrating function, connecting each individual and forming what McLuhan called a "global village of retribalized man." Unlike tribal man, however, moving beyond McLuhan's myth, humanity lives out the ephemeral process of technique, in a creation of realities made out of empty symbols that do not point beyond themselves, beyond the system.

Through the impact of technique, modern man comes to see himself as his own creation, as *Homo faber*.[70] In this role, humanity comes of age. Humanity of pretechnological culture is, thereby, not humanity at all. Civilization becomes equated with technology. As Ellul notes, this leads to some bizarre views of the past, for example, to those of Erich Von Däniken in *The Chariots of the Gods* (1970), which are "... side-splitting in ... [their] scientific pretense."[71] Selling over a million copies, it is the thesis of this book that the so-called mysteries of the past, such as the Saqqarra pyramid in Egypt, were really built by technologically superior spacemen from another planet. Von Däniken concludes that it would have been impossible to have built such grand edifices without the miracles of technique.

So far, I have suggested that technique may be regarded as the mysterious, the awe-inspiring, the center of being, the beginning and the future of time, and the principle of integration of the individual into the group. It remains to show how the sacred incorporates or unifies order with transgression, that is, it remains to indicate how the sacred is incorporated into societal rituals as well as how it becomes incarnate in an individual. The ritual, of course, makes this incarnation possible.

According to Ellul, sex is one transgression pole of technique.[72] Sex is desacralized when it is no longer considered a valuable activity, meaningful in and of itself. This is a feature of the debodying characteristic of technique noted in the transformation of the technical operation. Like the technical operation, "Sex is no longer a natural, free sphere of activity. It is an instrument of strife, a struggle for freedom."[73] Ellul notes that sex, during the late 1960s, functioned as political technique, pointing to the other pole of transgression—nation state/revolution.[74] With technique's creation of the docile body, neither sex nor politics are possible. Refering to a student takeover of an administration building, Ellul notes: "In May of 1968 I saw in a faculty council room a very significant inscription: 'This place has been desacralized. These chairs have been fucked on.'"[75] There has been a transgression but not a transcendence; this sacred is purely immanent. In addition to fornicating on chairs, students also wanted to join university committees, to help determine policy, a clear failure of imagination and a stunning indication of the fascination order and administration hold for even the most disenfranchised. Sex, like administration, further, is the subject for an endless proliferation of sex manuals and business success handbooks. Nothing is meaningful, even sex, unless it is done the one best way, in a correct performance.

The docile body appears in its purest form in its role as consumer. Following a clue left by Lévi-Strauss *Le Cru et Le Cuit* (1964) [*The Raw and the Cooked* (1969)], Ellul notes that consumption is connected to man's most primitive religious desires. The consumer, and his counterpart, the tourist—the consumer's consumer—pursues a sacralizing activity of taking in—buying and seeing—a self-contained system of sites and markers, honoring the space that technological rationality has laid out for it. Space itself becomes a technical phenomenon in the shopping center which combines consuming and touring. Sight-seeing, in addition to its honorific pose, helps to relieve the alienation caused by the former industrial society with its "museumization of work."[76] That is, alienating labor in an industrial society sets humans against themselves and each other by removing the laborer from an intimate relationship with the product of his or her own labor, by reducing the worker and laborers to functionaries, and by numbing the worker's senses with dull, repetitive tasks. This is resolved in the sight-seeing act, where the sacred and the profane, the technical and the bodily, are united. For example, the many displays in Chicago's Museum of Science and Industry, as well as a large picture window in a pizza parlor, enable passers-by to watch work being done. Productivity becomes sight-seeing, as machines do the work and as humans are reduced to mere spectators in the process. Sight-seeing as a full-time, sacralizing activity relieves the frustration and boredom of a life of seeming inactivity. In the shopping center, the great sacred space of our time, one is able to move about and be near the buying without actually having to buy. Sacred space, perhaps, rubs off.

Myths, as vivifications of the sacred, have to be viewed as unique to the culture in which they appear. These myths must appear as the culture's collective unconscious, represented by the mass media that are anonymous yet personal.

> Anonymity can no longer be assured by ancestral tradition in a society geared to the future and rejecting continuity with the past. The anonymity is now assured by the mass media. The someone who carries the story to all, the someone who is completely known and completely anonymous and is assimilated to the "no one" speaking in the myth, is, par excellence, the television announcer.[77]

The mass media do not, in themselves, produce myths but, rather, guarantee their authenticity.[78] The mass media and their cultural disruptions, resulting in the almost irrational return to the immediate, in the rejection of traditional, linear thinking, and in the loss of memory, serve to show that the sacral order has returned. The irrational, appearing in the logic of the sacred—a logic of identities without difference, a result of mind collapsing into its object—is very much a current reality.[79] This is a logic that hides behind official policy, a logic underneath the logic of technique. This sacred is vivified by the modern myths of history and science.[80]

History becomes mythical as it loses any sense of meaning outside of the flow of time itself. History becomes a mere accounting of events or of things that contributed to those events. It no longer begins with, for example, Christ's incarnation into the world, with humanity's discovery of a great truth. Greatness is denied in the realm of the merely finite. The meaning and structure of the world can now only come from history itself, and at this point, history becomes mythical inasmuch as the truth is simply nothing more than man's accounting of it. History has a meaning merely by having a structure.[81] Science, like history, becomes mythical when it believes in the absolute verity of its own accounts, when the scientist no longer finds his experiments verified by alleged truth, but when his experiments become truth.[82] As Ellul states:

> To the degree, in fact, to which objectivity stems from pure methodology, then becomes a state of consciousness, an attitude, an ethic, it becomes a value judgment, an exclusion of every other mode of apprehending truth. That relation to truth introduces us into the mythical. But more than that, objectivity presents itself as a value which synthesizes all science. It is just that to which the mythical discourse lays claim. ...[83]

Science, then, becomes mythical when it is reduced to scientific method and, therefore, to a technique, and when truth is reduced to the sensually immediate and cut off from a transcendental realm.

The Problem of the System

Technique, Ellul holds, is a form of desire to open up and to possess the natural object, the natural world, and moveover, to possess the truth itself. Toward this goal, technique replicated and simulated the natural world, building it on lines of a specific logic. These simulations are currently held in deep respect, in awe, in worship, much as nature was respected and worshiped in the pretechnological world. These simulations—technical phenomena— reveal a specific form: rationality, artificiality, automatism self-augmentation, monism, universalism, and autonomy. The result is the technological system, seeking always a totality and attempting to establish causal connections, the characteristics added in *The Technological System*. The system is constructed, however, according to a mathematical logic that abhors contradiction, seeks identities, and hungers after supreme and absolute coherence. But between the goal and the reality lies a great distance. Even mathematicians, following Gödel's insights, have come to suspect that a mathematical system cannot be completely consistent and coherent at the same time. Speaking, for example, of the counting numbers, which I can define as n plus 1, I notice that the numbers can never be completed. There will always be one more. To attempt to complete them is to arbitrarily assign an end to the series, that is, to leave a number out. Consistency and coherence are thus at odds in mathematics. There is still greater conflict in daily life.

As I have said in speaking of dialectical logic, my idea of the world never equals the world, which is either more or less than my idea of it. My vision of my friend as a great gourmand can never reconcile the fact that he hates oysters on the half-shell. As I define gourmand, so it must be. That is one approach. But, as with any legislation, the legislated may have other things in mind. My friend could tell me that he has chosen to monitor his cuisine from the standpoint of health, that eating bivalves from polluted waters is dangerous business. Or he could argue, on a more aesthetic note, that such food is simply the projection of some decadent cuisine, like the French cuisine, and that he has decided to give up all that up in favor of macrobiotics. I might resort to propaganda at this point, convincing my friend that I know best, that I know what he really desires. Technique has done just that: now the average citizen eats, in a TV dinner, an evolved version of the K-rations. There is always the danger of rebellion. There is the further danger inherent in any thought, in any position masquerading as the absolute. It may achieve what it really wants, discovering, however, that what it desires is insufficient, positing a range beyond desire itself.

If humanity's idea of the object could ever become identical with the object, the human would be a god. The technical system would work, as would any schema. The not-made would be the not-thought. Descartes's dilemma relating to the relationship between the mind and the body would be solved. The thought of the object and the object itself would be equal. What man thought of would be certain. Technique, indeed, assumes this godlike stance with its belief in the primacy of method. Consistent with Descartes's hope, technique assumes that truth, that the certain, will appear if it is put in line with a proper methodology. The society's honorific pose in front of this sacred assures the hegemony of technique. The true has become the made and the made is produced in the laboratory of technique. The technical system founders, however, on just this level.

In "La Technique, système bloqué" (1979),[84] Ellul argues that there are four very clear levels of breakdown: (1) pollution, which destroys the natural order's equilibrium, shows the fragility of the technical system, and reveals its dependence on the natural order, on the not-made (oil in water, plastics, and noise, are offered as kinds of pollution); (2) technique has created a congestion of clutter, an excess of information, as is typical in the newspaper or on the news broadcast, which has dislocated and disoriented the modern citizen, and has resulted in short attention spans and media-induced losses of memory; (3) the system is inundated by waste—the more one consumes the more one wastes—which is noticeable specifically on the governmental-military level where more is never enough; (4) technique is always on the verge of exhausting natural resources, nonrenewable items such as water and air. The object as the *other* of nature asserts itself. At this stage it is clear that the true is also the not-made, the not-intended. It matters little whether we strike "accident" from our vocabulary, as nuclear technicians have done. The problem works on many levels. First, there is a confusion with the intellectual and the real, as if what is rational is wholly real, a subversion of the notion of the true that is the whole, which includes the irrational, as Hegel had likely intended. Second, there is an intellectual problem with the notion of "system" itself.

Following Talcott Parson's definition in *The Social System* (1951), Ellul states that a system is both integrated and integrating, involving a model, an equilibrium, and a control.[85] A system must order and integrate, but it must also have an element serving as a model and a control. The position of the model and the control remain problematic. That is, a system tends toward a structure with no isolated elements. Elements within the system tend to combine among themselves, excluding outside elements to which it can only relate, if at all, as an other system. Systems repeat and replicate other systems, with elements repeating other elements. In the technical system, for example, technique is chosen automatically; other approaches are excluded. The technical system tends to become closed but is only able to relate to other technical systems. (Perhaps this level of technique explains why Third World countries are such problems for both the United States and the USSR.) But at the same time, within the technical system, there are evidences of breakdowns.

In addition to the above, we could add the problem of the Third World as a source of both terrorism and poverty. It is becoming clear that these countries are unable to establish themselves as law-abiding and prompt-paying citizens of an increasingly technical world. Crime, for example is also becoming a problem within the United States as a growing population of technical untrainables are herded into increasingly crowded jails, filled by the limitation of the system itself.

The problem is to determine the relationship of the meaning of the system to the system itself. If the system is defined simply in terms of one of the elements of the system, the system collapses, as the elements are meaninglessly multiplied into a bad infinity. If, however, the meaning is wholly outside the system, the system elevates to an impossible abstraction. Meaning must be both within and without the system at the same time. That is, as both Parsons and Ellul contend, the system must be able to incorporate feedback and true information, which is not always what the system wants to hear. As in mathematics, a system that is completely axiomatic cannot prove itself. Proof, here, may be understood both logically and existentially.

Georg Simmel, one of the founders of sociology, understood well the importance of "the stranger"—the outside element that defines, that incorporates and is incorporated by the social system—a role often historically played by the Jews.[86] The outsider is both outsider and insider, who the society often excludes; a society legislates normalcy by locking up, killing, or banishing those not fitting in. This outside element is necessary to the society's view of itself. Thus, it banishes these others at its own risk. It includes them at its own risk as well. The outsider is a transcendental element that calls the system into question by its very presence. What is done with the outsider depends upon the system's ability to handle "feedback." The technician's approach, Ellul has been maintaining, is to reduce the outsider to an element in the system. Meaning is thus made a member of the system and technique thereby *becomes* the sacred order. Traditionally, art, philosophy, and religion have played the roles of outsiders, of transcendental elements in the realm of knowledge. Ellul's claim, however, is that these, too, have been incorporated by the technical system, a move made easier by the humiliation of the symbol, of the word, which is my central concern in the next chapter. The word as distinct from the image, the bodily form of the technical phenomenon, points to the transcendental, to the outside, which may still be able to show the system to itself. The word, for Ellul, is not simply the spoken. The spoken, as distinct from the image, only points to this domain. What is most important is that the word represents the uncertain; the image, on the other hand, points to the certain. In fact, in the technical society, the certain becomes *the point*, the representation of sheer thereness, disconnected, disembodied being, the media decor. The spoken directs us to the realm of the symbol, which does not merely point but leads us in two directions: toward the object and back toward the subject. When the symbolizing function returns, the technical system has been defeated. This defeat will by definition not be a mass defeat, by definition. The technical system merely incorporates mass movements by turning them into the system or into other systems.

Ellul's approach is to stand against any direction the system can take. For example, he understands that when his critics argue there is no technical system, that is itself an idea promulgated by the system. That is, to claim that there are simply objects scattered about and that humanity can use them as they will, is to voice a commonplace created by the system that leads us to believe that all is relative, unconnected, and placed at humanity's disposal, providing that they apply a proper method.[87] When an inefficient method is applied, when one decides to act with no method, or to take up H. L. Mencken's advice that anything worth doing is worth doing badly, one finds out how relative things are. The necessity of the systemic nature of the system is reinforced in the obsession with using the computer in all facets of social life, giving it a prominent place in home and office. It does not matter that home computers at home are rarely used, as has recently been reported by news commentators. What matters is that they are there. In reality, the computer serves to link up the systems the technical society has already developed. With the full use of the computer, which is no mere adding machine, the technical system becomes more of a reality. That is, it enables the system to work more easily without the intervention of man, as it is now nearly able to do.[88]

Ellul's task is to desacralize the modern sacred that is technique and to return the symbolic dimension to the life of the individual. Ellul is himself an example of this embodied dimension of the outsider. Early in the 1940s he was able to see the *Reader's Digest* as an example of technique, as I mentioned in the last chapter. He was able to read the signs, a gift for which there is no technique, a vision that is both outside and inside the system. Ellul shows us how to work this vision. For example, in reading a French newspaper article that claimed that the washing machine would save France, Ellul found an important clue to developing his notion of the logic of technique.[89] Likewise, we might learn to see this article as equally significant: in *The Atlanta Constitution*, Thursday, 12 May 1983, it was reported that ten-year-old Stan Cox set out to build a model electric chair as a school project. He was inspired, he said, by the execution of convicted murderer John Louis Evans, III. The article reads:

> Stan's teacher, Sue Nelle Scruggs, said his model doesn't work, but you couldn't tell by looking at it. When you flip the switch, the chair lights up.
> The chair is about three feet high and is made of slats from crates, painted gray. It isn't strong enough to hold anyone, Stan said.
> The headpiece is made from a baseball cap, and the cuffs are made from an old belt.
> Mrs. Scruggs said her pupils are responsible for one class project each month and are permitted only a minimum of parental help with their projects. Stan got some help from an uncle, Jack Zeigler.
> "He helped me do some of the wiring and put the control box on the back," said Stan.
> But he said the design was his own, and it won him an award for the most creative project.
> The youngster said his project taught him how electrocution works and what a real electric chair looks like.
> Asked how he feels about capital punishment, he replied, "I believe in it."[90]

Here we may learn all we need to know about the logic of technique, by viewing this account as a modern Sufi story, finding the appropriate transcendental elements; and by not going to sleep, lulled by lethotechny. Here we see the modern young bricoleur, putting things together with the materials at hand, making sure that his creation looks as it should, that form follows function, that creativity is a matter of producing something very much within the society, and that morality is inherent in the technique. This is an account only possible within the world of technique but not understandable from the viewpoint of technique. It involves a transcendental, metaphysical perspective in the sense of receiving "News from nowhere," but knowing where, at the same time, it might be found. It involves being both outside and within the technical system that has been cut off from the sacred.

6

The Word and the Image:
The Discourse of Technique

On 8 December 1946 the Nuremberg War Crimes Trial convened. Among the many charges, it is to be shown that the Nazis had experimented on Jews: injecting them with fatal viruses; mutilating them and grafting on limbs; developing techniques for genocide and mass sterilization. This is not simply a charge against inhumanity. It is also an indictment of the improper practice of medicine. The prosecution states:

> To the German people we owe a special responsibility in these proceedings. ... This is a striking demonstration not only of the tremendous degradation of German medical ethics which Nazi doctrine brought about, but of the undermining of the medical art and thwarting of the techniques which the defendants sought to employ. The Nazis have, to a certain extent, succeeded in convincing the peoples of the world that the Nazi system, although ruthless, was absolutely efficient; that although savage, it was completely scientific; that although entirely devoid of humanity, it is highly systematic—that "it got things done." The evidence which this Tribunal will hear will explode this myth. The Nazi methods of investigation were inefficient and unscientific, and their techniques of research were unsystematic.[1]

Thus the Nazis are to be convicted of the greatest crime, the charge of inefficiency, of being unscientific. In this extraordinary document, the meaning of Ellul's claim that the Nazis won the war becomes clear. Where inefficiency is an atrocity, where unscientific and unsystematic investigation is a crime against humanity, technique is ensconced as the sacred, supported by the myths of science and history.

The modern state, for Ellul, is a concentration camp where suffering and torture are replaced by boredom, ennui, and anxiety, as all citizens submit to lives of perpetual surveillance in the greater interest of doing their jobs more efficiently.[2] Progress, it is believed, can be gained through scientific and effective management. Workers are watched, subjected to time study; administrators are watched, falling victims to the "suggestion box," to the questionnaire; consumers are watched by TV cameras, scrutinized as they shop, lest they steal, questioned as to which product they like best, asked to recommend future changes for the products they do not now buy. Finally, the police watch over everyone in a society where criminals cannot be recognized, where all are nearly "free" to do as they do. The most effective way to stop crime is to catch it before it happens, which involves keeping records on all citizens, having extensive systems of surveillance, and instituting "crime-watch" programs where citizens are encouraged to inform on each other. These are not the methods of Nazi Germany. These are the methods of practically all modern states, as all people, with great seriousness and urgency, attempt to do their jobs as well as possible, obeying the logic and the laws of technique.

Admittedly, this is not George Orwell's vision in *1984*, where the population is mostly ill-fed, living in dark and drab hovels, furnished mainly with a large television screen by means of which all movements are monitored by an ominous Big Brother. In our modern, well-lit interiors, the TV is watched but does not watch back, and most of the citizenry are tolerably well-fed with some form of TV dinner, seated in the moderate comforts of furniture bought on time from Sears. Orwell's world seems far from ours in external detail. It is easy to ignore or to reinterpret the interferences of the state as necessary evils and to overlook what could be interpreted as the overzealousness of employers and employees, saying: rules are rules, orders are orders, and where would we be without them? Note that a cliché is often used to disguise the transgressions against an individual by technique.

As I discussed in chapter 2, Ellul understands that the state, *le politique*, is taken up in the web of propaganda in the interests of *la politique*, in which the sensory real is transformed in a number of ways into the fleetingly ephemeral. On one level, all information is reduced to the fact, robbed of its context. The purpose of propaganda is to gain assent, not to invoke reason; so the context is ignored because it might provoke a dialectical response. It is one thing, for example, to know that a rate increase was given to a power company. This is a fact that is likely to appear in a newspaper. If the background surrounding this information were given, it might involve a questioning of that increase and of the judgments of those who granted it. Typically, a rate increase is announced and a judgment is made. This usually constitutes the news. In the process, language becomes ideology, as it becomes fact. That language and politics move together was for Ellul, and for Orwell, a common concern.

Unlike Orwell, however, Ellul understands that politics no longer exists, having become technique. He further understands that technique is a specific discourse, embodying the logic of technique, a notion that Orwell lacks. The cliché, Ellul believes, is illustrative of that discourse, possibly its fullest expression. As I will show, the cliché is more than bad linguistic manners, more than impoverished and tired thought. In one sense, the cliché is the language of an exhausted memory, of a subjectivity that no longer has a fix on its object. "Rules are rules," is the telling response to bureaucracy, at once a submission to that bureaucracy as well as its expression. The cliché is the result of a language and a consciousness that has lost the symbolic dimension. It is for this reason that the cliché is usually true—a fact—but also insignificant. The obviousness of the cliché often disguises its insignificance, or rather, hides its true significance. In the technical society, the cliché invariably points to technique.

For technique, the fact is the basis of all information. The fact, however, is reality decontextualized, and is well illustrated by nearly every news headline, followed by an equally decontextualized story. Typically, when contexts are sought, more facts are supplied, endlessly. Human memory finds itself at a loss, in a present cut off from the past. The past—the what is not—is by definition not a fact. Language and memory suffer as they are abused in a reality reduced to the fact. As I will show, the cliché is an attempt to provide a linguistic context that fails, as it substitutes repetition for remembrance. The cliché only reminds us of the absence of context and memory, a discursive tradition fed and nourished by common language, symbols, and culture. Language, however, because it is always an expression of culture, reveals in Ellul's analysis the incursions of technique. Technique, as I have been saying, is a symbology that denies its symbolic dimension. The cliché is evidence of this denial as well as an indication of its symbolic dimension.

Clichés in the technical society are often placed in the visual realm. For Ellul, technique eschews sound over sight, the uncertain (oral and narrational) for the certain (visual and the present.) The fact— the visual fact—supplants the need for the story. Stories, typically, are not told if they cannot be visualized. The importance of the announcer, the celebrity, the authority, follows from this understanding. The announcer, the celebrity, the authority all give life to the cliché; they embody the cliché. The authority allows us to forget that what we are hearing and seeing is an abstraction, made up, and manipulated, often for uncertain ends. The ends, as Ellul says, are often simply the ends of techniques itself, which has beome its own end. The television, whatever it advertizes, first and foremost advertize itself. It continually reminds us that reality begins with that "oval of vision."

Language and Politics

In *1984* Orwell hypothesized that the real force behind Oceana was its control over language objectified in the theory of Newspeak. This artificial language, constructed out of Oldspeak, consists of three vocabularies that obviate contradiction, that confound etymological significance with merely *ad hoc* expression. Newspeak extends only to the sensorily given, to that without context or tradition. Scientific and technical languages, however, are allowed.[3]

The A vocabulary consisted of mundane and simple words, some of which could be found in Oldspeak. Unlike Oldspeak, however, parts of speech were almost mechanically interchangeable. A noun could be a verb or an adjective or adverb, depending on place or suffix or prefix. Oppositions of words like "good" were formed with a prefix like "un." Good, thus, became ungood. Vocabulary B was the political vocabulary constructed from a kind of shorthand in which compound words were formed *ad hoc*, of which Minipax, Minitrue, Minilovely, are examples. Euphony was the overriding principle. The C vocabulary was the scientific and the technical, with no general word for *science*. A generalist perspective, necessary for political freedom, with roots in history, philosophy, and aesthetics, is forbidden.

Some years earlier, in "Politics and the English Language" (1946), Orwell stated the following concerns:

> Modern English, especially written English, is full of bad habits which spread by imitation and which can be avoided if one is willing to take the necessary trouble. If one gets rid of these habits one can think more clearly, and to think clearly is a necessary first step towards political regeneration: so that the fight against bad English is not frivolous and is not the exclusive concern of professional writers."[4]

Orwell sounds a bit like the crabby English teacher as he prescribes what he hoped would lead to lucidity and clarity of expression and, by implication, to just action. Specifically, in these interests he holds that we should avoid barbarisms, be on the lookout for the passive voice, and plumb instead for the active voice. We should move against verbosity, back off from scientific or foreign words, use short words and expressions where possible, and shrink from clichés.[5] These are essentially Cartesian thoughts, suggestions that might be found in Strunk and White's *Elements of Style*, proclaiming clarity and brevity as supreme virtues and believing that bad habits can be avoided if one is on guard.

This advice pales beside Orwell's own good example, however. In his "England Your England" (1941), we see exactly what Newspeak is not, although rules for it are surely not to be found in the above prescriptions. There are no rules for irony. He begins the essay: "As I write, highly civilized human beings are flying overhead trying to kill me."[6] This simplicity and brevity is quite strong contrasted with the enormity and the horror of the circumstance. There is no question that World War II, the rise of fascism, communism, and totalitarian forms of government are much on Orwell's mind, providing the backdrop for works such as *Animal Farm* and *1984*. His works, for many, were warnings against the confirmed rise of totalitarianism; and a restrictive and restricted language was taken as its barometer. The importance of his insights on language, however, should not be ignored, or reduced to the pronouncements of a style manual.

In United States the year 1984 was greeted largely with relief. One Illinois newspaper, the *Rockford Morning Star*, triumphantly announced that the United States had made it with no dictator at the helm and with freedom of speech, freedom of thought, and freedom of the press all intact. Freedom of language and expression was proof of the failure of Orwell's prophecy. It is common to say that our political freedoms are guaranteed so long as the press is free, allowing the individual voice to be heard. During 1984 many newspapers extolled that freedom in the face of Orwell's prognostication.

As if to confront Orwell directly, a special commemorative edition of *1984* was released late in 1983 in preparation for the "real" 1984, with a special preface by Walter Cronkite. He writes:

The [literary symbols] are familiar today, [*sic*] they were familiar when the book was first published in 1949. We've met Big Brother in Stalin and Hitler and Khomeini. We hear Newspeak in every use of language to manipulate, deceive, to cover harsh realities with the soft snow of euphemism. And every time a political leader expects or demands that we believe the absurd, we experience that mental process Orwell called doublethink. From the show trials of the pre-war Soviet Union to the dungeon courts of post-revolutionary Iran, *1984*'s vision of justice as

foregone conclusion is familiar to us all. As soon as we were introduced
to such things, we realized we had always known them.[7]

These are interesting reminders on many levels. First, Cronkite
values Orwell's text as a reminder; the images of Big Brother and
Newspeak are guides with which to guage political-intellectual
oppression. Cronkite, however, reminds us of what we already
know: Newspeak is a language of deception; Big Brother is the
embodiment of the dictator. These ideas have become commonplace found everywhere in magazine and newspaper articles. For
example, in the 30 June 1986 *Newsweek* the following headline
appears: "South Africa's '1984': Pretoria Imposes an Orwellian
Crackdown—and Defies the Press to Cover it."[8] There seems to be
a formula: an oppressive government restricts freedom of speech,
therefore, Orwell's *1984* applies. We are in the presence of an
interesting problem. Has Orwell's work become a cliché, something
we recite before the phenomenon, in place of understanding it? Is
South Africa a version of Orwellian oppression, or is *Newsweek*'s
reporting of it another form of Newspeak, signaling its own degree
of oppression, the reduction of a political problem to a cliché or to
a mere fact? Put in other terms, the problem lies in making the
distinction between repeating and remembering.

Remembering, for Ellul, involves the ability to make dialectical
distinctions, to say how something is both similar and different from
something else. The modern citizen, because of the barrage of media
images, goes to sleep numbed, and suffers from lethotechny. The
cliché abets this lessening of the ability to make distinctions, by
conflating epistemological and political significance. Ellul states:

Finally, any quest for true democracy demands that we question all our
clichés, all social evidence at present admitted without discussion, all
collective sociological presuppositions that permit us to be in agreement
at the most superficial level with our fellow citizens. These clichés are the
basic ideological drug insidiously slipped into our consciousness by our
society's actual development, designed to justify that society, and by
which we adjust to it without too much suffering. These stereotypes
provide the unconscious basis on which we build our glorious ideologies
and even our doctrines. They must be tracked down and exposed, so that
we can see in them our true social image: man is made for happiness; man
is good; everything is matter; history has a certain direction and follows
it inexorably; technology is neutral and under man's control; moral
progress inevitably follows material progress; nation is value; no more
words, but deeds; work is a virtue; the raising of the living standard is
a good in itself. And so on through all the thousands of aspects of our

judgment and consciousness. To attack the problem on this level is not just an intellectual game. . . .[9]

The cliché is the sign enabling us to see in only one direction. Clichés mean what they mean and nothing more. "Rules are rules," is the perfect example. There are no exceptions. Negatives cannot be formed. The cliché abides in the logic of the one dimension, a perfect law of identity, a fine extension of computer logic. Coke is the "real thing," and that is that. The logic of efficiency, the logic of technique, tells us that we must seek the one best way. The cliché is thus perfect language, perfectly repeatable and not to be questioned. It is more, for Ellul, than just a tired expression. It has a life and a force quite its own.

Cronkite tells us to see Big Brother in Hitler and Khomeini, but why not also see him in Nixon and Falwell? Why not see, as Orwell did, that Newspeak was not merely a form of lying but that it was also a matter of presenting facts robbed of their context. Hitler, for example, made great use of the fact. The objective of Leni Riefenstahl's filming of the Third Party Congress in 1934 was to make the cohesive unity of National Socialism into a fact. This very method of creating facts by manufacturing images is, of course, openly embraced today by both Democratic and Republican presidential nominating conventions in the United States, where the event is planned, orchestrated, and then broadcast. Party unity becomes a fact by becoming an image, a one-dimensional sign.

Next, we ask why Walter Cronkite writes a preface for the 1983 edition of *1984*. What is his particular form of expertise? He is, of course, a member of the press, but beyond that, who is he? We may find that we do not know. We do not have to know. He is a "celebrity." The celebrity is the one-who-is-seen, and as seen, he is known. As known, he becomes knowledgeable, *ipso facto*. The celebrity is another form of the fact, another one-dimensional sign. He appears in order to assuage doubt, to lend credibility to information. He is a sign that we no longer have to think, that that has been done for us, and that conclusions have already been safely and carefully drawn. The celebrity provides a certain "fixation of belief," to borrow a phrase from C. S. Peirce.

In one of his most recent works, *The Humiliation of the Word* (1985), Ellul tells us that in the modern age, full of doubts, anxieties, and incertitudes—reinforced in both life and literature—we need certainty. In our day, he insists, certainty comes from the visible.[10] Words that we see in print or see spoken from a moving, recognizable mouth before us—the TV commentator, the announcer, or the news analyst—embody that certainty. Their familiarity-made-visible quiets our fears and doubts. As one enters the fast-food parlor, one is first greeted by pictures of the food created in the laboratories of technique. In a similar way, Cronkite's Preface and the "Commemorative Edition" gold seal on the cover of the 1983 edition of *1984*, part of the packaging, invoke the certainty that now we are buying the "real thing."

The announcer, the celebrity, is one type of twentieth-century shaman, extolling the virtues of technique while at the same time representing them. The cliché, the formulaic utterance, lends weight to often empty expressions that take the place of thought, occurring in its absence and when memory is tired. Repetition replaces remembering. With the cliché we have no distance on our language. With the expression that is mindlessly repeated, chant-like, we experience language becoming the sacred in that the word becomes the object and the object identical with the word. However, most seriously, language has become a sacred because it has become a form of technique. We may remember that the prosecuters at the Nuremberg trials could not begin without embracing efficiency, without invoking the sacred of technique.

Language as Technique

Orwell's theory of Newspeak does not arise from a theory of technology or from a theory of society. Some such theory is implied, however, as we recall that words are to be interchangable, like machine parts; that they are not to reflect the past, a point of origin; that they are to be regarded as made up, as serving the exigencies of the moment; and that they are to be brief, efficient utterances, taking as little time as possible to say. The language of Newspeak suggests an industrial society ethos and aesthetics. Although Orwell is no theoretician of technique, he is an artist, writing out of a sense of and a feeling for the symbol that opposes the sign or the cliché. He realizes that if the word loses its power of ambiguity, its ability to say two quite different things at once, he could not effectively write "As I write this, highly civilized human beings are flying overhead trying to kill me." He says what he does not mean, and in doing so, extends his frame of reference, achieving the effect of irony. We go back and forth between both meanings, civilized people acting uncivilized. And yet, they are both civilized and uncivilized, and we experience the force of irony. However, the sign and the cliché, having only one meaning, are not ironic. We can treat them ironically. For example, a portrait could be painted of a stop sign functioning as a stop sign to extend its meaning, likely causing a laugh, with the realization that such things are not usually the subject of artistic vision. Here, the sign would no longer be a sign. Care would need to be taken to clarify the ironic intention, lest the portrait be regarded as simply a mistake. We could, in a like manner, say "Clichés are not worth a hill of beans," and if we meant it, we could not mean it, destroying the cliché. We would turn it into a joke and make it lose its one-dimensional direction. Orwell uses symbols that point beyond themselves and is aware that such symbols are impossible in Newspeak, a language of the sign and the cliché. Newspeak, in Orwell's work, achieves the symbolic dimension that language could never have. Ellul contends that the true symbol is dialectical, pointing always in at least two directions at once, indicating that what is, is always, as well, what it is not. The highly civilized people bombing Orwell cannot be highly civilized, and yet they are. They have airplanes, bombs, and techniques. And yet they are bombing other living beings. To find this funny, we would have to have a double sense of "civilized." Very likely, an air-force general would find nothing funny about this. Furthermore, true communication involves a dialectical movement between the known and the not known. The cliché tells us what we already know. It tells us nothing new, and thus there is not what Ellul calls real communication—the result of a tension between a signifier and a signified. When this tension collapses, as it does in language that is "clichégenic," communication as dialogue stops.

The silencing of dialectical tension, the inability of language and expression to produce opposition, is more than a matter of carving up the language, as some of Orwell's readers might think. As Ellul states:

> Tension between groups composing the entire society is a condition for life itself, or life susceptible to creation and adaptation in that society. It is the point of departure for all culture. There can be no culture in a unitary society; there can be only diffusion of knowledge developed and applied for the greatest good of the social body. To say this is no more than to affirm the reality of a certain dialectic movement in history. There, too, no key or universal system can be provided. There is no *necessary* dialectic. The possibility of this dialectic movement is the condition for life in societies. But this possibility is not always attained. One must not blindly believe that contradictions—still less the same contradictions—will arise under all circumstances. Man's dream— including the socialist dream—is to suppress these contradictions, i.e., to arrive at entropy, at the equilibrium of death.[11]

Communication, in its ideal sense, involves the attempt to say what cannot be said. It at least involves the ability to do this, to recognize when it is being done, and to realize the need for such a function of language. Signs have their place in language and communication, but when all becomes a sign, there can be no communication. Information flows when one person comes before another, sharing what he knows with one who lacks that information.[12] Two people cannot share what both have equally, an invocation of Leibniz's identity of indiscernibles; two people cannot be two unless they are different. This holds, as well, for what they know. It is the difference between subject and object that makes knowing as a dialectical phenomenon possible; it is the difference between two people that makes communication possible. The cliché abrogates this difference. The current American expression "you know," stuck at the end of nearly every sentence, says that we do not know, and moreover, that we are not interested in knowing. It is a sign that we are going on anyway, very likely an expression that arose out of telephone conversations in the absence of an embodied audience.

The cliché version of Orwell's notion of tyranny places before us the concept of the absolute dictator, the master of the overt power play, consciously manipulating language and everything else in his path. This dictator is before us as an *other*, a vile, loathesome beast. Hitler is a fine example. This dictator, though powerful, can be disarmed as he is beheld. The tyrany of technique, from Ellul's viewpoint, is more subtle. It is a form of consciousness and a form of language, of which the cliché is a symptom, but is not typically held as an object, any more than the cliché is seen as more than bad training. Technique, as I have been saying, is typically regarded as a means to be used either for good or for ill. Intentionality is held to be separate from technique and is therefore, in principle, able to judge technique. Ellul regards this as naive and wishful thinking, a manifestation of technique itself. Technique does not appear to consciousness because we cannot symbolize it, although it is a symbol. We cannot make it into an object of consciousness, because it has become consciousness's form. In *L'Empire du non-sens* (1980), he states:

It has become first of all the universal mediation, and because it is itself means, it is not the object of symbolization *as means*, but even more, it is also, by its own power, exclusive of all other systems of mediation (what was essentially symbolization). It is, in the second place, productive of community. The group's communion, today, no longer happens by a symbolic support but by a technical support (the play of media, for example). Finally, technique institutes a relation, non-mediated, non-distanced, with man. Man has felt strongly the need to establish a distance between himself and nature, but technique does not allow such an operation! It is, in appearance, the direct extension of the body. Who has said and repeated only that the tool is never anything more than the extension of the hand. Thus, now we pass from an organic world, where the symbolization was an adequate and coherent function of the milieu, to a technical system where the creation of symbols has neither place nor sense.[13]

Technique as a form of consciousness has become a world, but one that lacks place and sense; in it abstractions are embodied and the body is turned into an abstraction. For example, we wake up when the clock tells us to, eat when it is time, and leave for home when the clock of the workday runs out. The day is run according to abstract clock time and the body must follow. Time flies when we are having fun. The digital watch is a fine symbol of this fun. Clocks with hands used to stand in clear relation to sidereal time. The clock, what has become known as the "classic clock," was the mirror of a small universe, standing in symbolic relation to our own. The digital watch, though a symbol, is not consciously one: it is time itself, the perpetual now.

Technique is also a form of mediation, although it is not grasped as one. All instances of technique are results of contact with the natural phenomenon as *others*. Technical phenomena lose their phenomenal reality as made and become an ontological reality as the not-made, as realities and necessities. The real becomes the made. The not-made, that which prompts the making, as *other*, loses its ontological status. The made and the not-made are not understood to be in opposition. The Cuisinart, for example, is now a necessity in every well-run kitchen. Garage sales are good places to find these necessities, somehow become non-necessities. Unlike the natural phenomenon, the technical phenomenon belongs to the technical order, having its own logic, its own necessity. The natural object loses its necessity. Technical phenomena are rational, artificial embodiments, which proliferate automatically, produce other phenomena in geometric rather than arithmetic progression, possess their own ground of being, appear universally, having no cultural, traditional boundaries, and take on the characteristics of the sacred. They seem to be produced causally, and they always have the characteristics of an absolute finality. At this point reason looks in a mirror at itself. The object is no longer separate from the subject. The conceptual becomes the real and the real becomes the conceptual. All becomes discourse.

Recall that the technical phenomenon is in principle discursive, a matter easy to overlook in Ellul's formulation of technical rationality, for example, especially as it appears in the English edition. Ellul states:

> This rationality, best exemplified in systemization, division of labor, creation of standards, production norms, and the like, involves two distinct phases: first, the use of "discourse" in every operation, [under the two aspects the term can take (*on the one hand, the intervention of an intentional reflection and on the other hand, the intervention of means from one term to the other*).] This excludes spontaneity and personal creativity. Second, there is reduction of method to its logical dimension alone. Every intervention of technique is, in effect, a reduction of facts, forces, phenomena, means, and instruments to the schema of logic.[14]

The bracketed passage, my translation, omitted in Wilkinson's translation, emphasizes the discursive nature of technique. It is discourse, however, like the expression of mathematics. Mathematical discourse is not ordinary discourse inasmuch as it has no referents beyond the rules of the system that constructs it. Its meaning is totally systemic—the model technical discourse desires—where A is equivalent to A, where A is not *not-A*, and where A is either A or *not-A*. The development of artificial discourse thus moves in parallel with the development of technical phenomena. The cliché is ordinary language mirroring this form.

From the eighteenth-century notion of the book of nature to the twentieth-century mission given to the computer to divulge the language of this book, apparently written in mathematical code, there is a clear tradition. From Descartes's instinct that the truth cannot resist method to the attempts of Babbage, Turing, and von Neumann to quantify those methods mechanically, to create an artificial language giving access to nature's inner regions, to the thing-itself, we see the technical phenomenon and artificial language running hand in hand, plug in socket. Norbert Wiener, the founder of cybernetics, observed that the developments of navigation and clockmaking led almost of necessity to the desire for, and the possibility of, the automated factory, with the development of the computing machine.[15] Wiener also saw clearly the problems in such development. Like Ellul who in fact draws on his analysis, Wiener knew that significant information always contained a bit of disinformation, that artificial discourse could not hope to coordinate all factors unless it was capable of external modification. Wiener states:

> Just as entropy is a measure of disorganization, the information carried by a set of messages is a measure of organization. In fact, it is possible to interpret the information carried by a message as essentially the negative of its entropy, and the negative logarithm of its probability. That is, the more probable the message, the less information it gives. Clichés, for example, are less illuminating than great poems.[16]

If the technical system is to succeed, according to Wiener, disinformation, *otherness*, must be acknowledged. To acknowledge it, however, is to strain the system. The system tends to replicate itself, to stammer, and to produce clichés. On the assembly line the goal is to produce identical objects, *A*'s that are not *not-A*'s. Outside the line, if the process is to be controlled, these differences, malfunctions, must be noticed. That is, an *A* that is *not-A* must be observed. The machine must be tied to something beyond it for this information to be given. The computer serves this function. The computer, however, is a machine, having its own limitations, which engender another computer, another machine, a program, a programmer. If the system is merely repeated, all the flaws in the system will be repeated. Wiener has his finger on an essential problem: how does information transcend the system, through replication or through inspiration?

The cliché is not illuminating because we are told something we already know: *A* is *A*. Today is 98 degrees with 100 percent humidity at 10:00 A.M. This will be true at each moment we hear it, assuming we are reading the instruments correctly. There is nothing unique or memorable about this information, which is one of the reasons why the "weatherman" often becomes a "personality," taking on some guise to maintain audience interest. Furthermore, the temperature must be repeated as often as possible. We learn nothing true, unique, or memorable about the weather at any moment following the readings of instruments. Like the digital watch, the weather is a bad infinity. On the other hand, when T. S. Eliot tells us that "the evening is spread out against the sky like a patient etherized upon a table," we have information no machine could ever give us: we have in fact a contradiction—sky is patient—and a vision meteorologists could never glean from instrumentation. After hearing Eliot's view of the sky, of the evening, we are never the same. We can never forget this kind of evening; it occurs once in poetic history, and all are changed for having heard it. The weatherman's weather, what the machine can tell us, must ever be told; it can never be improved, never be completed. It can only be repeated.

It is Ellul's view that civilizations are created and sustained in and by poeticlike acts, in transcendental acts, from whence come our sense of the true, the beautiful, and the good. They are acts of freedom and must be appreciated from a free perspective. "Clichégenic" consciousness is an unfree consciousness. Clichés are not only not illuminating; they can be deadly.

The Cliché as Consciousness: The Appearance of the Authority

The cliché is a sign of a technical system in which nothing transcends it, although the transcendental is there as need and absence. It is there as the need for meaning, for a sense of origin, and for meaningful ritual. Much of modern life thwarts these needs, Ellul observes. We consume objects that are quickly thrown away, objects of mass production, made to be short-lived, to be of limited value. From these things we learn about value—temporary and quick. We interact during much of our day with strangers, for instance, going through a supermarket line often with little more than a nod of the head. Visits with friends on a normal day often occur on the phone, reduced to a small voice at a distance. Conversations among family members occur as time and the TV allow. Topics on television, like topics in the living room, last little longer than two to five minutes. The average news item lasts about as long as a block of commercials. Much of our life—conversations, friends, objects—appears to be in motion. The motion, however, rarely goes beyond the system. That is, our sense of meaning, significance, and ritual largely comes from the system itself. Our language, our gestures, and our interactions typically mirror the system or go on in spite of it. Simply, we often merely repeat the system.

In this regard, consider Hannah Arendt's account of the infamous Adolph Eichman. Originally written as a series of articles for *The New Yorker*, the book appeared as *Eichman in Jerusalem: A Report on the Banality of Evil* (1964), an ironic title at best. Arendt's portrait of Eichman is not of a vile and loathesome monster, but of a thoroughly modern citizen of the contemporary world with a faulty memory and a whole arsenal of stock phrases, of self-invented clichés. She writes:

Whether writing his memoirs in Argentina or in Jerusalem, whether speaking to the police examiner or to the court, what he said was always the same, expressed in the same words. The longer one listened to him, the more obvious it became that his inability to speak was closely connected with an inability to *think*, namely, to think from the standpoint of somebody else. No communication was possible with him, not because he lied but because he was surrounded by the most reliable of all safeguards against the words and the presence of others, and hence against reality as such.[17]

He had come to live in the cliché itself. His world was a world of words, merely abstract concepts. At one point, he says, "Officialese [*Amtssprache*] is my only language."[18]

Unable to fulfill his initial goal to become an engineer—he was an inadequate student—and relieved of his job as a traveling salesman for the Vacuum Oil Company, Eichman drifted into the National Socialist movement, escaping from boredom and a heightened sense of insignificance. He rose up through the ranks to become a "Jewish Expert," and to be given the responsibility for overseeing the mass deportation of the Jews in 1938. He saw his task in the following terms:

This is like an automatic factory, like a flour mill connected with some bakery. At one end you put in a Jew who still has some property, a factory, or a shop, or a bank account, and he goes through the building from counter to counter, from office to office, and comes out at the other end without any money, without any rights, with only a passport in which it says: "You must leave the country within a fortnight. Otherwise you will go to a concentration camp."[19]

In another explanation, he envisioned, ". . . an assembly line, at whose beginnings the first document is put, and then the other papers, and at its end the passport would have to come out as the end product."[20] This language seems to come out unconsciously, offered as an explanation and justification of his activity, as if morality were inherent in the technique, and now in the phrase.

During his service to Hitler, Eichman was obsessed with the concept of authority, which he understood as the manifestation of the professional. He states:

[Hitler]. . . may have been wrong all down the line, but one thing is beyond dispute: the man was able to work his way up from lance corporal in the German Army to Fuhrer of a people of almost eighty million. . . . His success alone proved to me that I should subordinate myself to this man.[21]

The efficient, the moral, the successful become coterminous, and Eichman sees his own actions as moving in line with these. It was all part of an assembly line. Eichman lived in a world of A's and *not-A*'s. Here was a job, and what could he do? Here was a Jew, and here were the railroad cars, here were product and the process. To judge the morality of the process, he would have had to have been outside the system. His language, like his moral view, is trapped in the mundane that is technique.

Dutch sociologist Anton Zijderveld, in *On Clichés: The Supersedure of Meaning by Function in Modernity* (1979), states:

> Again, only in society in which religion (i.e. that component in a culture which provides man with meaningful interpretation of the universe and of history) is totally superseded, or even stronger: brushed aside by magic (i.e. that component in a culture that provides man with techniques by which he can manipulate spiritual powers), will cliché formalism reign tyrannically. In such a society ... function would reign rampantly. It is safe to state that in most pre-modern societies function remained tied to meaning, while meaning remained tied to tradition through the institutions. Clichés did exist in these pre-modern societies but their functionality was conditioned by the power of institutional tradition.[22]

As modern institutions are made up, so is their language. Zijderveld makes the startling claim that the cliché has come to take the place of the institution. From Ellul's perspective, this is the result of all becoming a technical phenomenon, a concept, and hence a language. Zijderveld observes:

> It is typical of our age: science-without-universities, religion-without-churches, medicare-without-hospitals, performing arts-without-theatres or concert halls—all of them floating 'freely', 'creatively', liberated from tradition and traditional bonds. The individual is promised that thus he will discover his 'real' Self. But what such gnostic ideologies really promise, are swimming-pools-without-water.[23]

Actually, the water is provided by language, by the cliché. The TV minister is a fine example of religion without a church, The Word disembodied, the Bible reduced to endless clichés. Much of modern art, as Ellul notices in *L'Empire du non-sens*, as it attempts to "rejoin life," simply becomes "life," having no identifiable institution: artists become mechanics, technicians, practitioners of the "happening." The only distance between art and life is found in the concept, making the distinction between the artist and the connoisseur a slippery one. Ellul writes: "It is this mutual acknowledgment founded on the discernment of an intention which permits the differentiation of a piece of metal from that which an apprentice in a garage throws into the trashcan because it is broken or defective."[24] This is a problem because of the "clichégenic" nature of modern life and modern art, in which the judgment cannot transcend the process. Art is what artists do, and they do whatever they want, *n'importe quoi*.[25] They become the authority.

There is another sense in which Hitler, the master of the *n'importe quoi*, won the war. Hitler never tired of talking of the *Volk*, of nature's principle of the survival of the fittest, of the natural fitness of the Aryan race to rule, and yet this could only be brought about by the machinations of the individual, doing it for the good of all. In *Mein Kampf* he writes:

> The thinking of the one, therefore, will be determined by eternal truth, the actions of the other more by the practical reality of the moment. The greatness of the one lies in the absolute abstract soundness of his idea, that of the other in his correct attitude toward the given facts and their advantageous application; and in this the theoretician's aim must serve as his guiding star.[26]

The abstract theory, penetrating to the essence of things, the thing-itself, together with technical application is the key. But technique and theory are not enough. Myth and sentimentality, too, must be saddled up. Hitler writes:

> Since the day when I had stood at my mother's grave, I had not wept. When in my youth Fate seized me with merciless hardness, my defiance mounted. When in the long war years Death snatched so many a dear comrade and friend from our ranks, it would have seemed to me almost a sin to complain—after all, were they not dying for Germany? And when at length the creeping gas—in the last days of the dreadful struggle—attacked me, too, and began to gnaw at my eyes, and beneath the fear of going blind forever, I nearly lost heart for a moment, the voice of my conscience thundered at me: Miserable wretch, are you going to cry when thousands are a hundred times worse off than you![27]

It is tempting to see this only as bad style, and not as a kind of rampant sentimentality bred, for example, by the popular press, a mentality fostered in the shops, the factories and the workhouses, and the streets. The sentimental is the tragic side of the cliché, an expression of a mentality for which the mundane is reified, becoming the sacred, the holy, the absolute.

The "clichégenic" mentality, like technique itself, is universal. Consider the remarks of late Rand analyst and member of the

Defense Department's "Breakfast Group," Herman Kahn, in his influential book *On Themonuclear War* (1960). He discusses many of the problems of nuclear war, ". . . that are really problems in physics and engineering."[28] Although a "Doomsday Machine" is unthinkable, when it comes to protecting the lives of billions, Kahn states, ". . . I believe that both the United States and NATO would reluctantly be willing to envisage the *possibility* of one or two hundred million people dying from the immediate effects. . . ."[29] However, considering the worst, we ask.

> If we assume that people could survive the long-term effects of radiation, what would the standard of living in their postwar world be like? Would the survivors live as Americans are accustomed to living—with automobiles, television, ranch houses, freezers, and so on? No one can say but . . . I believe . . . the country would recover rather rapidly and effectively. . . .[30]

In discussing relations with the Soviet Union, Kahn often adopts some extraordinary rhetoric:

> In actual fact we do have some very strong cards to play, but if we do not know what these cards are we may be tricked out of playing them. If we refuse to accept a facesaving defeat and the Russians persist in rubbing our noses in the dirt. . . .[31]

Kahn, although on the winning team, like Hitler and Eichman, shows the moral-aesthetic perspective of the functionary, nicely exemplifying Zijderveld's understanding of the place of the cliché, and Ellul's understanding of the technical mentality, unable to separate itself from its language and its conceptualizations, which come to the same thing.

The cliché is the language of the modern authority, embodying the logic of technique and creating its own world. This idea was both understood and practiced by Thomas Kuhn in *The Structure of Scientific Revolution* (1962). Kuhn showed that the creation of a scientific revolution meant, among other things, getting the scientific community of a given period to speak a certain language. He spoke of this language as a "paradigm," a kind of model. In so saying, Kuhn established his own "paradigm." This very notion has established an untold amount of research across interdisciplinary lines—social scientists, philosophers, rhetoricians, physicists, historians. Many have used "paradigm" automatically, regardless of context, creating often very artificial distinctions. In simpler terms, it has become a cliché. Kuhn remarks that one of his critics found "paradigm" used twenty-two different ways.[32] This is, of course, its great value. Its "clichégenic" force has established Kuhn as a redoubted authority. It was almost a necessity that Kuhn's book be mentioned in this study. I do so, however, to try to see "paradigm" in a new light. The cliché, like our techniques, is used unconsciously, validated in and by the authority."

Ellul's goal is to dislodge the cliché from consciousness and, in turn, to disrupt the authority. Ellul remarks: "Today's discourse par excellence is that of Bouvard and Pecuchet. Everything must be left to the free choice of those who actually know nothing."[33] They do not know that they know nothing, not having obtained Socratic wisdom, the goal of Ellul's discourse. The invocation of Flaubert's novel is helpful with the points I have been making. Bouvard and Pecuchet, like today's authorities, retire from the everyday world to learn the truth of things. They enter the world of the technical authority, the "Empire of Non-sense." Deciding to become farmers, they discover the need to learn agriculture, which they find depends on chemistry. In learning about soil fertility, they are led to molecular biology, to physics, and so on. Flaubert concludes, at this point: "What amazed them more than anything was that earth, as an element, does not exist."[34] They learn firsthand what White-head called the fallacy of misplaced concreteness, that the results of analysis lead far beyond the matter at hand to abstractions that exist only for analysis, only in analysis.[35]

Bouvard and Pecuchet, to understand nature, reduce it to other elements; the earth becomes something they can no longer hold but something they can only think. To grasp these abstractions, they realize that machines are needed to reduce the earth, for example, to these elements. These machines, in turn, necessitate recourse to authorities and to other machines. The technical system within Flaubert's novel appears before our eyes. With the technical system, possibilities are endless, like the clichés that perpetuate it. Flaubert began this novel perhaps as early as 1853 with a study of the "*sottisier*," the cliché. He allegedly read some 1,500 books to complete this novel that he was never to finish. It remained incomplete, but the last section, called *The Book of Received Ideas*, a dictionary of clichés, is often published with *Bouvard and Pecuchet*, as it was to appear at the end of the projected volume.[36] It is appropriate that this volume was never completed, and that the book of clichés is there to remind us of this.

Bouvard and Pecuchet's explorations are our realities. The technical phenomenon has distanced us from our life-worlds and forced us to call in authorities at every step and turn, to use and depend on objects such as TVs and trashmashers that we can barely understand. Our automobiles, from time to time, lead us to the garage where we have to carry on technical discourse or pay out great sums of money, while we learn about the self-augmentation of techniques and about how costly such things are. For example, in the interests of making cars run more efficiently, carburetors have been replaced by fuel injectors, distributors by electronic circuitry, all of which are run by a computer, which generally cannot be repaired. If it breaks down it must be replaced. Ironically, as a result of these developments, the mechanic no longer knows how to work on cars. He becomes like the ordinary know-nothing, like most of us: he takes out the part, which he does not fully understand, and orders a new one. These developments, for example, make us all more dependent on the system. The authority does not understand the system by being apart from it. Understanding is neither required nor possible. The authority—the celebrity—is an expression of the system and not its master.

The Word and the Symbol: The Return to Symbolic Order

Orwell believed that language is a hope for freedom and for the future. A decadence of language foreshadows a decadence of culture and politics, and the cliché is symptomatic of this decadence. Language was for Orwell a means to an end, and the cliché, with its mindless repetitions does not pull its weight. Ellul agrees but with less optimism. Language is a crucial concern because, like politics, language has become an illusion, a veil that allows us to think that we really do communicate when in fact we say nothing at all. We repeat words and concepts that are no longer related to the life-world or to the cultural world. The cliché is evidence of this disregard. In fact, although Ellul does not discuss this, the cliché itself has become a cliché. Its origins and the significance of those origins have been lost.

According to *Oxford English Dictionary*, "cliché" enters English from the French in about 1832. "Cliché" originally refers to a stereotype block, a printer's cast or "dab." It is from the beginning related to the visual. Further, the word is tied essentially to an industrial process, making the notion that technical phenomena are clichés truly metaphorical. Cliché is a variant of *cliquer*, meaning "to click," probably referring to the sound of the lead pieces as they strike the mold. The auditory dimension in English is lost, as is its tie to industrialization, although we sense its connection. Now, of course, according to Eric Partridge in *A Dictionary of Clichés*, it refers to trite, hackneyed expressions, dead metaphors, pointless phrases, nauseating quotations, and well-worn foreign commonplaces such as *"bete noire."* It means "whatever," Ellul's sense of *"n'importe quoi."* I have not helped in this regard. I have deliberately made no attempt to use it consistently. Consistency here is not to the point. The point is that nearly all words are devalued in terms of tradition and significance in the bodily world. Words have lost their ability to refer, Ellul notes. A degree of inconsistency must be introduced.

Words no longer point to the man, to the object, but to the system. The structuralists are great offenders in this regard. In their attempts to understand language, they merely preside over its demise, ". . . with its crushing dominance by the synchronic element . . . reducing language to a relationship of structures."[37] With the ignoring of the diachronic, an element of the dialectic is taken out. Most important is Frederic Jameson's characterization of Saussure's definition of sign, the fundamental beginning point of structuralist analysis:

"The linguistic sign unites, not a thing and a name, but a concept and an acoustic image," the latter terms being then replaced by a new set, the "signifié" and the "signifiant," the signified and the signifier. The point is made further that the sign is wholly arbitrary, that its meaning rests entirely on social convention and acceptation and that it has no "natural" fitness in and of itself.[38]

The structuralists, however, offend no more than do most intellectuals who wish to turn reality into a concept and then confuse that concept with reality. Note that for Jameson the meaning of words is other words. Words thus exist in libraries and in dictionaries. This is their reality. They have become signs, having lost their symbolic relation to the dialectical other. Ironically, the intellectual's view of the world begins to assume the dimension of the factory, the character of mass production. Jameson seems to have understood this as well:

. . . Structuralism may be understood as a distorted awareness of the dawning collective character of life, as a kind of blurred reflection of the already collective structure of what is perhaps less the cybernetic than the mass-production commercial network into which our individual existences are organized. In this sense, the attack on the ego and on its pretensions is clearly an anti-idealistic impulse; it is, however, doubled with the relatively positivistic claim for the creation of a new type of objective science or semiology.[39]

The structuralists Jameson has in mind—and the ones Ellul attacks—are those who deny that the individual speaks and who affirm that it is instead language that speaks, those who deny the existence of the individual ego and who presuppose the mass ego, the "mass man," in their very characterization of language as anonymous, arbitrary, and without tradition.

Jameson's above critique in decidedly incarcerated prose occurs in the often cited text *The Prison-House of Language*. The title for this text is seemingly pulled from the following epigram attributed to Nietzsche: "We have to cease to think if we refuse to do it in the prison-house of language; for we cannot reach further than the doubt which asks whether the limit we see is really a limit. ..." Language is affirmed as a limit necessary to thought and to inquiry itself, a limit one ignores at great risk. I have discovered, however, that Jameson's quotation is taken from Erich Heller's essay "Wittgenstein and Nietzsche" in which Heller provides a quite loose and poetic translation of Nietzshe's actual words from *Der Wille zur Macht* that state: "*Wir hören auf zu denken, wenn wir es nicht in dem sprachlichen Zwange thun wollen*, wir langen gerade noch bei dem Zweifel an, hier eine Grenze als Grenze zu sehn."[40] Here, Nietzsche literally says: "*We cease to think when we refuse to do so under the constraint of language*; we barely reach the doubt that sees this limitation as a limitation." Heller has made a metaphor out of *Zwange*, constraint. Jameson has, apparently, copied Heller's translation without indicating the metaphor's origins (perhaps without knowing those origins). And literary critics have slavishly referred to the importance of this notion—the prison-house of language—with no sense of context or limitation. Jameson thereby adds force to the notion of the academic assembly line by example in its reduction of language to arbitrary nonreferential expression.

The admission, even the insistence, that language has a nonreferential, arbitrary character has been coupled with recent attempts to: (1) deny the usefulness of language as a form of communication and (2) reduce the word to a sign, an image. We are still not far from concerns of language as "clichégenic." This attack on language, Ellul notes, does not come from scientists or technicians, but from artists themselves, from the Dadaists, from the surrealists, from the absurdists. In his criticism of twentieth-century art in *L'Empire du non-sens*, Ellul observes that many modern artists, curiously, have adopted the clichés of political revolutionaries, an ironic stance for artists who would claim to transcend the state, the mundane. Ellul writes:

> In other words, one changes aesthetic formulas but one guards carefully the more run down at the heels of socio-political interpretations: one thinks of being, in effect, revolutionary in the theater in killing the word to advantage of bodily expression. It is a question of transmitting the emotions, upheavals, without having need of the word, of the logic of thought, of producing mediations all the more intense in that they are more limited, circumscribed, paralyzed by "sense" and clear consciousness. Pure loudness. Pure color ... movement. ... It is necessary that the theater no longer speak at all. The Rorschach is the model of the genre. "Spectacle reduces to gestures and murmurs." "The body without voice, voice without body." Silence and gesture. But how not to realize in the presence of the suppression of language to the advantage of this bodily expression that it is exactly the replica of what is produced in the world of the technician: there, all is movement. Technique is action. (And it is this that one speaks of as communication. ...) Technique is the transmission of a certain number of effects. At the moment when the study of language is carried to the summit, where the word is submitted to the most subtle, scientific analysis, it is brusquely suppressed to the benefit of the gesture that is the human replication of the mechanical, and no more. And we return to this theme when we reencounter the problem of the suppression of the senses, because, strictly speaking, technique has no sense. And it is here we are able to measure technique's most profound impact: those who seek the new most passionately have only one path, the transposing of the processes of technique into the human. Those who want to express, most profoundly, misery, suffering, free will, love, are reduced to suppressing what is specifically human—spoken language—to the benefit of more physical responses, directly produced by the influence of the machine.[41]

Language is reduced to one dimension by the machine—by the computer—to be followed by the artists. Flaubert feared the cliché. Modern artists embrace them. The theater of Robert O. Wilson, for example, is openly nontheater, with characters standing on stage for long periods of time in silence, their bodily gestures emptied of the significance of normal gesture.[42] The gesture of which Ellul speaks is the gesture of sheer thereness, the point directed at nothing in particular and toward all in general, toward the system that is technique.

The symbol, like the original cliché, had at least a double meaning, a meaning for sight and sound, as well as a meaning for action. The cliché is the denuded symbol of our age, although it had a symbolic determination in the nineteenth century. The symbol in our age has become a sign, as stated above, a pointing to the merely there. Marshall McLuhan in *From Cliché to Archetype* (1970) offers the following useful reminder:

> Many people confuse single objects with symbols. It helps to note the original meaning and structure of the term "symbol" as a juxtaposition of two things. Originally, parties to a contract broke a stick and each took a half. Upon completion of the relationship, the parties juxtaposed the two sticks, creating the *symbol*. It is from *symballein*, Greek for "throwing together."[43]

Technique disembodies language, reducing it to the sign, which is used alternately with "symbol." Only specialists make the distinction. The symbol is an activity, a moving back and forth in the manner that I have spoken of throughout this study. The symbol, for Ellul, involves motion, mediation, and memory, as the mind moves back and forth between the symbol and the symbolized, grasped in time by an individual in a specific culture, trying to find his own origins in space and time. Technical language moves endlessly forward, like the objects on the assembly line, with each object new but not unique, repeated but not memorable. Meaning becomes a matter of flipping switch on and off. The symbol in traditional cultures used to mean a prior agreement, a tradition, a sharing of a *sensus communis*. Modern symbols, signs, like the plays of the avant garde, signal that no agreement is possible, that nothing makes sense. The symbols of Robert O. Wilson's plays are nonsensical, a denial of tradition, the turning of the symbol into the sign, thereby expunging the dialectic. The word, for Ellul, is the symbol par excellence, and to abandon it is to abandon humanity.

The dialectic between the image and the word is another version of the dialectic that runs throughout Ellul's work, but it is taken up explicitly in *The Humiliation of the Word*. The basis of Ellul's dialectic is that the object never *is* the subject, nor is the subject ever the object. Human reality is always caught somewhere between being and nothingness, but it is never stranded in either category. Ellul's distinction between the word and the image begins with the recognition that both point to essentially different domains. All that is natural must be moved to the intellectual, to the circumscribing of method. This transformation occurs above all on the symbolic level. The symbol for Ellul is not merely an intellectual construct; it is a structure of conscious intention that is lived. This is the crux of the philosophical dimension that Ellul's American readers often do not understand.

Ellul's writing has proceeded from this awareness. His concerns have turned directly to processes of symbolization, not as they are taken up in current academic philosophy or in literary criticism, both of which he sees as furthering intellectual techniques. In his recent *The Humiliation of the Word*, he clearly unites his social and theological studies with an issue vital to philosophy since Plato: a concern for the relation between the word and the image. His approach at times seems phenomenological, that is, it follows nicely themes and matters analyzed by Sartre and Merleau-Ponty. But Ellul makes clear that he is not seeking the *truth* of consciousness. He is, instead, interested in the contemporary social obsession with images and with the audiovisual. His concerns proceed to more analytical dimensions.

He begins with the recognition that the word and the image point to two different domains.[44] Ellul sidesteps recent attempts to merge these dimensions; he is interested in their differences rather than in their similarities. The visual domain is essentially perspectivist, a point of view which is given for modern man (the primitive might see it in quite another way). For example, I as viewer am situated over and against the object, a here and now. As a viewer, the object appears as a being-there, to which I may direct a point, a gesture. As a *there* it is a certainty, a totality as a that-which-is-before-me. It is, however, as a before-me, a limited totality.[45] It disappears or ceases to be a certainty as I turn my head, as my attention wanders, as the light changes, or as it moves away. It becomes a *certainty then*, a no longer true now, a truth out of time, to be brought back by fortune, fate, intention, or memory. A photograph, a movie, is only another present, another image, another ripple in the Heraclitean stream. The image as a mere present to which I may point suggests or encourages sequentiality, leading always to another moment. Each moment, however, is a distinct totality and only leads to the next moment because of its inherent lack of total meaning.[46] It is only a totality in the moment, what Hegel called a bad infinity. It is, further, a totality out there, inherently estranged or separated from the viewer. It is always a not-mine, that which I must make mine.

The word, on the other hand, points away from the certain, however much it seeks such a location. And, it is always mine. Further, a sound requires with almost gravitational necessity a turn of the head, a "gaze" directed.[47] A strange sound is always accompanied by anxious eyes. Sound is as ambiguous as sight is certain, and the word shares this characteristic, even though the printed word tries to make light of this. There is, of course, deception in both domains of sight and sound, although perceptual error is always greeted with surprise. It is no accident that "sight gags" are typical forms of contemporary comedy, guaranteeing delight and wonder. Sound offers, as a rule, uncertainty; irony and ambiguity here are everyday occurrences. Sound and, by implication, the word provide an all-around and not a being-there, which is the province of sight.

Sound, because of its uncertainty, is dialectical; sight is non-dialectical, merely logical. Ellul states:

> Thus visual reality is clearly non-contradictory. You can *say* that a piece of paper is both red and blue. But you cannot *see* it as both red and blue at the same time. It is either one or the other. The famous principle of noncontradiction is based on visual experience of the world, just as the principle of identity is. Declaring that two opinions cannot both be true, when one denies what the other affirms, has to do with vision, which involves instantaneousness. But language involves duration. Consequently what is visual cannot be dialectical. Knowledge based on sight is of necessity linear and logical. Only thought based on language can be dialectical, taking into account contradictory aspects of reality, which are possible because they are located in time.[48]

Sight and sound are the existential dimensions of the dialectic. They both need each other; certainty must be checked by ambiguity, and ambivalence must be allowed the ability to decide. When one sense predominates, the dialectic stops. Sight, agreeing with Spengler, is in the domain of technique. It is no accident that a main feature of the contemporary decor is the video. The remains of music are reduced to noise and enter the realm of space through sheer volume and dissonance.

According to Ellul, the incursions of technique, producing, revealing, and reflecting a nondialectical consciousness, have the profoundest and most disturbing effect on human language. In language the human maintains humanity and remains free of artificial necessity. For Ellul, only God can determine necessity, and He too opts for freedom and choice: He offers grace and redemption for transgression. Thus, freedom involves a kind of irony, a distance from the world that, through the building of symbolic bridges, makes that world. Ellul, the ironic Christian, understands God and humanity to be engaged in an adventure. God's creation was at first total, final, but God allows man to challenge even that.[49] At stake is everything, and language—not in the form of Nietzsche-Jameson's "prison-house"—provides the rules and the limits of the game. It is sad that this irony is lost in the translation of *La Technique ou l'enjeu de siècle*, literally, *Technique or the Wager of the Century*, to *The Technological Society*. Here we may think—and this is the

function of irony, a movement between symbol and symbolized—of
Pascal's wager, whereby he allowed that we could either bet on the
infinity of the world, a false infinity with no beginning and no end,
or wager on the real infinity—God.[50]

What is crucial to human language is the dimension of the spoken
word, increasingly obviated in written language, without which there
could not be technique. Ellul states:

> Human spoken language is characterized precisely by these elements we
> have mentioned: overflowing of limits, going beyond, and destructuring
> what can be conveyed in tactile or visual language. Its essential aspects
> are breadth of meaning, ambiguity, and variation in interpretation. A
> sign in human language does not correspond to a thing. A word calls up
> echoes, feelings intertwined with thoughts, reasons mingled with
> irrationality, motives that lead nowhere, and uncoordinated urges. This
> specificity is what matters. . . .[51]

"Language" has increasingly come to mean "written language."
Literacy is often defined in terms of our abilities to manipulate witten
language. These abilities invariably lead to abilities with logic and
what has come to be characterized as linear reasoning.[52] Oral
language, on the other hand, suggests the realm of the story, the
narrative, the word appearing in the dialogical discourse between
human beings where disagreement, ambiguity, and ambivalence
conjoin to produce meaning in process. The fact, in this realm, is
untruth, babble (Babel), the province of individual reality. Truth,
the whole, is what is beyond all fact, relieving this strain, promising
clarity, certainty, and resolution. However, it is Ellul's view that this
daytime labor, the noise of fact gathering and arguing, is really the
snorings within a terminal sleep.

Ellul and the Philosophy of Technique

I have outlined Ellul's case around the notion of dialectic,
although it is likely to convince few philosophers or savants within
the social sciences. Many distinctions, the life-blood of those
disciplines, have been avoided. Although Ellul sketches a specific
development within Western societies, clearly not all communities
were in the stage of *la société* by the eighteenth century. This can no
doubt be documented. Not all societies had advanced to the level of
la technique by the nienteenth century. Societies that might reach
a relatively high technical state have been known to fall to barbar-
ism, a fact well documented by Spengler. The development within

societies, moreover, does not follow the smooth diachronic plan that
Ellul has suggested. There are, using terms of current value, diachronic and synchronic lapses in Ellul's schema.

Further, Ellul's analyses of sight and sound may easily be judged
simplistic. For example, sight and sound may overlap to the point
of being nearly indistinguishable, as in an explosion or, perhaps,
in the experience of the thundering sky, which enabled the first
communities to form a notion of a god and to engage in poetic action
to form those communities. The claim that sight is inherently logical
is challenged by the maze of signs engulfing an overcrowded
expressway. There are indeed any number of philosophical
distinctions that might be raised: contradictions arise when we
wonder how a symbol can be nonsymbolic, when we question how
propositions can be meaningful but not subject to argumentative
analysis, or when we speak of an unconscious mode of consciousness. And then, there is the matter of the Christian perspective, the
problem of how there can be an absolute creation that is still
somehow being finished, of how there can be an infinite God, in
principle unknowable, who yet can speak and be revealed through
biblical revelation.

I have not confronted these problems directly. My concern has not
been to argue with Ellul. It would, in his defense, be possible to see
that the diachronic and synchronic concerns of a materialistic,
socially oriented, historical analysis are technical concerns, matters
of interest to a technological society, interested in telling history in
terms of its own development; history as the adventures of great men
and movements has become the chronicling of material acquisition,
the pouring over of documents and statistics with the hope of
somehow finding meaning behind the detail. The demand for
archival documentation may be less a search for historical truth and
more a manifestation of *la technique.*

The observation that much of the contemporary landscape has
become a confusing visual display does not provide a counterclaim
to the proposition the sight is logic; it is, instead, its affirmation.
It may confirm Ellul's thesis that the logic of logic breaks down
in the human community; the visual, making the claim to logic,
proliferates in the absence of dialectical meaning, in the absence of
the word, the narrative dimension. Further, it is clear that the current
concern for logic and argumentation, for contradiction, in the form
it has taken, is post-Cartesian. True, Plato and Aristotle provide
much of the rationale for the view of man as *Homo logicus*, but their
inquiries took them to the *agora*, to the discovery of many logics and
to the metaphysical depths or heights that supported them. That

metaphysics has fallen from professional philosophical favor, again supports Ellul's claim. And I will make no effort to judge Ellul's theology, an area where I hope to maintain an amateur's status. Answering these problems I leave to the work of others.

Instead, I have taken seriously Ellul's claim that technique, while co-opting the natural sacred, has become the new sacred. As he writes in *The New Demons*:

> An overvaluing of the ephemeral transformed into law everlasting, the transformation of everything into an object of consumption, absorption in living standards, a giddy frenzy attempting to feed on all the possibilities in order to attain thereby to true existence and to transcend the human condition—that is what is being expressed by every argument for our society. We walk on the moon. We fly at Mach 3. We split the atom. We create life. We are going beyond the human condition. The techno-consumer is the shaman of our society. But it is a shamanism made available to spiritual nothingness with a bank account.[53]

I have taken this claim as dialectical, which reveals technique as a mentality, expressing a specific subject-object relationship, embodied in a world of sight and sound, grasped in symbolic activity. Ellul opposes sacral consciousness to religious consciousness. In the sacred, thought becomes tired, falling to an identity with the object. The cliché, the authority, the decadence of language, the reification of the particular into the universal, all constitute evidence for this claim. They do not prove the claim. There is no proof involved; proof is a concern, for technical consciousness. Ellul has instead provided us with a way to understand.

Ellul's vision is possible because he takes a stance outside the technical system. He takes the position of the religious person who believes both that the Word of God is transcendent and that it is revealed. He opts for a view, contradictory at best, that he takes to be an absolutely revealed transcendent. God, however, is only revealed to us in our attempts to understand Him, to make Him speak. God has been silent, Ellul claims, and it is the Christian's job to make Him speak.

First, however, the word must learn to speak again, having in modern times been reduced to a sound and light show. Religious consciousness, in Ellul's view, is engaged in a pure dialectic with God, the Wholly Other. With the sacred, God becomes the Wholly Immanent, and thus not God at all. As technique becomes the sacred force, all becomes ephemeral, tied to the technical phenomenon. The technical is the result of a reduction of the natural to the rational and the artificial, to the qualities of automatism, self-augmentation, monism, universalism, and autonomy.[54] That is, technical choices are made automatically, creating a system that produces other objects by the nature of the system itself, making the universal incursions of technique into other cultures disruptive. The values of technique—efficiency according to a mathematics-like precision—coopt all other values. These are not fixed categories. They are what Ellul calls the characteristics of the technical phenomenon, and they must be understood in dialectical relationship. Thus, Ellul's notion of technique is not "clichégenic," although it could become a cliché. Florman's notion of Ellul as a *technophobe* is a clear cliché. With this notion, Florman and his followers no longer have to think.

The notion of technique has to be grasped and worked out by each reader. There are no rules for this. They have to be made up as one goes. For example, I have taken Ellul's method to be that of an ironist. Only Michel Cornu has also seen this.[55] I have suggested that Ellul's power is in his ability to see things as *Other*. For example, his notion of technique amounts to seeing reason in this form as inherently irrational, to understanding politics as no longer politics, language as no longer language, work as no longer work, etc. In fact, Ellul takes each of the contemporary commonplaces and inverts them. This is Ellul's method, the method of no method. Ellul's method is not merely ironic, however. It is grounded in a cosmic view, in seeing God as the ultimate resolution, although that view is not available to humankind. It is a matter of faith and prayer.

My perspective, however, is different from Ellul's, although in some respects also similar. I take seriously his notion of discourse, both as neglected in the modern age and yet as offering hope, although not exclusively in the Christian sense. In *The Humiliation of the Word*, Ellul writes:

The word *discourse* itself contains part of the explanation of this tendency [to reduce the word to an image]. Discourse implies a long process: an indirect approach and a kind of winding movement involving successive approximations that irritate lazy modern people. Visual representation is the easy, efficient, quick path. It allows us to grasp a totality in a single glance, without any need to break up a thing and to analyze it. Explanation and precise formulation are no longer necessary when a person has been able to grasp all at once what the issue is. It is much easier to let oneself be captivated or impressed by an image than to follow an oral demonstration. It is easier not only intellectually, but we could almost say it is easier because of our temperament: a line of reasoning or a demonstration are efficacious only if they are in accord with the person who listens to them. The rigor of spoken thought must find its counterpart in a similar rigor in the listener. In order for the word to become truly demonstrative, a kind of asceticism and interior discipline are required. These cannot be acquired all at once.[56]

I have tried to take this position with respect to Ellul's own words. By the oral word—sadly I have never heard Ellul's—he means the word not reduced to the image. The ironic word is such a word. The metaphor is a beginning of such a notion, and the poet is, perhaps, the key to metephor. For Ellul, it is the poet using "traditional language" who holds the key, a notion that may be abstracted from the whole of his work but is found explicitly in no one work. I do not offer my view of the whole as the whole. I just take this as a beginning to viewing the whole as a whole.

In traditional language, the context is given by the community, by tradition, or by the body; in technical discourse the context is always made up out of abstractions. In technical discourse, the word has only a systemic and contextual meaning that eschews the individual speaker or reduces words to the ravings of the merely individual, for example, to the discourse of the mad, which so fascinates many French intellectuals from Lacan to Foucault. In traditional language, the individual is always subordinate to the discourse that gives life and direction inasmuch as the individual can separate from it. That is, words must be seen as strivings. In technical discourse the *"n'importe quoi"* holds. Words are whatever one wants to make them. Words become a matter of fashion. "Upscale" once used to refer to consumer goods; now it is used in film criticism and food service. Traditional language provides humanity with a condition of freedom, while for technique language becomes a prison in which we are trapped. For Ellul, the modern expression for the ideal is: "You're coming through loud and clear."[57] Language is thus reduced to noise and to image.

Ellul does not try to prove that technique exists as he understands it. He is simply interested in presenting an understanding of it that is dialectically grounded in a way that the Cartesian philosopher is not likely to approve. Ellul does not try to come through loud and clear. His works must be read and not consulted. His concern is to disturb what he feels has become the modern balance through words. His concern is ethical, political, and philosophical at once. He writes:

This reasonable man, without whom human democracy cannot exist, is the one who at the same time can restore to language its true reason and to its communicative substance and who will seek neither a metalanguage, nor a "point zero" in language, nor an expression of the inexpressible, nor an original language opposed to artificial rhetoric. To be sure, we know that this reasonable language is artificial. And so? That only means that it must be maintained as a modest utensil, irreplaceable and reliable. You want absolute language? The word in itself? Here too, I repeat: I do not apply value judgments, but judgments of fact. To lay oneself open to mystical and hypnotic language is to provide a total opening to propaganda action upon oneself. The more that language loses its content and reasonable structure, the more man is delivered to propaganda's delirium.[58]

Language exists in a *sensus communis*, before another human being. Clarity is a matter of achievement, a labor of the negative. Language is the tool, fallible and not absolute, either as a medium of freedom or as a medium of enslavement. It is only a mediation pointing two ways: toward the speaker and toward the object. This mediation is never resolvable except in myth and in propaganda.

The answer to technique is for Ellul the word, both image and sound, transcendent and particular. This is a sense that certain artists understand—I include philosophers and any other practitioners of the transcendental arts, although hardly all artists or philosophers dare these domains—which points to this use of the word. Orwell's image of Big Brother and Newspeak so point—if we can keep from going to sleep, if we can maintain our memories. Kafka, that cartographer of the labyrinths of modern society, knew this sense. He knew the trivialities that haunt the visual domain when he refused to allow his publisher to include a drawing of the insectlike Gregor Samsa in *Die Verwandlung* (1915). John Updike observes: "In this age that lives and dies by the visual, *The Metamorphosis* stands as a narrative absolutely literary, able to exist only where language and the mind's hazy wealth of imagery intersect."[59] The *Ungeziefer*, literally vermin, is not a bug specifically. He is not an insect. Nor is he merely Gregor. He is also you and I. Gregor, like us, has been transformed by his milieu—it is not just that he is a salesman, awakening in a drab room with a picture of a woman cut from a magazine on the wall, a man drowning in a job of tedium and regularity. These words of Kafka, truly literary images, force our minds to move back and forth, to construct the whole of Gregor's condition, and to see it in relation to our own in space and time. The meaning of the work is forever beyond us, but still we read and listen as long as we can, until we too become wholly the *Ungeziefer*.

Ellul's words are crucial. His notion of technique as a metaphor has given me much pause, caused me to spend the last ten years of my life seeing my own age and myself in relation to this understanding. Over these last ten years his words, true or false, have always remained interesting. Consider these words:

> The most explicit and the best-explained word still brings me inevitably back to mystery. This mystery has to do with the other person, whom I cannot fathom, and whose word provides me with an echo of his person, but only an echo. I perceive this echo, knowing that there is something more. This is the mystery I feel as I recognize spontaneously that I do not understand well or completely what the other person says. There is a mystery for me in my own lack of comprehension, as I become aware of it. How am I going to react? How can I respond? I sense a whole area of mystery in the fact that I am not very sure I understood correctly. I am not very sure about answering. I am not very sure of what I am saying.[60]

This lack of certainty, Ellul states, will provide a distance from the word, from the object, from the person, and from the institution and allow the reflection and recollection of whatever totalities are available. Ellul's words invoke a mystery couched in paradox and irony that, when properly heard, remain a challenge to technique—the sacred of our age—numbly worshipped in a ritual that has become repetition as we hang from the device.

Notes

Preface

1. Jacques Ellul, *La Technique ou l'enjeu du siècle* (Paris: Armand Colin, 1954); Jacques Ellul, *The Technological Society*, trans. John Wilkinson (New York: Alfred A. Knopf, 1965), xiii, hereinafter cited as *TS*.

2. See, for example, D. P. Verene, "Kant, Hegel, and Cassirer: The Origins of the Philosophy of Symbolic Forms," *Journal of the History of Ideas* 30 (1969): 33–46.

3. R. G. Collingwood, *An Essay on Metaphysics* (Oxford: Clarendon Press, 1939), 17–77. Also see Collingwood's *Speculum Mentis or the Map of Knowledge* (Oxford: Clarendon Press, 1924), which is his most complete statement of his philosophy of culture.

4. Ernst Cassirer, *Philosophie der Symbolischen Formen*, 3 vols. (Darmstadt: Wissenschaftliche Buchgesellschaft, 1923–29); Ernst Cassirer, *The Philosophy of Symbolic Forms*, trans. Ralph Manheim, 3 vols. (New Haven: Yale University Press, 1953, 1957), 2: xvi, hereinafter cited as *PSF*. Also see Cassirer's discussion of technique and Ernst Kapp's *Philosophie der Technik* in *PSF*, 214–318.

5. Jacques Ellul, *Le Vouloir et le faire: Recherches éthique pour les chrétiens*, Nouvelle Série Théologique, no. 18 (Geneva: Labor et Fides, 1964); Jacques Ellul, *To Will and to Do: An Ethical Research for Christians*, trans. C. Edward Hopkin (Philadelphia: Pilgrim Press, 1969), 2. All references will be to the English translations of Ellul's works where possible. In few cases have I changed or added to translation, indicating in the text where I have done so, and citing the French text. When not available, I have provided my own translations.

6. See David Lovekin, "Jacques Ellul and the Logic of Technology," *Man and World* 10 (1978): 251–72; idem, "Degenerate Travel: The World of the Tourist in Technological Society," in *Essays in Humanity and Technology*, ed. David Lovekin and Donald Phillips Verene (Dixon, Ill.: Sauk Valley College, 1978), 167–89; idem, "Giambattista Vico and Jacques Ellul: The Intelligible Universal and the Technical Phenomenon," *Man and World* 15 (1982): 407–16.

7. Katherine C. Temple, "The Task of Jacques Ellul: A Proclamation of Biblical Faith as a Requisite for Understanding the Modern Project," Ph.D. diss., McMaster University, 1976.

8. Darrell J. Fashing, *The Thought of Jacques Ellul: A Systematic Exposition* (New York: Edwin Mellen Press, 1981).

9. *Jacques Ellul: Interpretive Essays*, ed. Clifford Christians and Jay M. Van Hook (Urbana, Chicago, and London: University of Illinois Press, 1981), hereinafter cited as *Essays*. Also see my review in *Technology and Culture* 23 (1982): 694–96.

10. Etienne Dravasa, Claude Emeri, and Jean-Louis Seurin, *Religion, société, et politique: Mélanges en hommage à Jacques Ellul* (Paris: Presses Universitaires des France, 1983).

Introduction

1. Jacques Ellul, *Le Système technicien* (Paris: Calmann-Lévy, 1977), 86; Jacques Ellul, *The Technological System*, trans. Joachim Neugroschel (New York: Continuum, 1980), 74, hereinafter cited as *System*.

2. Jacques Ellul, *Les Nouveaux possédés* (Paris: Arthème Fayard, 1973); Jacques Ellul, *The New Demons*, trans. C. Edward Hopkin (New York: Seabury Press, 1975), hereinafter cited as *Demons*.

3. See Preface, n. 1.

4. Jacques Ellul, *La Parole humiliée*, (Paris: Editions du Seuil, 1981); Jacques Ellul, *The Humiliation of the Word*, trans. Joyce Main Hanks (Grand Rapids, Mich.: William B. Eerdmans, 1985), hereinafter cited as *Humiliation*.

5. Jacques Ellul, *L'Empire du non-sens: L'Art et La société technicienne* (Paris: Presses Universitaires de France, 1980), hereinafter cited as *L'Empire*.

6. Jacques Ellul, "Symbolic Function, Technology, and Society," *Journal of Social and Biological Structures* 3 (July 1978): 207–18, hereinafter cited as "Symbolic Function."

7. For the most comprehensive bibliography of Ellul's work, see the extraordinary: Joyce Main Hanks, *Jacques Ellul: A Comprehensive Bibliography* (Greenwich, Conn. JAI Press, 1984).

8. Jacques Ellul, *Sans feu ni lieu: Signification biblique de La Grand Ville* (Paris: Gallimard, 1975); Jacques Ellul, *The Meaning of the City*, trans. Denis Pardee (Grand Rapids, Mich.: William B. Eerdmans, 1970), hereinafter cited as *Meaning*.

9. *System*, 176.

10. Jacques Ellul, *L'Histoire des institutions*, 5 vols. (Paris: Presses Universitaires de France, 1955–80).

11. René Descartes, *The Discourse on Method*, in *The Philosophical Works of Descartes*, trans. Haldane and Ross, 2 vols. (New York: Dover Publications, 1955), 1: 84–85.

12. *TS*, 19–22, 42.

13. Jacques Ellul, *La Subversion du christianisme* (Paris: Editions du Seuil, 1984); Jacques Ellul, *The Subversion of Christianity*, trans. Geoffrey W. Bromiley (Grand Rapids, Mich.: William B. Eerdmans, 1986), 21, hereinafter cited as *Subversion*.

14. Ibid., 15, 17.

15. Ibid., 59.

16. Jacques Ellul, "On Dialectic," in *Essays*, hereinafter cited as "Dialectic."

17. *Humiliation*, 22.

18. Ibid., 10–11.

19. Ibid., 37.

20. Ibid., 63–70.

21. René Descartes, *Meditations on First Philosophy*, trans. Laurence J. Lafleur (New York: Bobbs-Merrill Co., 1986), 31.

22. *TS*, 43.

23. René Descartes, *Meditations sur la philosophie premiere, dans Laquelle est demonstrée L'existence de Dieu et L'immortalite de l'âme*, in *Oeuvres et Lettres*, ed. Andre Bridoux (Paris: Editions Gallimard, 1953), 272.

24. Jacques Ellul, "Developments in Technology and the Philosophy of the Absurd," in *Research in Philosophy and Technology*, ed. Paul T. Durbin, (Greenwich, Conn.: JAI Press, 1984), 7:90.

25. Ibid., 92.

26. Ibid., 94.

27. Ibid., 95.

28. Ibid.

29. Ibid., 78, 96–97. Also see "Dialectic," 298–99, 308.

30. "Dialectic," 294–95.

31. *System*, 12.

Chapter 1. Ellul and the Critics

1. William Stringfellow, "Introduction," in Jacques Ellul, *The Presence of the Kingdom*, trans. Olive Wyon and with an Introduction by William Stringfellow (New York: The Seabury Press, 1967), 2, hereinafter referred to as *Presence*.

2. John Wilkinson, "The Divine Persuasion: An Interview on Jacques Ellul with John Wilkinson," in *Introducing Jacques Ellul*, ed. James Holloway (Grand Rapids, Mich.: William B. Eerdmans, 1970), 168, hereinafter referred to as *Introducing*.

3. Ibid.

4. *TS*, iii. Note that this "Statement from the Publisher" is not in the first American edition.

5. Ibid., iv.

6. Ibid., v.

7. Ibid., vi.

8. Ibid., viii.

9. Eugene S. Ferguson, *Bibliography of the History of Technology* (Cambridge: MIT Press, 1968), 205.

10. See Hanks, *Comprehensive Bibliography*, 168–70, upon which I base my count.

11. Howard Falk, "Review of *The Technological Society*," *Technology and Culture* 6 (Summer 1965): 532.

12. Ibid.

13. Ibid.

14. Ibid., 533.

15. Ibid.

16. Ibid., 534–35.

17. Victor Ferkiss, *The Technological Man: The Myth and the Reality* (New York: Mentor Books, 1969), 35, 36–37.

18. Alvin Toffler, *Future Shock* (New York: Random House, 1970), 233–36.

19. Samuel Florman, "In Praise of Technology," *Harpers*, November 1975, 68.

20. Samuel Florman, *The Existential Pleasures of Engineering* (New York: St. Martin's Press, 1976), 57–73.

21. Ibid., 58–60.

22. Ibid., 63.

23. Ibid., 62.

24. Ibid.

25. Ibid., 68.

26. Ibid., 71.

27. Daniel Lerner, "Review of *Propaganda*," *American Sociological Review* 29 (1964): 793–94.

28. Rupert Hall, "An Unconvincing Indictment of the Evils of Technology," *Scientific American* 212 (1965): 128.

29. Ibid.

30. Charles Silberman, "Is Technology Taking Over," *The Myths of Automation* (New York: Harper and Row, 1966), 212.

31. Ibid.

32. *TS*, 259.

33. Jacques Ellul, *Exégèse des nouveaux lieux communs* (Paris: Calmann-Lévy, 1966); Jacques Ellul, *A Critique of the New Commonplaces*, trans. Helen Weaver (New York: Alfred A. Knopf, 1968), 10–11, hereinafter cited as *Commonplaces*.

34. Ibid. A chapter is devoted to each commonplace.

35. Melvin Kranzberg and Carrol W. Pursell Jr., "The Importance of Technology in Human Affairs," in *Technology in Western Civilization*, ed. Melvin Kranzberg and Carroll W. Pursell Jr., 2 vols. (New York, London, Toronto: Oxford University Press, 1967), 1: 4.

36. Ibid.

37. Ibid., 11.

38. Melvin Kranzberg, "Introduction: Trends in the History and Philosophy of Technology," in *The History and Philosophy of Technology*, ed. George Bugliarello and Dean B. Doner with an introduction by Melvin Kranzberg (Urbana: University of Illinois Press, 1979), xxiv.

39. Ibid.

40. Christopher Lasch, "The Social Thought of Jacques Ellul," *Introducing*, 63.

41. Ibid., 64.

42. Ibid., 80–86.

43. Ibid., 64.

44. Ibid., 63.

45. Ibid., 68–74.

46. Langdon Winner, *Autonomous Technology: Technics-Out-of-Control as a Theme in Political Thought* (Cambridge: MIT Press, 1977).

47. Ibid., 123.

48. Ibid., 177.

49. Ibid., 130.

50. Ibid., 323.

51. Ibid., 327.

52. David Lovekin, "Jacques Ellul and the Logic of Technique," *Man and World: An International Journal of Philosophy* 10 (1977): 251–72.

53. Winner, *Antonomous Technology*, 65.

54. Ibid.

55. Ibid., 331.

56. Ibid., 218.

57. Carl Mitcham and Robert Mackey, "Jacques Ellul and the Technological Society," *Philosophy Today* 15 (Summer 1971): 117–19.

58. Jacques Ellul, "The Relationship between Man and Creation in the Bible," in *Theology and Technology: Essays in Christian Analysis and Exegesis*, ed. Carl Mitcham and Jim Grote (Lanham, New York, London: University Press of America, 1984), 142, hereinafter referred to as *Theology and Technology*.

59. Ibid., 140.

60. *Humiliation*, 22–26.

61. Ibid., 10–11.

62. Ibid., 155–82.

63. Jacques Ellul, "Technique and the Opening Chapters of Genesis," *Theology and Technology*, 132–34.

64. *Subversion*, 44–45.

65. *Humiliation*, 10–11. Also see *Subversion*, 23, 44–46.

66. *Subversion*, 9–10.

67. Ibid., 11, n. 6.

68. Ibid., 15.

69. *Humiliation*, 269.

70. Gene Outka, "Discontinuity in Ellul's Ethics," *Essays*, 182.

71. Ibid., 209.

72. Ibid., 203.

73. Ibid., 178.

74. Ibid., 182–88.

75. *TS*, xxvii.

76. *Commonplaces*, 9–13.

77. Arthur F. Holmes, "Ellul on Natural Law," *Essays*, 238–41.

78. Ibid., 238.

79. Ibid., 244.

80. Ibid., 241.

81. Daniel B. Clendenin, *Theological Method in Jacques Ellul* (Lanham, New York, London: University Press of America, 1987), 5–28.

82. Ibid., 43–54.

83. Ibid., 120.

84. Ibid., 30–42.

85. Ibid., 39.

86. Ibid., 135.

87. *Subversion*, 71.

88. Ibid., 44.

89. Norman O. Brown, "Jacques Ellul: Beyond Geneva and Jerusalem," in "Contested Domain," *Democracy* 2 (Fall 1982): 119–20.

90. Ibid., 120.

91. Ibid., 126.

Chapter 2. Ellul and the Problem of a Philosophy of Technology

1. *TS*, xxxii–xxxiii.

2. Blaise Pascal, *Pensées* in *Oeuvres Completes*, texte établi, présénté et annoté par Jacques Chevalier (Paris: Editions Gallimard, 1954), 1213.

3. Ibid., 1215.

4. *TS*, xxxii–xxxiii.

5. Ibid., xxxiii.

6. *System*, 18–19.

7. Peter Gay, *The Weimar Culture: The Outsider as Insider* (New York and Evanston: Harper and Row, 1968), 63.

8. Heinrich von Kleist, "On the Puppet Theater," *An Abyss Deep Enough: Letters of Heinrich von Kleist with a Selection of Essays and Anecdotes*, ed., trans., and intro. by Phillip B. Miller (New York: E. P. Dutton, 1982), 212.

9. Ibid.

10. Ibid., 213.

11. Ibid., 214.

12. Ibid., 216.

13. Ernst Kapp, *Grundlinien einer Philosophie der Technik* (Braunschweig: Westerman, 1977).

14. See Hans-Martin Sass, "Man and his Environment: Ernst Kapp's Engineering Experience and his Philosophy of Technology and Environment," in *German Culture in Texas*, ed. Glen E. Lich and Dona B. Reeves (Boston: Twayne, 1979), 82–99.

15. Ibid., 86.

16. Ibid., 96.

17. Friedrich Dessauer, "Technology in Its Proper Sphere," trans. William Carroll, in *Philosophy and Technology: Readings in the Philosophical Problems of Technology*, ed. Carl Mitcham and Robert Mackey (New York and London: The Free Press, 1983), 324–30.

18. Ibid., 328.

19. Ibid.

20. Ibid., 321.

21. Ibid.

22. Ibid., 334.

23. Ernst Cassirer, *An Essay on Man* (New Haven and London: Yale University Press, 1979), 27.

24. For the best book-length discussion of the structure of Cassirer "system" of symbolic forms, see John Michael Krois, *Cassirer: Symbolic Forms and History* (New Haven and London: Yale University Press, 1987).

25. Ernst Cassirer, *The Myth of the State* (New Haven and London: Yale University Press, 1946), 282.

26. *PSF*, 2: xiv.

27. Ibid., 214–15.

28. Ibid., 215.

29. Ibid., 216–17.

30. Ernst Cassirer, "Form and Technik," *Symbol, Technik, Sprache*, ed. Ernst Wolfgang Orth and John Michael Krois, intro. by Josef M. Werle (Hamburg: Felix Meiner Verlag, 1985), 39–91.

31. Ernst Cassirer, *Zur Logic der Kulturwissenschaften* (Darmstadt: Wissenschaftliche Buchgesellschaft, 1942); Ernst Cassirer, *The Logic of the Humanities*, trans. Clarence Howe (New Haven and London: Yale University Press, 1961), 117–58. Also see *PSF*, 1: 177–86.

32. Cassirer, *The Myth of the State*, 277–96.

33. Cassirer, *An Essay on Man*, 228.

34. *PSF*, 3: 40–41.

35. Jacques Ellul, *Metamorphose du bourgeois* (Paris: Calmann-Lévy, 1967), 235–36. My translation.

36. Carl Mitcham, "What Is the Philosophy of Technology?" *International Philosophical Quarterly* 25 (March 1985): 73–88.

37. Ibid., 83.

38. Ibid., 73.

39. Ibid., 83.

40. Steven L. Goldman "The Techné of Philosophy and the Philosophy of Technology," *Research in Philosophy and Technology*, ed. Paul T. Durbin (Greenwich, Conn.: JAI Press, 1984), 115–44.

41. Ibid., 124.
42. Ibid., 136.

Chapter 3. Ellul and the Consciousness of Technique

1. *TS*, xxv.
2. See *La Technique ou l'enjeu du siecle: "La conscience technique,"* 49; *"l'etat d'esprit,"* 31; *"d'une intention technique,"* 44.
3. *TS*, 19–22.
4. Ibid., 19. See *System*, 79.
5. Ibid., 20.
6. Ibid., 131.
7. *System*, 105.
8. Jacques Ellul, *Politique de Dieu, politique de l'homme* (Paris: Nouvelle alliance, Eclitions Universitaires, 1966); Jacques Ellul, *The Politics of God and the Politics of Man*, trans. and ed. Geoffrey W. Bromiley (Grand Rapids, Mich.: William B. Eerdmans, 1972), 16, hereinafter cited as *Politics*.
9. *System*, 12.
10. Ibid., 331, n. 7.
11. *Metamorphose du Bourgeois*, 237. My translation.
12. "Dialectic," 299.
13. *Humiliation*, 63.
14. Ibid., 65.
15. Ibid., 107.
16. *Politics*, 23–40.
17. Ibid., 25–27.
18. Ibid., 29–30.
19. Ibid., 35–38.
20. Ibid., 34.
21. *Meaning*, 17–18.
22. "Symbolic Function," 209.
23. Ibid., 210.
24. Jacques Ellul, *Living Faith: Belief and Doubt in a Perilous World*, trans. Peter Heinegg (San Francisco: Harper and Row, 1983), 277, hereinafter cited as *Faith*.
25. *Subversion*, 45.
26. "Dialectic," 296.
27. G. W. F. Hegel, *Hegel's Science of Logic*, trans. A. V. Miller (London and New York: Humanities Press, 1969), 138.
28. Ibid., 139.
29. Ibid., 149; see also G. W. F. Hegel, *Wissenschaft der Logic*, ed. Georg Lasson, 2 vols. (Hamburg: Felix Meiner Verlag, 1971) 1: 138–39.
30. Ibid., 151.
31. G. W. F. Hegel, *Phenomenology of Spirit*, trans. A. V. Miller (Oxford: Clarendon Press, 1977), 493; see also G. W. F. Hegel, *Phänomenologie des Geistes*, ed. Johannes Hoffmeister, 6th ed. (Hamburg: Felix Meiner Verlag, 1952), 563–64.
32. Donald Phillip Verene, *Hegel's Recollection: A Study of Images in the Phenomenology of Spirit* (Albany: State University of New York Press, 1985), 14–26.

33. Ibid., 70–79.
34. Hegel, *Phenomenology of Spirit*, 131.
35. Ibid., 135.
36. Verene, *Hegel's Recollection*, 70–74.
37. "Dialectic," 306–7.
38. *Subversion*, 59.
39. "Symbolic Function," 211.
40. Ibid.
41. Ibid., 212.
42. Ellul, *L'Histoires des institutions*, 1: 220–21. My translation.
43. *Demons*, 55.
44. "Symbolic Function," 211.
45. *Demons*, 130.
46. "Symbolic Function," 213–14.
47. Ibid.
48. Jacques Ellul, "Histoire: Les Trois Ages," *Le Monde* 11–12 (March 1979): 2.
49. Jacques Ellul, *The Ethics of Freedom*, trans. and ed. Geoffrey W. Bromiley (Grand Rapids, Mich.: William B. Eerdmans, 1976), 355.
50. *Time*, 10 February 1986), 25.
51. Ibid., 29.
52. Ibid.

Chapter 4. Historical, Social, and Intellectual Dimensions of Ellul's Thought

1. Jacques Ellul, "Problems of a Sociological Method," trans. Daniel Hofstadter, *Social Research* 43 (1976): 7.
2. *Faith*, 277.
3. Ibid., 228.
4. Ibid., 229.
5. Ibid., 187–188. In the simplest terms, the transcendent is "... the one who is never an object" (ibid., 189). Religions err, Ellul believes, when they create sacred orders by turning their gods into objects.
6. "On Dialectic," 295.
7. Ibid., 296.
8. Ibid.
9. Jacques Ellul, *A temps et à contretemps: Entretiens avec Madeleine Garrigou-Lagrange* (Paris: LeCenturion, 1981); *An Introduction to the Thought of Jacques Ellul*, trans. Lani K. Niles, based on interviews by Madeline Garrigou-Lagrange (San Francisco: Harper & Row, 1982), hereinafter cited as *Season*.
10. Jacques Ellul, *Perspectives on Our Age: Jacques Ellul Speaks on His Life and Work*, trans. Joachim Neugroshel, ed. William H. Vanderberg (New York: The Seabury Press, 1981), hereinafter cited as *Perspectives*.
11. Jacques Ellul, *L'Illusion Politique* (Paris: Robert Laffont, 1965); Jacques Ellul, *the Political Illusion*, trans. Konrad Kellen (New York: Vintage Books, 1967), hereinafter cited as *PI*. *Perspectives*, 23.
12. It is not unttil Hanks's *Jacques Ellul: A Comprehensive Bibliography* that Ellul's corpus was really known.
13. *Season*, 14.

14. *Perspectives*, 7.

15. *Season*, 4–5; *Perspectives*, 1.

16. *Season*, 6.

17. Ibid., 5.

18. *Faith*, 117.

19. *Season*, 17.

20. Ibid.

21. Ibid., 13–14.

22. Ibid., 7.

23. Ibid., 10.

24. *Perspectives*, 12.

25. *Season*, 12.

26. Ibid.

27. Ibid., 4.

28. Ibid., 20.

29. Ibid.

30. Ibid., 21.

31. Jacques Ellul, *Etude sur l'evolution et la nature juridique du Mancipium* (Bordeaux: Delmas, 1936).

32. *Season*, 22.

33. *Perspectives*, 5.

34. Ibid., 5–12.

35. Ibid., 15.

36. Ibid., 14.

37. *Season*, 14.

38. Ibid., 15.

39. *Perspectives*, 15.

40. *Season*, 17–18.

41. Ibid., 17.

42. *Perspectives*, 17.

43. Ibid., 8–9.

44. *Season*, 80.

45. Ibid., 79.

46. *Faith*, 100–101.

47. Jacques Ellul, "Preface," in Nelly Viallaneix, *Ecoute, Kierkegaard: Essai sur la communication de la parole*, vol. 1 (Paris: Cerf, 1979), iii. My translation.

48. Jacques Ellul, "Between Chaos and Paralysis," *Christian Century* 85 (1968): 747–50.

49. *Faith*, 45.

50. *Season*, 59–60.

51. *Perspectives*, 18.

52. Jacques Ellul, "Une introduction à la penseé de Bernard Charbonneau," *Ouvertures: Cahiers de Sud-ouest* 7 (1985): 40–41, hereinafter cited as "Une introduction." My translation.

53. See *Season*, 33–43, for an account of this period.

54. Jacques Ellul, "Pourquoi Je me suis séparé de Mounier," *Réforme* 265 (1950): 7. My translation.

55. "Une introduction," 42–43.

56. Ellul, "Pourquoi," 7.

57. *Perspectives*, 20.

58. Ibid., 20–21.

59. *Season*, 49.
60. Ibid., 48.
61. Ibid., 51.
62. Ibid.
63. Ibid., 50.
64. Ibid., 53–54.
65. Ibid., 56.
66. Jacques Ellul, *Le fondement théologique du droit*, Cahiers Théologiques de l'Actualité Protestante, nos. 15/16 (Neuchâtel 1: Delachaux and Niestlé, 1946); Jacques Ellul, *The Theological Foundation of Law*, trans. Marguerite Wieser (New York: Doubleday, 1960), 27–30, hereinafter cited as *Law*. For an excellent study of this work see Mark Aultman, "Technology and the End of Law," *The American Journal of Jurisprudence* 17 (1972): 46–79.
67. *Law*, 34.
68. Ibid., 31.
69. Ibid., 104.
70. *Presence*, 117–36.
71. This refers to the importance of otherness, a key to my understanding of Ellul.
72. Jacques Ellul, *Propagandes* (Paris: A. Colin, 1962); Jacques Ellul, *Propaganda: The Formation of Men's Attitudes*, trans. Kondrad Kellen and Jean Lerner (New York: Alfred A. Knopf, 1965), hereinafter cited as *Propaganda*.
73. *Political Illusion*, 2.
74. *PI*, 6–7.
75. *PI*, xiii–xvi.
76. *PI*, xiii–xxi.
77. Ellul develops this notion thoroughly in *Autopsy of a Revolution*, trans. Patricia Wolf (New York: Alfred A. Knopf, 1971).
78. See especially Michel Foucault, *Surveiller et Punir: Naissance de la Prison* (Paris: Gallimard, 1975); Michel Foucault, *Discipline and Punish: The Birth of the Prison*, trans. Alan Sheridan (New York: Vintage, 1979), and Michel Foucault, *L'Histoire de folie* (Paris: Libraire Plan, 1961); *Madness and Civilization: A History of Insanity in the Age of Reason*, trans. Richard Howard (New York: Vintage, 1973).
79. *PI*, 29.
80. *PI*, 27.
81. *PI*, 27–29.
82. *PI*, 28.
83. *PI*, n. 4.
84. *PI*, 39.
85. *PI*, 39–40.
86. Maurice Merleau-Ponty, *Humanism and Terror*, trans. John O'Neill (New York: Beacon Press, 1969), xx.
87. Ibid.
88. Ibid.
89. *PI*, 36.
90. See Karl Japers, *Man in the Modern Age*, trans. Eden and Cedar Paul (New York: Anchor Books, 1957).
91. Jacques Ellul, "Victoire d'Hitler?" *Réforme* 14 (1945): 2.
92. Jacques Ellul, "Le Temps Mepris," *Réforme* 52 (1946): 3.
93. *Propaganda*, 178–92.

94. *PI*, 49–50.

95. Claude Lévi-Strauss, *Totemism*, trans. Rodney Needham (Boston: Beacon Press, 1963), 89.

96. Michael Jacobson, *The Eater's Digest: The Consumer's Factbook of Food Additives* (New York: Doubleday, 1969).

97. Jean Anthelme Brillat-Savarin, *Physiology of Taste: or Meditations on Transcendental Gastronomy*, trans. M. F. K. Fisher (New York: The Heritage Press, 1949), 1.

98. *PI*, 113.

99. As quoted in David Welch's *Propaganda and the German Cinema: 1933–1945* (Oxford: Clarendon Press, 1983), 148.

100. *PI*, 124.

101. *PI*, 61–62.

102. *PI*, 115.

103. See my "Degenerate Travel: The World of the Tourist in Technological Society," in *Essays in Humanity and Technology*, ed. David Lovekin and Donald Phillip Verene (Dixon, Ill.: Sauk Valley College, 1978).

104. *PI*, 215.

105. Ibid.

106. *Seasons*, 130.

Chapter 5. The Technological Phenomenon and the Technical System

1. *TS*, 79.

2. Siegfried Giedion, *Mechanization Takes Command* (New York: Oxford University Press, 1948). Giedion traces the "rationalization" of such processes as the bodily movement of factory workers by Frank B. Gilbreth and of such objects as the Yale lock and the barber's chair.

3. Tom Wolf, *The Right Stuff* (New York: Farrar, Strauss, Giroux, 1979), 244.

4. Claude Lévi-Strauss, *The Savage Mind*, trans. George Weidenfeld (Chicago: University of Chicago Press, 1966), 22.

5. Ibid., 32.

6. C. J. Jung, "Flying Saucers: A Modern Myth," *Collected Works of C. G. Jung*, vol. 10, trans. R. F. C. Hull (Princeton: Princeton University Press, 1964), 328.

7. Mircea Eliade, *Myths, Dreams and Mysteries: The Encounter between Contemporary Faiths and Archaic Realities*, trans. Philip Mairit (New York: Harper Torchbooks, 1967), 234.

8. David Lovekin, "Jacques Ellul and the Logic of Technology," *Man and World* 10 (1977): 251–67.

9. *TS*, 19.

10. *Perspectives*, 33.

11. *TS*, 4.

12. *TS*, 77–147.

13. *System*, 123–204. Also, *Le Système technicien*, 137–224.

14. Ibid.

15. *TS*, 437.

16. *TS*, 78–79. See also *La technique*, 73–74.

17. *TS*, 19.
18. *TS*, 19–20.
19. *TS*, 20–21.
20. *TS*, 146.
21. Ibid.
22. *TS*, 21.
23. Giedion, *Mechanization Takes Command*, 93.
24. *System*, 18.
25. *TS*, 83.
26. *TS*, 80.
27. *TS*, 74.
28. *TS*, 43.
29. See René Descartes, *Philosophical Works of Descartes*, trans. and ed. Haldane and Ross (New York: Dover, 1955), 87–93.
30. *Meditations*, in ibid., 157.
31. *TS*, 86.
32. *TS*, 86.
33. *TS*, 93.
34. *TS*, 90–91.
35. *TS*, 17.
36. *TS*, 39.
37. *TS*, 113.
38. *TS*, 95.
39. *TS*, 97.
40. *TS*, 96.
41. *System*, 164.
42. *TS*, 131.
43. Mao Tse Tung, *Selected Works of Mao Tse Tung*, ed. Bruno Shaw (New York: Harper Colophon Books, 1970), 88.
44. *TS*, 130.
45. *TS*, 131.
46. *TS*, 392–93.
47. *System*, 177.
48. Ibid.
49. *TS*, 141–142.
50. *System*, 129.
51. Ibid.
52. *TS*, 142.
53. *Myths, Dreams and Mysteries*, 138.
54. Peter Worsley, *The Trumpet Shall Sound* (New York: Schocken Books, 1968), 131–145.
55. Umberto Eco, *Travels in Hyperreality*, trans. William Weaver (New York: Harcourt Brace Jovanovich, 1986), 3–58.
56. *System*, 149.
57. *New Demons*, 51–52.
58. Ibid., 52.
59. Ibid., 57.
60. Ibid., 67.
61. Ibid., 64.
62. Ibid., 93.
63. Ibid., 97.

64. Ibid., 96–97.

65. Ibid., 121.

66. Ibid., 50–52, 70–74.

67. Ibid., 73–74.

68. Donald Phillip Verene, "Technique and the Directions of the Human Spirit: Laughter and Desire," in *Essays in Humanity and Technology*, 99.

69. Ibid., 108.

70. *New Demons*, 74.

71. Ibid., 135.

72. Ibid., 91.

73. Ibid., 77.

74. Ibid., 71.

75. Ibid., 77.

76. See Lovekin, "Degenerate Travel," 183.

77. *New Demons*, 97.

78. Ibid.

79. Ibid., 97.

80. Ibid., 98–109.

81. Ibid., 99–101.

82. Ibid., 100–101.

83. Ibid., 102.

84. Jacques Ellul, "La Technique, système bloqué," *Pour* 64 (1979): 16–17.

85. *System*, 77.

86. Georg Simmel, "The Stranger," in *The Sociology of Georg Simmel*, trans., ed., and intro. by Kurt H. Wolf (New York: The Free Press of Glencoe, 1950), 402–8.

87. *System*, 93–105.

88. Ibid.

89. *Presence*, 24.

90. *Atlanta Constitution*, 12 May 1983, 16A.

Chapter 6. The Word and the Image:
The Discourse of Technique

1. Alexander Mischerlich and Fred Mielke, *Doctors of Infamy*, trans. Heine Norden (New York: Henry Schuman, 1949), xix–xx.

2. *TS*, 101.

3. George Orwell, *1984*, with preface by Walter Cronkite and an afterword by Erich Fromm (New York: New American Library, 1983), 246–56.

4. George Orwell, *A Collection of Essays by George Orwell* (New York: Doubleday Anchor, 1954), 163.

5. Ibid., 174–77.

6. Ibid., 257.

7. Orwell, *1984*, 1–2.

8. *Newsweek*, 30 June 1986, 13.

9. *PI*, 239.

10. *Humiliation*, 5–12.

11. *PI*, 217.

12. *PI*, 207–9.

13. *L'Empire*, 69. My translation.

14. *TS*, 79.

15. Norbert Wiener, *The Human Uses of Human Beings* (New York: Avon Books, 1967), 105–221.

16. Ibid., 31.

17. Hannah Arendt, *Eichman in Jerusalem: A Report on the Banality of Evil*, (New York: Viking Press, 1964), 49.

18. Ibid., 48.

19. Ibid., 46.

20. Ibid., 45.

21. Ibid., 126.

22. Anton Zijderveld, *On Clichés: the Supersedure of Meaning by Function in Modernity* (London, Boston, Henley: Routledge & Kegan Paul, 1979), 46.

23. Ibid., 43.

24. *L'Empire*, 42. My translation.

25. Ibid., 58.

26. Adolph Hitler, *Mein Kampf*, trans. Ralph Manheim (Boston: Houghton Mifflin, Co., 1971), 211.

27. Ibid., 204.

28. Herman Kahn, *On Thermonuclear War*, 2d ed. (Princeton: Princeton University Press, 1961), 331.

29. Ibid., 149.

30. Ibid., 74.

31. Ibid., 222.

32. Thomas Kuhn, *The Structure of Scientific Revolution* (Chicago: University of Chicago Press, 1970), 181.

33. *New Demons*, 149.

34. Gustav Flaubert, *Bouvard and Pechuchet*, trans. A. J. Krailsheimer (New York: Penguin Books, 1976), 69.

35. For instance, we can conclude, following Sir James Jeans's insights, that everything contains space between it, inasmuch as everything is made up of molecules, atoms, and what not. If this is true, then it is theoretically possible to drive a car through a brick wall, given enough tries. If one attempts this, and if one drives fast enough, likely there will only be one try. That is, there will be only one try if we are driving a real car through a real brick wall. The analytical car will go through the analytical wall an indefinite number of times. With analysis, there is no end to the possibility. In the actual world, apart from analysis, the choices seem to be more limited.

36. Flaubert, *Bouvard*, 8–9.

37. *Humiliation*, 159.

38. Frederic Jameson, *The Prison House of Language* (Princeton: Princeton University Press, 1972), 30.

39. Ibid., 196.

40. Friedrich Nietzsche, *Gesammelte Werke*, Musarion-Ausgabe, IX (Munich, 1926), 34. For Heller's translation see Erich Heller, "Wittgenstein and Nietzsche," *The Artist's Journey Into the Interior* (New York and London: Harcourt Brace Jovanovich, 1976), 219.

41. *L'Empire*, 55–56. My translation.

42. Ibid., 196.

43. Marshall McLuhan, *From Cliché to Archetype* (New York: Viking Press, 1970), 36.

44. *Humiliation*, 5–47.
45. Ibid., 5–12.
46. Particularly note: "The image contains within itself a deep contradiction. It is not ambiguous: it is coherent, reliable, and inclusive; but it is insignificant. It can have innumerable meanings, depending on culture, learning, or the intervention of some other dimension. For this reason I must learn to see before looking at the image. After seeing it, I must learn to interpret it. The image is clear, but this clarity does not imply certainty or comprehension. My certainity is limited to this directly perceived reality that my sight reveals to me" (*Humiliation*, 8). See also 9–11.
47. Ibid., 13–15.
48. Ibid., 10–11, n. 3.
49. Ellul's theology is characterized by this ironic distance between man and God. Of particular interest in this regard is parts 3 and 4 of *Hope in the Time of Abandonment*, trans. C. Edward Hopkin (New York: The Seabury Press, 1973), 167–301. Very specifically, note: "A contradiction? Precisely. Logically unsolvable, but it creates a biblical dialectic which makes man's relation to God not a repetition, a fixity, a ritual, a scrupulous submission, but a permanant invention, a new creation of the one with the other, a challenge, a love affair, an adventure whose outcome can never be known in advance" ("On Dialectic," 299).
50. Pascal, *Pensées, sect II*, "Le Noeud," en *Oeuvres Completes* (Paris: Gallimard, 1954), 1210–28.
51. *Humiliation*, 3.
52. Marshall McLuhan championed this notion in *Understanding Media: The Extensions of Man* (New York: McGraw Hill, 1964). It became almost immediately a cliché, with no one clear about exactly what it meant.
53. *Demons*, 145.
54. For a particularly interesting short summary of the notion of the artificial, see Jacques Ellul, "Nature, Technique, and Artificiality," trans. Katharine Temple, in *Research in Philosophy and Technology*, vol. 3 (Greenwich, Conn.: JAI Press, 1980), 263–83.
55. Michel Cornu, "Ironie et humour selon Kierkegaard," *Les Études Philosophiques* 2 (1979): 217–28. Cornu notes Ellul's ironic method in *Hope in the Time of Abandonment*, 284–306. Cornu, however, does not develop a theory of Ellul's notion of irony.
56. *Humiliation*, 133.
57. Ibid., 163.
58. *PI*, 236.
59. John Updike, "Reflections: Kafka's Short Stories," *The New Yorker*, 9 May 1983, 129.
60. *Humiliation*, 25.

Bibliography

Works by Jacques Ellul

For a complete bibliography of Ellul's works see Joyce Main Hanks. *Jacques Ellul: A Comprehensive Bibliography*. Greenwich, Conn.: JAI Press, Inc. 1984. I have adopted Professor Hank's approach of listing Ellul's works chronologically to give the historical direction of Ellul's thought.

1936

Etude sur l'évolution et la nature juridique du Mancipium. Bordeaux: Delmas, 1936.

1945

"Victoire d' Hitler?" *Réforme* 12 (1945): 1, 3.

1946

Le Fondement théologique du droit. Cahiers Theologiques de l'Actualite Protestante, nos. 15/16. Neuchâtel: Delachaux a Niestle, 1946. English trans.: *The Theological Foundation of Law.* Translated by Margerite Wiesner. Garden City, N.Y.: Doubleday, 1960.
"Le Temps du Mepris." *Réforme* 52 (1946): 1, 3.

1947

"Note sur le proces de Nurmeberg." *Verbum Caro* 3 (1947): 97–112.

1948

Présence au monde moderne: Problèmes de la civilization post-chrétienne. Geneva: Roulet, 1948. English trans.: *Presence of the Kingdom.* Translated by Olive Wyon. New York: Seabury Press, 1967.

1950

"Engagement et dégagement." *Reforme* 253 (1950): 1, 3.
"Le Bible et la ville." *Foi et Vie* 48 (1950): 2.
"La femme et les esprits." *Foi et Vie* 294 (1950): 2.

1952

Le Livre de Jonas. Paris: Cahiers Bibliques de *Foi et Vie*, 1952. English trans.: *The Judgment of Jonah.* Translated by Geoffrey W. Bromiley. Grand Rapids, Mich.: Eerdmans, 1971.
"La Science Politique." *Le Monde*, 10 April 1952, 7.
"Propagande et democratic." *Revue Francaise de Science Politique* 2 (1952): 474–504.

1954

L'Homme et l'argent. Neuchâtel: Delachaux a Niestle, 1954. English trans.: *Money and Power.* Translated by LaVonne Neff. Downers Grove, Ill.: Inter-Varsity Press, 1984.

La Technique ou l'enjeu du siècle. Paris: Armand Colin, 1954. English trans.: *The Technological Society.* Translated by John Wilkinson. New York: Alfred A. Knopf, 1964.

1955

L'Histoires des institutions. 5 vols. Paris: Presses Universitaires de France, 1955–80.

1956

"L'Intellectuel et la technique." *Profils* 14 (1956): 24–32.

1957

"Information et propagande." *Diogène* 18 (1957): 69–90. English trans.: "Information and Propaganda." *Diogenes* 18 (1957): 61–77.

1958

"Mythes modernes." *Diogène* 23 (1958): 29–49. English trans.: "Modern Myths." *Diogenes* 23 (1958): 23–40.

1960

"La Technique et les premier chapitres de la Gènese." *Foi et Vie* 59 (1960): 97–113. English trans.: "Technique and the Opening Chapters of Genesis." Translated by Greta Lindstrom and Katharine Temple. In *Theology and Technology*, edited by Carl Mitcham and Jim Grote. Washington, D.C.: University Press of America, 1984.

"Technique et civilisation." *Free University Quarterly* (Amsterdam) 7 (1960): 72–84.

1961

"Essai sur la signification philosophique des réformes actuelles de l'enseignement du droit." *Archives de Philosphie du Droit* 6 (1961): 1–18.

1962

Propagandes. Paris: A. Colin, 1962. English trans.: *Propaganda: The Formation of Men's Attitudes.* Translated by Konrad Kellen and Jean Lerner. New York: Knopf, 1965.

"The Technological Order." Translated by John Wilkinson. In *Philosophy and Technology: Readings in the Philosophical Problems of Technology* edited by Carl Mitcham and Robert Mackey. New York: The Free Press, 1972.

1963

Fausse Présence au mond moderne. Paris: Les Bergers et les Mages, 1963. English trans.: *False Presence of the Kingdom.* Translated by C. Edward Hopkin. New York: Seabury Press, 1972.

"Le Sacré dans le monde moderne." *Le Semeur* 2 (1963): 24–36.

1964

Le Vouloir et le faire: Recherches éthiques pour les chrétiens; Introduction (première partie). Nouvelle Série Théologique, no. 18. Geneva: Labor et Fides, 1964. English trans.: *To Will and to Do: An Ethical Research for Christians.* Translated by C. Edward Hopkin. Philadelphia: Pilgrim Press, 1969.

1965

L'Illusion politique: Essai. Paris: Robert Laffont, 1965. English trans.: *The Political Illusion.* Translated by Konrad Kellen. New York: Knopf, 1972.

"The Biology of Technique." *Nation* (May 1965): 567–68.

1966

Exégèse des nouveaux lieux communs. Paris: Calmann-Lévy, 1966. English trans.: *A Critique of the New Commonplaces.* Translated by Helen Weaver. New York: Knopf, 1968.

Politique de Dieu, politiques de l'homme. [Coll. Nouvelle Alliance.] Paris: Editions Universitaires, 1966. English trans.: *The Politics of God and the Politics of Man.* Translated by Geoffrey W. Bromiley. Grand Rapids, Mich.: Eerdmans, 1972.

"The Artist in the Technological Society." Translated by Roger Clark. *Structurist* 6 (1966): 35–41.

1967

Histoire de la propagande. Que Sais-Je?, no. 1271. Paris: Presses Universitaires de France, 1967.

Métamorphose du bourgeois. Paris: Calmann-Lévy, 1967.

"Le Facteur déterminant des problèmes et de l'evolution de la société contemporaine: La Technique." *Sciences* 48 (1967): 28–46.

1968

"Technique, Institutions and Awareness." *American Behavioral Scientist* 2, no. 6 (1968): 38–42.

"The Psychology of a Rebellion—May–June, 1968." *Interplay: The Magazine of International Affairs* 2 (1968): 23, 27.

1969

Autopsie de la révolution. Paris: Calmann-Lévy, 1969. English trans.: *Autopsy of Revolution.* Translated by Patricia Wolf. New York: Knopf, 1971.

Violence: Reflections from a Christian Perspective. Translated by Cecelia Gaul Kings. New York: Seabury, 1969. French edition: *Contre les violents.* Paris: Le Centurion, 1972.

"L'Inadaptation des jeunes, signe d'une société." *Economie et Humanisme* 185 (1968–69): 26–34.

"Comment nommer la société actuelle? Enquête." *Recherche Sociale* 23–24 (1969): 64–65.

1970

The Meaning of the City. Translated by Dennis Pardee. Grand Rapids, Mich.: Eerdmans, 1970. French edition: *Sans feu ni lieu: Signification biblique de la Grand Ville.* Paris: Gallimard, 1975.

Prayer and Modern Man. Translated by C. Edward Hopkin. New York: Seabury, 1970. French edition: *L'Impossible Prière.* Paris: Le Centurion, 1971.

"Mirror of These Ten Years." Translated by Cecelia Gaul Kings. *Christian Century* 87 (1970): 200–204.

"From Jacques Ellul." *Katallagate: Be Reconciled* 2 (1970): 3–4.

1971

Jeunesse délinquante: Une Expérience en province. With Yves Charrier. Paris: Mercure de France, 1971.

"Losing Faith in Technology." *Playboy* 18 (1971): 55–56.

1972

De la révolution aux révoltes. [Liberté de l'Esprit.] Paris: Calmann-Lévy, 1972.

L'Espérance oubliée. Paris: Gallimard, 1972. English trans.: *Hope in the Time of Abandonment.* Translated by C. Edward Hopkin. New York: Seabury, 1973.

"Conformism and the Rationale of Technology." In *Can We Survive Our Future?*, edited by G. R. Urban and Michael Glenny. New York: St. Martin's Press, 1972.

1973

Les Nouveaux Possédés. Paris: Arthème Fayard, 1973. English trans.: *The New Demons.* Translated by C. Edward Hopkin. New York: Seabury, 1975. "With a View toward Assessing the Facts." Translated by Leonard Mayhew. *New York Times,* (July 1, 1973), 13E.

"Search for an Image." *Humanist* 33 (1973): 22–25.

1974

"Spéculation et bureaucratie: L'Aquitaine vicitime de ses aménageurs." *Le Monde,* (17 March 1974), 19.

"De la mort." *Foi et Vie* 73 (1974): 1–14.

"Interviews with Jacques Ellul: October 20, 24, and 30, 1973." In David Charles Menninger, "Technique and Politics: The Political Thought of Jacques Ellul." Ph.D. diss., University of California, Riverside, 1974.

1975

L'Apocalypse: Architecture en mouvement. Paris: Desclée, 1975. English trans.: *Apocalypse: The Book of Revelation.* Translated by George W. Schreiner. New York: Seabury, 1977.

Ethique de la liberté. 2 vols. Geneva: Labor et Fides, 1973–75. English trans.: *The Ethics of Freedom.* Translated and edited by Geoffrey W. Bromiley. Grand Rapids, Mich.: Eerdmans, 1976.

Trahison de l'Occident. Paris: Calmann-Lévy, 1975. English trans.: *The Betrayal of the West.* Translated by Mathew J. O'Connell. New York: Seabury, 1978.

1976

"La Technique considérée en tant que système." *Les Etudes Philosophiques* 2 (1976): 147–66.

"Problems of Sociological Method." Translated by Daniel Hofstadter. *Social Research* 43 (1976): 6–24.

1977

Le Système technicien. Paris: Calmann-Lévy, 1977. English trans.: *The Technological System.* Translated by Joachim Neugroschel. New York: Continuum, 1980.

1978

"Symbolic Function, Technology and Society." *Journal of Social and Biological Structures* 1 (1978): 207–18.

1979

"La Technique, système bloqué." *Pour* 64 (1979): 13–21.

"Histoire: Les Trois Ages." *Le Monde* (11–12 March 1979), 2.

"An Aspect of the Role of Persuasion in a Technical Society." Translated by Elena Radutsky and Charles Stern. *ETC: A Review of General Semantics* 36 (1979): 147–52.

"Remarks on Technology and Art." Translated by Daniel Hofstadter. *Social Research* 46 (1979): 805–33.

"Preface." In Nelly Viallaneix. *Ecoute, Kierkegaard: Essai sur la communication de la parole.* Vol. 1. Paris: Cerf, 1979.

1980

L'Empire du non-sense: L'Art et la société technicienne. Paris: Presses Universitaires de France, 1980.

La Foi au prix du doute: "Encore quarante jours. . . ." Paris: Hachette, 1980. English trans.: *Living Faith: Belief and Doubt in a Perilous World.* Translated by Peter Heinegg. San Francisco: Harper and Row, 1983.

"Le Travail." Theme issue, *Foi et Vie* 79 (1980): 1–82.

"The Ethics of Nonpower." Translated by Nada K. Levy. In *Ethics in an Age of Pervasive Technology,* edited by Melvin Kranzberg, 204–12. Boulder, Colo.: Westview Press, 1980.

"Nature, Technique, and Artificiality." Translated by Katharine Temple. In *Research in Philosophy and Technology.* Vol. 3, 263–83. Greenwich, Conn.: JAI Press, 1980.

1981

A temps et à contretemps: Entretiens avec Madeleine Garrigou-Lagrange. Paris: Le Centurion, 1981. English trans.: *In Season, Out of Season: An Introduction to the Thought of Jacques Ellul: Based on Interviews by Madeleine Garrigou-Lagrange.* Translated by Lani K. Niles. San Francisco: Harper and Row, 1982.

La Parole humiliée. Paris: Seuil, 1981. English trans.: *The Humiliation of the Word.* Translated by Joyce Main Hankes. Grand Rapids, Mich.: Eerdmans, 1985.

Perspectives on Our Age: Jacques Ellul Speaks on His Life and Work. Edited by William H. Vanderburg. New York: Seabury, 1981.

"Epilogue: On Dialectic." Translated by Geoffrey Bromiley. In *Jacques Ellul: Interpretative Essays,* edited by Clifford G. Christians and Jay M. Van Hook. Urbana: University of Illinois Press, 1981.

"The Ethics of Propaganda: Propaganda, Innocence, and Amorality." Translated by D. Raymond Tourville, *Communication* 6 (1981): 159–75.

1982
Changer de révolution: L'Ineluctable Proletariat. Paris: Seuil, 1982.

1984
"The Latest Developments in Technology and the Philosophy of the Absurd."
Translated by Carl Mitcham and Katharine Temple. *Research in Philosophy and
Technology.* Vol. 7. Greenwich, Conn.: JAI Press, 1984.

Critical Literature on Ellul

Aultman, Mark. "Technology and the End of Law." *American Journal of
Jurisprudence* 17 (1977): 46–79.

Benello, C. George, "Technology and Power." In *Jacques Ellul: Interpretive
Essays,* edited by Clifford Christians and Jay M. Van Hook, 91–107. Urbana:
University of Illinois Press, 1981.

Boli-Bennett, John. "The Absolute Dialectics of Jacques Ellul." In "Symposium
on Jacques Ellul." In *Research in Philosophy and Technology,* vol. 3, edited by
Paul T. Durbin, 171–201. Greenwich, Conn.: JAI Press, 1980.

Bromiley, Geoffrey W. "Barth's Influence on Jacques Ellul." In *Jacques Ellul:
Interpretive Essays,* edited by Clifford Christians and Jay M. Van Hook, 32–51.
Urbana: University of Illinois Press, 1981.

Brown, Norman O. "Jacques Ellul: Beyond Geneva and Jerusalem." In *Democracy*
2 (Fall 1982): 119–26.

Buchanan, Scott. "*La Technique* (Review)." *George Washington Law Review*
33 (1965): 821–23.

Burke, David John. "Jacques Ellul: Theologian and Social Critic." Ph.D. diss.,
Washington State University, 1980.

Byrne, Edmund F. "C. Christians and J. M. Van Hook, eds., *Jacques Ellul:
Interpretive Essays* (Review)." *Nature and System* 3 (1981): 184–88.

Cerezuelle. "Doubts Concerning the Religious Origins of Technological Civilization." Translated by Katherine Temple and edited by Carl Mitcham. In
Research in Philosophy and Technology, vol. 6, edited by Paul T. Durbin,
161–70. Greenwich, Conn.: JAI Press, 1983.

_____. "Fear and Insight in French Philosophy of Technology." Translated by
Simon Inkle and K. Temple. In *Research in Philosophy and Technology,* vol. 2,
edited by Paul T. Durbin, 53–75. Greenwich, Conn.: JAI Press, 1979.

_____. "From the Technological Phenomenon to the Technological System." In
"Symposium on Jacques Ellul," *Research in Philosophy and Technology,* vol. 3,
edited by Paul T. Durbin, 161–70. Greenwich, Conn.: JAI Press, 1980.

Christians, Clifford G., coauthor. "Jacques Ellul's Contributions to Critical Media
Theory." *Journal of Communications* 29 (1979): 83–93.

_____. Coeditor. *Jacques Ellul: Interpretive Essays.* Urbana: University of Illinois
Press, (1981).

_____. "Jacques Ellul's *La Technique* in a Communications Context." Ph.D.
diss., University of Illinois, 1974.

_____. "Ellul on Solution." In *Jacques Ellul: Interpretive Essays,* edited by
Clifford Christians and Jay M. Van Hook, 147–73. Urbana: University of Illinois
Press, 1981.

———. "Jacques Ellul's Concern with the Amorality of Contemporary Communications." *Communications: International Journal of Communications Research* 3 (1977): 62–80.

Clark, David. "The Mythic Meaning of the City." In *Jacques Ellul: Interpretive Essays*, edited by Clifford Christians and Jay M. Van Hook, 260–90. Urbana: University of Illinois Press, 1981.

Clendenin, Daniel B. *Theological Method in Jacques Ellul.* Lanham, New York, London: University Press of America, 1987.

Cornu, Michel. "Ironie et humour selon Kierkegaard." *Les Etudes Philosphiques* 2 (1979): 217–28.

Cox, Harvey. "The Ungodly City: A Theological Response to Jacques Ellul." *Commonweal* 94 (1971): 351–75.

———. *The Seduction of the Spirit: The Use and Misuse of People's Religion.* New York: Simon and Schuster, 1973.

Crick, Bernard. "*Violence* [review]." *Political Quarterly* 42 (1971): 229–32.

De Rubertis, Kim. "In Defense of Dubos and Ellul." *Civil Engineering* 42 (1972): 51–53.

Donnelly, Thomas G. "In Defense of Technology." *Christian Century* 90 (1973): 65–69.

Dupuy, Gabriel. *Urbanisme et technique: Chronique d'un Mariage de raison.* Paris: Centre de Recherche d'Urbanisme, 1978.

Dravasa, Etienne, Claude Emeri, and Jean-Louis Seurin, eds. *Religion, société et politique: Mélanges en hommage à Jacques Ellul.* Paris: Universitaires de France, 1983.

Eller, Vernard. "Ellul and Kierkegaard." In *Jacques Ellul: Interpretive Essays*, edited by Clifford Christians and Jay M. Van Hook, 52–66. Urbana: University of Illinois Press, 1981.

———. "Four Who Remember: Kierkegaard, the Blumhardts, Ellul, and Muggeridge." *Katallagete: Be Reconciled* 3 (1971): 6–12.

Falk, Howard. "*La Technique* [review]." *Technology and Culture* 6 (1965): 532–35.

Fasching, Darrell J. "The Apocalypse of Freedom;: Christian Ethics in the Technological Society." Ph.D. diss., Syracuse University, 1978.

———. *The Thought of Jacques Ellul: A systematic Exposition.* New York: Edwin Mellen Press, 1981.

Ferkiss, Victor C. "*Le Système technicien* [review]." *American Political Science Review* 75 (1981): 739–40.

———. *The Technological Man: The Myth and the Reality.* New York: Braziller, 1969.

Florman, Samuel C. "Anti-Technology: The New Myth." *Civil Engineering* 42 (1972): 68–70.

———. *The Existential Pleasures of Engineering.* New York: St. Martins Press, 1976.

———. "In Praise of Technology." *Harpers* 251 (1975): 53–72.

Gendron, Bernard. *Technology and the Human Condition.* New York: St. Martins, 1977.

Gill, David. "Jacques Ellul: Prophet in the Technological Wilderness." *Catholic Agitator* (1976): 3–4.

Grant, George P. *Technology and Empire.* Toronto: House of Anansi, 1969.

Hall, Rupert. "An Unconvincing Indictment of the Evils of Technology." *Scientific American* 212 (February 1965): 125–28.

Harrington, Michael. "I Am Not a Marxist, I Am Marx." *Nation* 213 (1971): 694–96.

Holloway, James Y., ed. *Introducing Jacques Ellul.* Grand Rapids, Mich.: Eerdmans, 1970.

Holmes, Arthur. "A Philosophical Critique of Ellul on Natural law." In *Jacques Ellul: Interpretive Essays*, edited by Clifford Christians and Jay M. Van Hook, 229–50. Urbana: University of Illinois Press, 1981.

Lasch, Christopher. "A Profusion of Information." *Nation* 202 (4 April 1966): 397–98.

_____. "The Social Thought of Jacques Ellul." In *Introducing Jacques Ellul*, edited by James Holloway, 21–33. Grand Rapids, Mich.: Eerdmans, 1970.

Lerner, Daniel. "Propaganda [review]." *American Sociological Review* 29 (1962): 793–94.

Lipset, Seymour Martin. "Forcing a Free Choice." *New York Times Book Review*, 6 March 1966, p. 47.

Lovekin, David. "Artifacts, Politics, and Imagination: From Vico to Marx." In *Research in Philosophy and Technology*, vol. 5, edited by Paul T. Durbin, 67–75. Greenwich, Conn.: JAI Press, 1982.

_____. "Degenerate Travel: The World of the Tourist in Technological Society." In *Essays in Humanity and Technology*, edited by David Lovekin and Donald Phillip Verene, 167–89. Dixon, Ill.: Sauk Valley College, 1978.

_____. "Giambattista Vico and Jacques Ellul: The Intelligible Universal and the Technical Phenomenon." *Man and World* 10 (1982): 252–72.

_____. "Technology and the Denial of Mystery: The Sacralization of the Familiar." In *From Artifact to Habitat: Studies in the Critical Engagement of Technology*, edited by Gayle L. Ormiston. Bethlehem, Pa.: Lehigh University Press, 1990.

_____. "Technology as the Sacred Order." In "Symposium on Jacques Ellul," *Research in Philosophy and Technology*, vol. 3, edited by Paul T. Durbin, 203–22. Greenwich Conn.: JAI Press, 1980.

McLuhan, Marshall. "Big Transistor Is Watching You." *BookWeek* 5 (28 November 1965): 25–26.

Marty, Martin E. "Introduction: Creative Misuses of Jacques Ellul." In *Jacques Ellul: Interpretive Essays*, edited by Clifford Christians and Jay M. Van Hook, 3–13. Urbana: University of Illinois Press, 1981.

Menninger, David. "Technique and Politics: The Political Thought of Jacques Ellul." Ph.D. diss., University of California, Riverside, 1974.

_____. "Jacques Ellul: A Tempered Profile." *Review of Politics* 37 (1975): 235–46.

_____. "Marx in the Social Thought of Jacques Ellul." In *Jacques Ellul: Interpretive Essays*, 17–31.

Merton, Robert K. "Foreword." In Ellul's *The Technological Society*, translated by John Wilkinson v–viii. New York: Alfred A. Knopf, 1969.

Meynaud, Jean. *Technocracy.* Translated by Paul Barnes. New York: The Free Press, 1968.

Miller, Duane R. "The Effect of Technology upon Humanization in the Thought of Lewis Mumford and Jacques Ellul." Ph.D. diss., Boston University, 1970.

Mitcham, Carl, coauthor. *Bibliography of the Philosophy of Technology.* Chicago: University of Chicago Press, 1973.

_____, coauthor. "Introduction: Technology as a Philosophical Problem." In *Philosophy and Technology: Readings in the Philosophical Problems of Technology*, edited by C. Mitcham and R. Mackey, 1–30. New York: The Free Press, 1972.

_____, coauthor. "Jacques Ellul and the Technological Society." *Philosophy Today* 15 (1971): 102–21.

_____. "Philosophy of Technology. In *Guide to the Culture of Science, Technology, and Medicine*, 309–12. New York: The Free Press, 1980.

Muller, Herbert J. *The Children of Frankenstein: A Primer on Modern Technology and Human Values.* Bloomington: Indiana University Press, 1970.

Nisbet, Robert. "The Grand Illusion: An Appreciation of Jacques Ellul." *Commentary* 50 (1970): 40–44.

Outka, Gene. "Discontinuity in the Ethics of Jacques Ellul." In *Jacques Ellul: Interpretive Essays*, edited by Clifford Christians and Jay M. Van Hook, 177–228. Urbana: University of Illinois Press, 1981.

Pickrel, Paul. "Heading Toward Postcivilization." *Harpers* 229 (October 1964): 122–28.

Rapp, Friedrich. *Analytical Philosophy of Technology.* Translated by Stanley Carpenter and Theodor Langenbruch. Boston: D. Reidel, 1981.

_____. "Philosophy of Technology." In *Contemporary Philosophy: A New Survey*, vol. 2 edited by Guttorn Floisted, 361–412. The Hague: Martinus Nijhoff, 1982.

Schickel, Richard. "Marx Is Dead." *Harpers* 244 (1972): 96–101.

Shriver, Donald, W., Jr. "Man and His Machines: Four Angles of Vision." *Technology and Culture* 13 (1972): 531–55.

Silberman, Charles E. "Is Technology Taking Over." In *The Myths of Automation*, 96–114. New York: Harper & Row, 1966.

Sklair, Leslie. "The Sociology of Opposition to Science and Technology: With Special Reference to the Work of Jacques Ellul." *Comparative Studies in Society and History* 13 (1971): 217–35.

Stanley, John. "The Uncertain Hobbesian: Ellul's Dialogues with the Sovereign and the Tradition of French Politics." In *Jacques Ellul: Interpretive Essays*, edited by Clifford Christians and Jay M. Van Hook, 69–90. Urbana: University of Illinois Press, 1981.

Stanley, Manfred. *The Technological Conscience: Survival and Dignity in an Age of Expertise.* Chicago: University of Chicago Press, 1981.

Stringfellow, William. "Introduction." In Jacques Ellul's *The Presence of the Kingdom*, translated by Olive Wyon, 1–6. New York: Seabury Press, 1967.

Stritch, Thomas. "Trahison de l'Occident (Review)." *Review of Politics* 41 (October 1979): 582–85.

Sullivan, Robert. "Jacques Ellul: Toward Understanding his Political Thinking." *Journal of Church and State* 24 (1982): 13–28.

Temple, Katharine. "The Task of Jacques Ellul: A Proclamation of Faith as Requisite for Understanding the Modern Project." Ph.D. diss., McMaster University, 1976.

_____. "The Sociology of Jacques Ellul." In "Symposium on Jacques Ellul,"

Research in Philosophy and Technology, vol. 3, edited by Paul T. Durbin, 23–61. Greenwich, Conn.: JAI Press, 1980.

Theobald, Robert, "The House that Homo Sapiens Built." *Nation* 11 (October 1964): 249–52.

Toffler, Alvin. *Future Shock*. New York: Random House, 1970.

Vahanian, Gabriel. "Jacques Ellul and the Religious Illusion." In Darrell J. Fasching, *The Thought of Jacques Ellul: A Systematic Exposition*, xv–xxxviii. Translated by Charles Courtney. New York: Edwin Mellen Press, 1981.

Vance, Rupert. "*La Technique* (Review)." *Social Forces* 46 (1968): 416–17.

Van Hook, Jay. "The Politics of Man, the Politics of God, and the Politics of Freedom." In *Jacques Ellul: Interpretive Essays*, edited by Clifford M. Christians and Jay M. Van Hook, 128–46. Urbana: University of Illinois Press, 1981.

Verene, Donald Phillip. *Hegel's Recollection*. New York: SUNY Press, 1985.

———. "Technique and the Directions of Human Spirit: Laughter and Desire." In *Essays in Humanity and Technology*, edited by David Lovekin and Donald Verene, 87–113. Dixon, Ill.: Sauk Valley College, 1978.

———. "Technological Desire." In *Research in Philosophy and Technology*, vol. 7, edited by Paul T. Durbin, 99–112. Greenwich, Conn.: JAI Press, 1984.

———. "Technology and the Ship of Fools." In *Research in Philosophy and Technology*, vol. 5, edited by Paul T. Durbin, 281–98. Greenwich, Conn.: JAI Press, 1982.

Wilkinson, John. "The Divine Persuasion: An Interview with John Wilkinson about Jacques Ellul." In *Introducing Jacques Ellul*, 161–83. Grand Rapids, Mich.: Erdmans, 1970.

Winner, Langdon. *Autonomous Technology: Technics-Out-Of Control as a Theme in Political Thought*. Cambridge: MIT Press, 1977.

Other Works Cited in the Text

Arendt, Hannah. *Eichman in Jerusalem: A Report on the Banality of Evil*. New York: Viking Press, 1964.

Brillat-Savarin, Jean Antheleme. *Physiology of Taste: Or Meditations on Transcendental Gastronomy*. Translated by M. F. K. Fisher. New York: The Heritage Press, 1949.

Cassirer, Ernst. *An Essay on Man*. New Haven and London: Yale University Press, 1979.

———. "Form und Technik." In *Symbol, Technik, Sprache*, edited by Wolgang Orth and John Michael Krois. Introduction by Josef M. Werle. Hamburg: Felix Meiner Verlag, 1985.

———. *The Myth of the State*. New Haven and London: Yale University Press, 1946.

———. *Philosophie der Symbolishen Formen*. 3 vols. Darmstadt: Wissenschaftliche Buchgesellschaft, 1923–39. *The Philosophy of Symbolic Forms*. Translated by Ralph Mannheim. 3 vols. New Haven: Yale University Press, 1953–57.

_____. *Zur Logic der Kulturwissenschaften.* Darmstadt: Wissenschaftliche Buchgesellschaft, 1942. *The Logic of the Humanities.* Translated by Clarence Howe. New Haven and Longon: Yale University Press, 1961.

Collingwood, R. G. *An Essay on Metaphysics.* Oxford: Clarendon Press, 1939.

_____. *Speculum Mentis or the Map of Knowledge.* Oxford: Clarendon Press, 1924.

Descartes, René. *The Discourse on Method.* In *The Philosophical Works of Descartes.* Translated by Haldane and Ross. 2 vols. New York: Dover Publications, 1955.

_____. *Meditations sur la philosophie premiere, dans laquelle est demonstrée l'existence de Dieu et l'immortalite de l'âme.* In *Oeuvres et Lettres,* edited by André Bridoux. Paris: Editions Gallimard, 1953. *Meditations on First Philosophy.* Translated by Laurence J. Lafleur. New York: Bobbs-Merrill Co., 1986.

Dessauer, Friedrich. "Technology in Its Proper Sphere." Translated by William Carroll. In *Philosophy and Technology,* edited by Carl Mitcham and Robert Mackey, 317–34. New York and London: The Free Press, 1983.

Eco, Umberto. *Travels in Hyperreality.* Translated by William Weaver. New York: Harcourt Brace Jovanovich, 1986.

Eliade, Mircea. *Myths, Dreams and Mysteries: The Encounter Between Contemporary Faiths and Archaic Realities.* Translated by Philip Mairit. New York: Harper Torchbooks, 1967.

Foucault, Michel. *L'histoire de folie.* Paris: Librairie Plon, 1961. *Madness and Civilization: A History of Insanity in the Age of Reason.* Translated by Richard Howard. New York: Vintage, 1973.

_____. *Surveiller et Punir: Naissance de la Prison.* Paris: Gallimard, 1975. *Discipline and Punish: The Birth of the Prison.* Translated by Alan Sheridan. New York: Vintage, 1979.

Gay, Peter. *The Weimar Culture: The Outsider as Insider.* New York and Evanston: Harper and Row, 1968.

Giedion, Siegfried. *Mechanization Takes Command.* New York: Oxford University Press, 1948.

Goldman. Steven L. "The Technè of Philosophy and the Philosophy of Technology." In *Research in Philosophy and Technology,* vol. 7, edited by Paul T. Durbin, 115–44. Greenwich, Conn.: JAI Press, 1984.

Hegel, G. W. F. *Phanomenology des Geistes.* Edited by Johannes Hoffmeister. 6th ed. Hamburg: Felix Meiner Verlag, 1952. *The Phenomenology of Mind.* Translated by A. V. Miller, with an Introduction by J. N. Findlay. Oxford: Clarendon Press, 1977.

_____. *Wissenschaft der Logic.* Edited by Georg Lasson. 2 vols. Hamburg: Felix Meiner Verlag, 1971. *Hegel's Science of Logic.* Translated by A. V. Miller. London and New York: Humanities Press, 1969.

Hitler, Adolph. *Mein Kampf.* Translated by Ralph Mannheim. Boston: Houghton Miffflin Co. 1971.

Jacobson, Michael. *The Eater's Digest: The Consumer's Factbook of Food Additives.* New York: Doubleday, 1969.

Jameson, Frederic. *The Prison House of Language.* Princeton: Princeton University Press, 1972.

Jaspers, Karl. *Man in the Modern Age.* Translated by Eden and Cedar Paul. New York: Anchor Books, 1957.

Jung, C. G. "Flying Saucers: A Modern Myth." In *Collected Works of C. G. Jung*, vol. 10, translated by R. F. C. Hull, 308–433. Princeton: Princeton University Press, 1964.

Kahn, Herman. *On Thermonuclear War*. Princeton: Princeton University Press, 1961.

Kapp, Ernst. *Grundlinien einer Philosophie der Technik*. Braunschweig: Westerman, 1977.

Kleist, Heinrich von. "On the Puppet Theatre." In *An Abyss Deep Enough: Letters of Heinrich von Kleist with a Selection of Essays and Anecdotes*, translated and edited by Phillip B. Miller, 211–17. New York: E. P. Dutton, 1982.

Kranzberg, Melvin. "Introduction: Trends in the History and Philosophy of Technology." In *The History and Philosophy of Technology,* edited by George Bugliarello and Dean B. Doner, xii–xxxi. Urbana: University of Illinois Press, 1979.

Kranzberg, Melvin, and Pursell, Carroll W., Jr. "The Importance of Technology in Human Affairs." In *Technology in Western Civilization*, edited by Melvin Kranzberg and Carroll W. Pursell, Jr., 3–11. 2 vols. New York and London: Oxford University Press, 1967.

Krois, John Michael. *Cassirer: Symbolic Forms and History*. New Haven and London: Yale University Press, 1987.

Kuhn, Thomas. *The Structure of Scientific Revolution*. 2d ed. Chicago: University of Chicago Press, 1970.

Lévi-Strauss, Claude. *The Savage Mind*. Translated by George Weidenfeld. Chicago: University of Chicago Press, 1966.

_____. *Totemism*. Translated by Rodney Needham. Boston: Beacon Press, 1963.

Mao Tse Tung. *Selected Works of Mao Tse Tung*. Edited by Bruno Shaw. New York: Harper Colophon Books, 1970.

McLuhan, Marshall. *From Cliché to Archetype*. New York: Viking Press, 1970.

_____. *Understanding Media: The Extensions of Man*. New York: McGraw Hill, 1964.

Merleau-Ponty, Maurice. *Humanism and Terror*. Translated by John O'Neill. New York: Beacon Press, 1969.

Mischerlich, Alexander, and Mielke, Fred. *Doctors of Infamy*. Translated by Heine Norden. New York: Henry Schuman, 1949.

Orwell, George. *1984*. With a preface by Walter Cronkite and an afterword by Erich Fromm. New York: New American Library, 1983.

_____. "Politics and the English Language." In *A Collection of Essays by George Orwell*, 156–71. New York: Doubleday Anchor, 1954.

Pascal, Blaise. *Pensées*. In *Oeuvres Completes*, edited by Jacques Chevalier. Paris: Editions Gallimard, 1954.

Sass, Hans-Martin. "Man and His Environment: Ernst Kapp's Engineering Experience and his Philosophy of Technology and Environment." In *German Culture in Texas*, edited by Glen E. Lich and Dona B. Reeves, 82–273. Boston: Twayne, 1979.

Simmel, Georg. "The Stranger." In *The Sociology of Georg Simmel*, translated by Kurt H. Wolf, 402–8. New York: The Free Press, 1950.

Updike, John. "Reflections: Kafka's Short Stories." *New Yorker*, 9 May 1983, 129.

Welch, David. *Propaganda and the German Cinema: 1933–1945*. Oxford: Clarendon Press, 1983.

Wiener, Norbert. *The Human Uses of Human Beings.* New York: Avon Books, 1967.

Wolf, Tom. *The Right Stuff.* New York: Farrar, Strauss, Giroux, 1979.

Worsley, Peter. *The Trumpet Shall Sound.* New York: Schocken Books, 1968.

Zijderveld, Anton. *On Clichés: The Supersedure of Meaning by Function in Modernity.* London, Boston, Henley: Routledge and Kegan Paul, 1979.

Index